palgrave macmillan law masters

legal theory

340.1 M

D0314861

If you would like to comment on this book, or on the series generally, please write to lawfeedback@palgrave.com.

palgrave macmillan law masters

legal theory

ian mcleod

Visiting Professor of Law
Stirling Law School
University of Stirling

Sixth edition

This edition first published 2012 by PALGRAVE MACMILLAN

Palgrave Macmillan in the UK is an imprint of Macmillan Publishers Limited, registered in England, company number 785998, of Houndmills, Basingstoke, Hampshire RG21 6XS.

Palgrave Macmillan in the US is a division of St Martin's Press LLC, 175 Fifth Avenue, New York, NY 10010.

Palgrave Macmillan is the global academic imprint of the above companies and has companies and representatives throughout the world.

Palgrave® and Macmillan® are registered trademarks in the United States, the United Kingdom, Europe and other countries.

ISBN 978–0–230–36204–8   paperback

This book is printed on paper suitable for recycling and made from fully managed and sustained forest sources. Logging, pulping and manufacturing processes are expected to conform to the environmental regulations of the country of origin.

A catalogue record for this book is available from the British Library.

10 9 8 7 6 5 4 3 2 1
21 20 19 18 17 16 15 14 13 12

Printed and bound in Great Britain by TJ International, Padstow

Contents

Preface

This edition continues with the same intention as its predecessors, namely to combine an introduction to many of the topics commonly encountered in courses on Legal Theory or Jurisprudence, with, wherever possible, practical illustrations drawn from substantive law.

The emphasis on practical application stems from my experience of teaching the subject within a semesterized system. More particularly, when law is taught in units of eleven or twelve weeks (or thereabouts), students have little opportunity for that leisurely reflection which might enable at least some of them to make the connections between legal theory and substantive law for themselves; and it is my experience that law students relate best to legal theory when they can see the point of it all in terms of substantive law. Similarly, I hope that students who come to legal theory from the study of disciplines other than law (such as philosophy and politics), may find their perceptions of their subjects enhanced by seeing how they relate to practical aspects of law.

The most significant single piece of updating in this edition is its introduction to Dworkin's *Justice for Hedgehogs*, which shows every sign of being as influential for at least the next quarter of a century as his *Law's Empire* has been over the last one. Other matters I have noted include the appearance of the second edition of Finnis's *Natural Law and Natural Rights*, the finalization of the Director of Public Prosecutions' policy on assisted suicide and the report of the *Commission on Assisted Dying*.

I am grateful to Lady Hale for allowing me to reproduce a passage from the text of her lecture on *Leadership in the Law: What Is A Supreme Court For?* (which was delivered at City University on 30 April 2008) and to Oxford University Press for permission to quote extensively from H.L.A. Hart's *The Concept of Law*, 2nd edn, 1994. I am also grateful to Davina Hehir (of Dignity in Dying) for answering questions and to Durham University for allowing me to use its library.

I am also grateful to Ian Kingston for processing my eighteenth typescript in seventeen years and especially for suffering my inefficiency with more than good grace.

My principal acknowledgment must, as always, be to my wife Jacqui, who continues to provide editorial assistance as well as being unbelievably patient and supportive generally. She understands fully what the Roman poet Juvenal meant when he replied to the question 'Is writing an art or a craft?', with 'Neither: it is a disease'.

I have tried to be up-to-date to 1 April 2012.

Ian McLeod

Table of cases

Chapter 1

The nature of legal theory: from laws to law

1.1 Introduction

This chapter begins with a discussion of the relationship between *law* and *legal theory*, and continues by clarifying some basic problems of terminology and methodology. It then considers the importance of context in legal theory, the dangers inherent in classifying legal theories and the extent (if any) to which we can have knowledge of moral matters, before concluding with an explanation of why it is useful to study legal theory, both from the perspective of legal practice and within the wider context of the academic study of law.

1.2 Law and legal theory

Most courses of study within the field of law involve an analysis of the content of a specific part of the whole legal system. Provided you know the basic terminology of the legal system you are studying, the title of a typical course gives a reasonably accurate indication of the scope of the subject matter involved. Thus English lawyers will know what aspects of legal doctrine they can expect from a course on *tort*, while Scots lawyers will know what they can expect from a course on *delict*; and comparative lawyers will know that, broadly speaking, the two subjects are the same.

It is not surprising, therefore, that law students develop an expectation that the scope of both the courses they study, and the textbooks which support those courses, will be defined by reference to specific areas of law. Of course, the treatment of the legal content may vary. Some courses will be taught and studied *contextually*, with the legal doctrines being examined within the social and economic context of the real world; others will proceed on the so-called *black letter* basis, which means that the cases and statutes containing the legal doctrines will be subjected to purely textual analysis, with little or no reference to the practical context within which those doctrines function.

Other variations are possible. For example, the packaging and labelling of courses may change from time to time. What was once commonly known as *constitutional and administrative law* has become widely (but not universally) known as *public law*. Similarly, the established textbook unities of *contract* and *tort* may be merged and expanded by the addition of *restitution* to form the new subject of *obligations*. Nevertheless, irrespective of the ways in which courses are labelled, taught and studied, the general proposition remains that practically the whole of the law curriculum is presented in terms of areas of law which are (or are at least perceived to be) doctrinally coherent.

Legal theory is different. One immediately apparent difference is that legal theory is painted on a larger canvas; or, to change the metaphor into a more appropriately verbal one, it asks bigger questions. So, for example, criminal lawyers will ask questions such as *what is the definition of theft?* Legal theorists, on the other hand, will ask questions such as *what is it that makes the prohibition on theft (along with a great many other prohibitions) into a matter of law, whereas many other forms of dishonesty are left solely in the realm of morality?*

In a nutshell, therefore, legal theory involves a progression from the study of *laws* to the study of *law*.

1.3　A question of terminology: *jurisprudence*, *legal philosophy*, or *legal theory*?

Although this book is called *Legal Theory*, you will find that some other books (and the courses for which they are used) bear other titles, such as *Jurisprudence*, *Legal Philosophy* or the *Philosophy of Law*. Closer examination of the contents of both books and courses, however, will generally show that the choice of title often reflects nothing more substantial than the personal preference of the person making the choice. All that need be said here is that this book uses the expression *legal theory* in a relatively broad sense to include discussion of not only the nature of *law*, but also the nature of *rights* and *justice*, and the use of *law* to *enforce morality*.

If justification for this use of *legal theory* is required, it may be provided on two bases.

First, all these topics discussed are clearly theoretical in nature, and those which do not directly address the nature of law itself are so closely involved with the nature of law that it would be both unrealistic and unhelpful to consign them to separate consideration elsewhere.

Secondly, it is a peculiarly Anglo-American idea to treat *legal theory* as being more or less synonymous with *jurisprudence*. In French, for example, the word *jurisprudence* means the body of law developed through the decisions of the courts. This explains the use of the phrase *Strasbourg jurisprudence* to identify the *law* contained in the European Convention on Human Rights as developed by the European Court of Human Rights at Strasbourg. The phrase *théorie générale du droit*, on the other hand, reflects the theoretical nature of that kind of material which, in Anglo-American usage, is called *jurisprudence*.

1.4　The sources of legal theory

It is, of course, trite to say that the primary sources of English law are cases and statutes, together with any relevant sources of European Community (now Union) law. Admittedly, as we shall see more or less throughout this book, one of the central concerns of legal theory is whether *law* may properly be limited to formal texts of any kind, or whether it also incorporates elements drawn from other sources. However, for the present purposes, the essential point is that judicial and legislative texts are, in practical terms, the primary sources of legal doctrine, with scholarly works being no more than aids to understanding those sources.

For the student of legal theory, on the other hand, the primary sources are frequently not cases and legislative enactments, but the works of legal theorists. Furthermore, legal theorists are not necessarily lawyers, because the subject matter is inextricably linked with both philosophy and political theory. As Friedmann puts it,

> 'all legal theory must contain elements of philosophy – man's reflections on his position in the universe – and gain its colour and specific content from political theory – the ideas entertained on the best form of society.' (*Legal Theory*, 5th edn, 1967, p. 4.)

More particularly:

> 'Before the nineteenth century... the great legal theorists were primarily philosophers, churchmen and politicians'

and

> 'the new era of legal philosophy arises mainly from the confrontation of the professional lawyer, in his legal work, with problems of social justice.
>
> 'It is, therefore, inevitable that an analysis of earlier legal theories must lean more heavily on general philosophical and political theory, while modern legal theories can be more adequately discussed in the lawyer's own idiom and system of thought. The difference is, however, one of method and emphasis. The modern jurist's legal theory, no less than the scholastic philosopher's, is based on *ultimate beliefs whose inspiration comes from outside the law itself.*' (Emphasis added. *Ibid.*)

Some support for the part of this analysis which relates to the pre-20th century period can be found in Oliver Wendell Holmes' pointed comment on the leading English legal theorist of the 19th century, that 'the trouble with Austin was that he did not know enough English law'. (*The Path of the Law* (1897) 8 Harv LR 457, at p. 475. Austin's *command theory* of law is discussed in Chapter 4.)

The most practical consequence of the fact that many legal theorists are not lawyers is that some of the skills required to read and evaluate texts drawn from non-legal disciplines may not come easily to law students, whose habits of conceptualizing, and whose expectations of language and those who use it, have been conditioned by the protracted study of legal texts. One of the characteristics which the other academic disciplines may possess, when contrasted with law, is a greater dependence on *soft concepts*, in the sense that the concepts are, in their very nature, incapable of the degree of precise verbal formulation which would enable their exact content and limits to be easily identified. It follows that some law students, who are often used to working with harder (using the term *harder* in the sense of *more precise*) concepts, may well find that it takes time to adapt to some aspects of the academic discipline involved in legal theory. However, this adaptation is part of the mind-broadening process of education, and must be accepted as a valuable part of the academic challenge which the subject presents.

1.5   The importance of context in legal theory

1.5.1   Introduction

Having established the nature and sources of legal theory, we must move on to consider one of the most basic points of all, namely that all legal theories must be seen within their own context or contexts.

1.5.2   Theories in context

Introduction

There are many contexts within which legal theories may be viewed. While acknowledging that there is significant overlap between them, it will nevertheless be useful to identify, and comment briefly upon, three of the most basic contexts.

First, we will consider the importance of the historical context within which a theory is formulated. Secondly, we will turn to the cultural context of which a theory forms part. Finally, we will consider the context of the particular question to which a theory is offered as an answer.

The historical context

At the risk of stating the obvious, all legal theorists work within the intellectual climate of their age; and this is equally true whether they belong to, or react against, the mainstream of contemporary ideas. While this fact necessarily governs the scope of each theorist's world-view, on a more positive note it also gives succeeding generations the opportunity to benefit from the work of their predecessors. As Isaac Newton recognized of his own position within the field of physical science, if he had been able to 'see further than other men' it was because he had been able to 'stand on the shoulders of giants'.

The cultural context

Although the existence of a legal system is one of the characteristics of all human societies, and therefore legal theory is, to this extent, cross-cultural, it will nevertheless be apparent that what is meant by words such as *rights*, *freedom* and *justice* will vary substantially from one culture to another. The factors which govern these differences will themselves vary, but will typically include the economic basis of each society (for example, capitalist and socialist societies will obviously take different approaches to the question of property rights) and the status of religion within each society.

By way of overlap with the historical context, it will be obvious that, even within a single culture, attitudes may undergo fundamental changes with the passage of time. For example, in *Bird v Holbrook* (1828) 4 Bing 628, which involved a claim in respect of an injury caused by a spring-gun, Best CJ said '... Christianity... has always been held to be... part of the law of England'.

Similarly, as recently as the second half of the 19th century, the Court of Exchequer Chamber held that a person who had agreed to let a room was entitled to refuse to proceed with the letting when he discovered that the room was to be used by the Liverpool Secular Society for a lecture which would question Christian doctrine. The basis of the court's decision was that since Christianity was part of English law, it followed that the intention had been to use the room for an unlawful purpose. (*Cowan v Milburn* (1867) LR 2 Exch 230.)

However, by the early part of the 20th century judicial attitudes had changed. In *Bowman v Secular Society Ltd* [1917] AC 406, the House of Lords upheld the legality of a legacy to a company whose objects were 'to promote... the principle that human conduct should be based upon natural knowledge and not upon super-natural belief, and that human welfare in this world is the proper end of all thought and action'. More particularly, Lord Sumner, having discussed *Bird v Holbrook* (above), and having pointed out that 'spring-guns, indeed, were got rid of, not by Christianity, but by Act of Parliament', observed that 'the phrase "Christianity is part of the law of England" is really not law; it is rhetoric'. He explained the change of legal principle thus:

> 'The words, as well as the acts, which tend to endanger society differ from time to time in proportion as society is stable or insecure in fact, or is believed by its reasonable members to be open to assault. In the present day, meetings or processions are held lawful which a hundred and fifty years ago would have been deemed seditious, and this is not because the law is weaker or has changed, but because the times have changed, society is stronger than before. In the present day reasonable men do not apprehend the dissolution or the downfall of society because [the Christian] religion is publicly assailed by methods not scandalous.'

It may seem that the culture-specific aspect of legal theory poses problems for students who hold strong personal views. In reality, however, as you will see in Section 1.7 (below), all that is required is that you should be willing to discuss all the possible views in an intellectually rigorous and critical fashion. Nevertheless, the fact remains that your view of legal theory, and of all the topics that fall within its scope, can never be more than one part of your wider world-view.

Of course, it may be argued that the ideal work on legal theory would be cross-culturally comprehensive. Perhaps. But practical constraints of time, expertise and the size of the resulting book are such that attainment of this ideal is unlikely. Furthermore, the attempt may be counter-productive. As Oliver Wendell Holmes says, having read the Appendix on the subject of *possession* in Stephen's *Criminal Law*, the author was 'not the only writer whose attempts to analyse legal ideas have been confused by striving for a useless quintessence of all systems, instead of an accurate anatomy of one'. (*Op. cit.*, p. 475.)

The context of the question which is being answered

Quite apart from the historical and cultural contexts within which legal theories are formulated and criticized, the different answers given by legal theorists need to be assessed in the context of the questions which they are considering. For example, the classification of legal theories into *natural law* and *positivist* categories (which is outlined in Chapter 2 as a preliminary to considering some of the major theories within each category in subsequent chapters), may in some cases represent a genuine disagreement as to the nature of law itself. Alternatively, in some cases, the differences between the answers will flow simply from the fact that different questions are being asked, namely '*what is it that makes a statement into a statement of law?*' and '*what is it that makes law into good (in the sense of morally desirable) law?*'. This is important because a theorist who is giving detailed consideration to one question may well give no attention whatever to some other question, which is equally interesting but simply outwith the scope of the instant inquiry. In this context, it may be useful to remember that legal theory is a branch of philosophy, because:

> 'Philosophy may be pre-eminently a subject where insight into one aspect of things tends to blind us to other aspects, and we should try to draw upon other people's insights positively in order to advance our own halting and necessarily personal, but not therefore necessarily wrong, grasp on things.' (T.L.S. Sprigge, *The Rational Foundations of Ethics*, 1990, p. 5.)

1.6   The danger of classifying legal theories

Books and courses on legal theory will inevitably classify the legal theories with which they deal, even if only into the natural law and positivist categories. However, the process of classification must never be allowed to obscure the fact that all schemes of classification are only convenient shorthand to indicate generalities rather than specifics, and they must therefore be seen only as an aid to, and not as a substitute for, understanding.

It may be valuable to recall the ancient Greek legend of Procrustes, who claimed to have a bed into which anyone would fit exactly. And indeed everyone did fit Procrustes' bed, but only after he had stretched on a rack those who were naturally too short, and amputated the bodily extremities of those who were naturally too tall. The relevance of this tale in the present context is that there is often a temptation to treat the classifications of legal theory as a set of Procrustean beds into which every insight and every argument must be fitted, no matter what distortion of the material may be necessary. It will be obvious that this temptation must be resisted, since distorting the material in this way will necessarily distort your understanding of it.

The problem is that avoiding the kind of distortion which results from forcing ideas into Procrustean beds may deprive you of the comfortable support of a pre-existing framework and leave you with the corresponding need to develop your own 'halting and necessarily personal, but not therefore necessarily wrong, grasp on things'. (The phrase is repeated from Sprigge's comment quoted above.) The 'halting' nature of your 'grasp on things' may, of course, leave you holding positions which cannot be reconciled with each other. In other words, you may be open to the charge of inconsistency. However, unless you have a perfect understanding of the whole of legal theory, the only way to avoid the charge of inconsistency is either to abandon the study of the subject altogether (and thus avoid inconsistent understanding by having no understanding whatsoever), or to claim an understanding which is limited to an area of the subject which is small enough to enable you to avoid inconsistency. A more realistic alternative is simple acceptance that inconsistency is the price to be paid for the intellectual honesty of avoiding Procrustean beds; or, putting it the other way round, in the famous phrase of the American poet Ralph Waldo Emerson, 'a foolish consistency is the hobgoblin of little minds'.

1.7   Moral argument

1.7.1   Introduction

Legal theorists adopt many different approaches to the analysis of law, justice and morality, some of which will support, and some of which will contradict, your most basic personal beliefs and values. To take one of the most obvious examples, you may consider abortion to be, in some situations at least, perfectly legitimate; or you may consider it to be either never permissible, or permissible only in the most exceptional of circumstances. In other words, you will be talking the *moral* language of *right* and *wrong*.

More particularly, you may ask: 'how can we debate moral matters in the same way as we debate factual matters, when the former are ultimately only matters of opinion?'. This is an enormous question to which philosophers working in that part of philosophy, which is often known as *ethics* as well as *morality*, have offered very many answers. While it would be impossible to provide a full-scale survey of ethics here, it may be useful to outline, very briefly, three ways of arguing that absolute moral knowledge *is* possible, and that therefore such matters are *not* simply matters of opinion. We will then consider two further arguments. One of these rejects the possibility of moral knowledge altogether. The other constitutes a sort of half-way house by accepting the possibility of moral knowledge while nevertheless rejecting the idea that such knowledge can be *absolute*.

Before turning to the arguments themselves, it must be said that some arguments which claim to demonstrate the existence of absolute moral knowledge are based on the idea of *duty*, some on the idea of *consequences*, and some on the idea of *virtue*.

1.7.2 Arguments based on duty

Arguments based on *duty* (which in the technical vocabulary of philosophy are known as *deontological* arguments) may be broadly divided into those which rest on religion and those which do not.

Taking the religious response first, the argument is likely to be along the following lines: 'my god has revealed his (or her) truth to me (typically through a holy book, by communicating through prophets or through transcendental experience) and his (or her) truth is therefore the ultimate fact on which I base my entire life. If the truth of this fact cannot be demonstrated in the same way as the truth of "ordinary" facts can be demonstrated, that is because the ultimate facts relating to god and to his (or her) existence are not "ordinary" facts'. While believers will, of course, be wholly satisfied with this type of answer, unbelievers will remain unmoved. Two points may be made in passing.

First, some believers do claim to be able to prove the existence of their god by means of rational argument. However, the most strikingly common characteristic of such proofs is that they are much more effective at bolstering the beliefs of those who are already convinced than at delivering others from their unbelief.

Secondly, it is a common observation that religion breeds disagreement. Sometimes these disagreements are based on disputes as to the legitimacy of religious authority (as is the case in Christianity between Roman Catholicism and Protestantism). Sometimes they are based on different interpretations of holy texts and doctrines. However, whatever the source of any particular disagreement between believers, the unbeliever will commonly point out that the wide range of opinions, even within a single religion, is a curious characteristic of any system which claims to deliver ultimate truth.

Even those who believe in a god have to confront a problem which has been recognized since at least the time of Plato (c. 429–347 BCE). Does their god approve of what is good; or is what is good good because their god approves of it? If the former, it follows that the quality of goodness existed before their god approved of its manifestations; which leads to the conclusion that the source of goodness, as distinct from its recognition, lies outside the activities of their god. If the latter, then (at least in the case of an all-powerful god) the quality of goodness is arbitrary, in the sense that their god could have conferred his or her approval differently in the first place and could change his or her mind at any time subsequently.

Those who find religious answers unsatisfactory may seek purely rational answers to the moral questions. One of the most influential examples of such answers is provided by the German philosopher Immanuel Kant (1724–

1804). In particular, Kant argues that the only thing which is absolutely and unconditionally good is the good will, with all other things which are conventionally regarded as being good (such as wealth and health) being good only to the extent that they are used in the pursuit of good ends. Clearly, this leads us to the question of how we can identify the good will. Kant's answer is that there is a pre-existing moral law, which humans, being rational and possessed of free will, can identify by using their reason and which they need to identify in order to know how they should exercise their free will.

> '[Kant] takes the existence of an ordinary moral consciousness for granted.... It is the moral consciousness of this ordinary human nature which provides the philosopher with an object for analysis.... The philosopher's task is... to ask what character our moral concepts and precepts must have to make morality as it is possible.... Science is what it is, morality is what it is, and there's an end on't.' (Alasdair MacIntyre, *A Short History of Ethics*, 2nd edn, 1998, p. 191.)

It is important to realize that, for Kant, the moral law simply *is*, and our intellectual endeavours merely lead us to its discovery. In other words, we do *not* create it.

These ideas lead Kant to identify a universal moral law, which he proceeds to call the *categorical imperative*. This is *categorical* because it is *unconditional* or *absolute*, rather than *conditional* or *contingent*, and is *imperative* because it commands obedience. Despite the fact that the categorical imperative is a single idea, Kant formulates it in two ways. One formulation is that you should *make the maxim of your action such that it could be the maxim of a general action*. In other words, the *maxim* (or *motive* or *justification*) on which you rely must be such that everyone else could also rely on it; or, even more simply, it must be capable of being *universalized*. The other formulation is that *people must be treated as ends in themselves and not as mere means to ends*.

Many people find Kant's ideas attractive because they make a rational framework available to those who either have no religious belief, or at least regard whatever belief they – and other people – may have, as being purely subjective. However, Kant's ideas are not unproblematic. Two points may usefully be made.

First, Kant argues that the moral quality of an act (or, in other words, whether an act is performed with a good will) depends *solely* on the maxim underlying it. So, for example, I act morally if I perform an act of charity because I think I am under a duty to do so. On the other hand, I act immorally if I act out of self-interest (for example, giving large sums of money to charity in the hope of obtaining a knighthood), or even if I act simply out of compassion (despite the fact that many other systems of morality would rank compassion very highly).

Secondly, Kantian morality may lead to results which offend many people's intuitions. For example, we have a duty to tell the truth, because social life would be impossible if everybody considered themselves to be at liberty to tell lies whenever it suited them to do so. Therefore, telling the truth is morally good, even if – to take a standard example – it means telling a homicidal maniac where he will find someone whom he wishes to kill. (The case of *R v Registrar-General ex parte Smith* [1991] 2 All ER 88, discussed at p. 58, provides a good example of a decision which would have gone the other way if the court had been thinking along Kantian lines.)

1.7.3 Arguments based on consequences

If you conclude that duty-based approaches are less than wholly satisfactory, you may be tempted by *consequentialist* alternatives, which hold that moral quality depends on *consequences* rather than *duties*. So, if we return to the homicidal maniac example, the consequence of telling a lie as to the whereabouts of the intended victim are better than the consequences of telling the truth, and therefore, to that extent at least, it is morally better to lie than to tell the truth.

We will give more detailed consideration to some aspects of consequentialism in Chapter 10, but the general idea may be illustrated as follows. If a highway authority finds itself with limited resources and many towns and villages needing by-passes to be built, should it not prioritize those schemes which will provide the greatest benefit? In other words, do not the consequences indicate the best way for public money to be allocated? However, we must consider three standard objections to consequentialism.

First, it may be argued that at least some consequentialist conclusions are counter-intuitive and must, therefore, be wrong. For example, consequentialism may be used to justify scapegoating an innocent minority for the benefit of the majority. (See p. 166.)

Secondly, the fact that the future is inevitably uncertain makes it impossible to identify all the possible consequences of all possible acts in order to choose the one with the most beneficial consequences.

Thirdly, consequentialism may require us to evaluate comparisons in ways which are difficult or even impossible. For example, adapting the example of by-pass building, the issue may be whether even a single by-pass should be built. Suppose experience shows that high-speed traffic on by-passes produces a relatively small number of relatively serious accidents, while low-speed traffic in town and village centres produces more, but less serious, accidents. Although, of course, there will be many factors to take into account, consequentialism requires us to say whether (taking some hypothetical figures) two fractured skulls a year are better or worse than a hundred broken legs. (Admittedly, those who analyse law in economic terms (see pp. 167–171) will try to calculate the answer in terms of the cost of state benefits, lost working days and so on. However, quite clearly, there are some consequences which cannot be convincingly valued in purely financial terms.)

1.7.4 Arguments based on virtue

If you find neither arguments based on *duty*, nor those based on *consequences*, sufficiently compelling, you may be attracted to arguments based on *virtue*, which may be seen as being both distinct from, yet in a sense complementary to, the other two types of argument. The origins of such arguments may be traced back to Aristotle's *Nichomachean Ethics*, which approaches the question of morality in terms of the kind of values, qualities and activities which enable human beings to flourish. While this approach is, in essence, conceptually distinct from arguments based on duty, it can nevertheless be seen as one way of identifying what an individual's duty should be in specific circumstances. Similarly, while virtue theory is, in essence, distinct from arguments based on consequences, it can nevertheless be seen as one way of identifying consequences (both favourable and unfavourable) in the sense that values, qualities and activities which promote human flourishing are better than those which do not do so.

A major difficulty with virtue theory is that there is no universally agreed list of virtues, the pursuit of which will promote human flourishing, although there may be some obvious candidates for inclusion, such as charity, modesty, industriousness, courage and loyalty. However, even some virtues which may appear, at first sight, to be universally acceptable may, on closer examination, prove problematic. For example, while most people would accept that charitable giving is virtuous, even this apparently obvious identification of virtue may conceal serious and legitimate disputes. Pursuing the same example, does virtue lie in, say, giving money to an alcoholic who is living rough, rather than giving the same money to a charity dedicated to providing shelters and other facilities which may increase the chances of such derelicts reclaiming control over their own lives? Similarly, since we are using the word *virtue* in the sense of the promotion of human flourishing, can we say that it includes the enjoyment of good food and drink; or is all such consumption which exceeds the needs of the body merely gluttonous? In short, may not the intuitively attractive appeal to virtue become all too easily nothing more than a device to provide a cloak of respectability for our individual preferences and prejudices?

In terms of the legal theories discussed in this book, the effects of virtue theory may be discerned in John Finnis' theory of natural law (see Chapter 6). Although it must be emphasized that Finnis does not explicitly rest his argument on virtue theory, he does rely heavily on certain things which he identifies as *basic forms of human flourishing* or *human goods*. While these do not, in themselves, generate moral obligations, they are nevertheless an integral part of an argument which does claim to do so. Dworkin's theory based on value provides another comparator. (See pp. 127–134.)

1.7.5   Arguments rejecting moral knowledge altogether

One argument which rejects the possibility of moral knowledge altogether is known as *emotivism*. As the name suggests, the content of the argument is essentially that statements that purport to be about morality are, when properly understood, nothing more than statements of emotion. So, if I say abortion is wrong, all I really mean is that I disapprove of it, while if I say it is right all I really mean is that I approve of it. It is obvious, therefore, why emotivism is sometimes called the *boo–hurray* theory.

Attractive though emotivism may be to those who are perplexed by the difficulties flowing from both duty-based and consequentialist arguments, it nevertheless also offends some of our most basic intuitions. Is it really impossible to say, for example, that human sacrifice, or genocide, is wrong? Can we really do no more than express our personal disapproval?

A further common objection to any argument that rejects the possibility of having knowledge of morality, and therefore the possibility of making statements about morality, is that the statement that we cannot make statements about morality is itself a statement about morality. In other words, that statement is *self-refuting*.

However, there is an equally standard reply to this objection, which is based on Bertrand Russell's *Theory of Types*. The argument may be summarized thus:

> 'A principle must be accepted by which any expression which refers to *all* of some type must itself be regarded as being of a different and higher type than that to which it refers. Thus there is a hierarchy of types and a rule that they cannot be mixed.' (J.C. Hicks, *The Liar Paradox in Legal Reasoning* [1971] CLJ 275 at p. 279.)

Whether you find this convincing depends on whether you fall within that category of people for whom 'this procedure of proposing a new rule... appears... to be an *ad hoc* manoeuvre and therefore an evasion of the problem rather than a fundamental solution of it'. (*Ibid.*)

1.7.6　Arguments rejecting absolute moral knowledge

Even if you are unwilling to embrace emotivism, you may be tempted by *relativism*. The central idea of relativism is that what is morally right and wrong depends on the society in the context of which the question is being asked. So, for example, monogamy may be right in a Judaeo-Christian society, but polygamy may be right in other societies with other religious beliefs and values.

This approach is comforting to those who are unhappy with the kind of cultural imperialism which leads those in a politically dominant position to impose their values on others (or, if unable to do so, at least to judge others by reference to their own values). However, once again, the argument offends some of our most basic instincts. Even if we have no real problem with polygamy, and even if we are willing to stretch a point in order to accept that there are (or may have been) societies in which human sacrifice need not be regarded as immoral, are we really willing to say the same about genocide? Could Auschwitz and Belsen ever be morally acceptable?

1.7.7　Conclusion

As we have seen, all the views we have considered are open to significant objections. Nevertheless, most people find themselves (perhaps more than anything else as a matter of temperament or background, or both) inclined to favour one rather than the others, even though this means having to live with substantial counter-arguments; and some people even manage to do so with a striking degree of self-confidence. However, two final points may usefully be made.

First, in purely academic terms, it is important to have at least some grasp of the various possible arguments.

Secondly, many people accept that (whichever way their personal inclinations may lead them) this is an area in which an element of self-doubt is an integral part of any intelligent position. Those who are inclined to accept this view may well recall Oliver Cromwell's entreaty to the General Assembly of the Church of Scotland: 'I beseech you, in the bowels of Christ, think it possible you may be mistaken'. (*Letter of August 3, 1650.*) (It is, of course, a nice irony that his precise choice of words indicates how difficult it can be to distance yourself from your own personal beliefs.) Alternatively, or additionally, they may recall Tennyson's view (see *In Memoriam, xcv*) that

There lives more faith in honest doubt,
Believe me, than in half the creeds,

the spirit of which applies equally to the secular context as to the religious one within which it was written. Or they may simply be among those who find Procrustean beds even more uncomfortable than inconsistency. (See p. 6.)

Finally, surely nobody would doubt that an absolute conviction that you are right is no guarantee that you are so. As Oliver Wendell Holmes puts it, 'certitude is not the test of certainty. We have been cocksure of many things that were not so'. (*Natural Law* (1918) 32 Harv LR 40 at p. 40.) Doubting the possibility of certainty anyway, he continues:

'I do not see any rational ground... for being dissatisfied unless we are assured... that the ultimates of a little creature on this little earth are the last word on the unimaginable whole.' (*Op. cit.*, p. 43.)

1.8 Why study legal theory?

The discussion of the nature of legal theory which you have just read, and any number of similar discussions which you may read elsewhere, will leave many students saying 'So what? How will all this help me when I am a lawyer?'. You may even pray in aid Cotterrell's comment that 'no-one could suggest that legal theory has at any time been necessary to help the lawyer earn a living in everyday practice'. (*The Politics of Jurisprudence*, 2nd edn, 2003, p. 223.) But the key word here is *necessary*, for there can be equally little doubt that cases do arise where practitioners with a knowledge of legal theory are better equipped than those who lack it. (See in particular but by no means exclusively, the cases discussed in Chapter 11, dealing with the relationship between law and morality.) Indeed, it may even be argued that *without* a knowledge of legal theory there is a sense in which you cannot credibly claim to be a lawyer, as distinct from someone who knows some laws: 'while legal science is capable of being intelligently learnt, legal facts are capable only of being committed to memory'. (T.E. Holland, *The Elements of Jurisprudence*, 13th edn, 1924, p. 4.)

In similar vein, Holmes, having noted that the English meaning of *jurisprudence* 'is confined to the broadest rules and most fundamental conceptions', adds that 'one mark of a great lawyer is that he sees the application of the broadest rules'. He proceeds to illustrate this basic truth with a practical anecdote.

> 'There is a story of a Vermont justice of the peace before whom a suit was brought by one farmer against another for breaking a churn. The justice took time to consider, and then said that he had looked through the statutes and could find nothing about churns, and gave judgment for the defendant.... If a man goes into law it pays to be a master of it, and to be a master of it means to look straight through all the dramatic incidents and to discern the true basis [for predicting what the court will do if the matter ever comes before it].' (*The Path of the Law* (1897) 8 Harv LR, pp. 474–475.)

Developing this point requires a return to the comment which concluded Section 1.2, that the study of legal theory takes you beyond *laws* and into *law*. Making the point more explicitly in relation to professional practice, the value of a knowledge of legal theory lies in the fact that it provides a principled overview of law as a whole, which enables practitioners to relate a large number of individualized statements of legal doctrine to, and evaluate them in the light of, each other. Practitioners with a knowledge of legal theory will be able to construct arguments, and counter opposing arguments, with more confidence, and with a greater likelihood of success, than would otherwise be the case. As Holmes puts it:

> 'The remoter and more general aspects of the law are those which give it universal interest. It is through them that you not only become a great master in your calling, but connect your subject with the universe and catch an echo of the infinite, a glimpse of its unfathomable process, a hint of the universal law.' (*Op. cit.*, p. 478.)

More polemically, if less poetically, members of the critical legal studies movement (which is considered further in Chapter 9) regard a knowledge of legal theory as being unequivocally essential to practitioners. Thus Alan Thomson challenges the view (which he takes to be prevalent among both students and practitioners), that legal theory is marginal, and that the only thing which really matters, even for a radical lawyer, is to be a good lawyer:

> 'Critical legal theory must... make explicit the implicit theory on which the existing legal rules, institutions and practices are based, with the aim of showing that since that theory cannot support what it claims it can, the world could be otherwise... [and] ... critical legal theory attempts to reconnect law with everyday political and moral argument, struggles and experiences, with all their attendant incoherences,

uncertainties and indeterminacies. Most importantly, in rejecting a view of law as the expression of reason, critical legal theorists reveal, in different ways, law as the expression and medium of power.' (*Foreword: Critical Approaches to Law: Who Needs Legal Theory?*, in Ian Grigg-Spall and Paddy Ireland (eds), *The Critical Lawyers' Handbook*, 1992, pp. 2–3.)

Ronald Dworkin, who is by no stretch of the imagination a member of the critical legal studies movement, goes even further than Thomson, arguing that legal theory and legal practice are, in fact, two aspects of a single, seamless, whole. (See p. 121.)

Finally, however, although it is easy to justify the study of legal theory by reference to the demands of legal practice, it is not necessary to do so:

'It is perfectly proper to regard and study the law simply as a great anthropological document. It is proper to resort to it to discover what ideals of society have been strong enough to reach that final form of expression, or what have been the changes in dominant ideals from century to century. It is proper to study it as an exercise in the morphology and transformation of human ideas.' (Oliver Wendell Holmes, *Law in Science and Science in Law* (1899) 12 Harv LR p. 444.)

Summary

▶ Legal theory involves a progression from the study of *laws* to the study of *law*.

▶ Differences of terminology between *legal theory, jurisprudence* and *legal philosophy/ philosophy of law* are largely matters of personal taste.

▶ The study of legal theory involves the use of sources other than the law, including works on philosophy and political theory.

▶ All legal theories must be seen in the context of the historical period and the culture within which their authors were working, as well as within the context of the questions which their authors were seeking to answer.

▶ Legal theories are classified in a variety of ways, but all classificatory schemes are only aids to understanding and not substitutes for it.

▶ There is no universally accepted way of identifying what is morally right and what is morally wrong, but three of the major approaches to these questions involve theories that are either duty-based, consequence-based or virtue-based.

▶ Legal theory can be relevant to practitioners of law when it makes them think about the basis of what they are doing. It also has its own intrinsic value as a branch of the study of ideas.

Further reading

Cotterrell, Roger, *The Politics of Jurisprudence: A Critical Introduction to Legal Philosophy*, 2nd edn, 2003

Friedmann, W., *Legal Theory*, 5th edn, 1967

Hicks, J.C., *The Liar Paradox in Legal Reasoning* [1971] CLJ 275

Holland, T.E., *The Elements of Jurisprudence*, 13th edn, 1924

Holmes, Oliver Wendell, *Law in Science and Science in Law* (1899) 12 Harv LR 443

Holmes, Oliver Wendell, *Natural Law* (1918) 32 Harv LR 40

Holmes, Oliver Wendell, *The Path of the Law* (1897) 8 Harv LR 457

MacIntyre, Alasdair, *A Short History of Ethics*, 2nd edn, 1998 (republished 2002)

Sprigge, T.L.S., *The Rational Foundations of Ethics*, 1990

Thomson, Alan, *Foreword* in Grigg-Spall, Ian and Ireland, Paddy (eds) *The Critical Lawyers' Handbook*, 1992

Chapter 2

An overview of the relationship between law and morality

2.1 Introduction

Pausing only to repeat the warning against the dangers of being seduced into Procrustean beds (see p. 6), this chapter begins with an overview of two of the historically standard classifications of legal theories, namely *natural law* and *positivism*. At this stage, all that need be said is that the distinction between these two schools of legal theory centres on their differing views of the extent, if any, to which law depends on morality. The chapter then considers the opposite side of the same coin, namely the extent, if any, to which morality depends on law, before discussing the functions of law. The final part of the chapter presents a famous (but fictitious case), which serves to bring into focus a variety of arguments about the nature of law and the judicial function, including many of the elements which have been introduced in the earlier parts of the chapter.

Much of the material which is introduced in this chapter will be referred to again throughout this book, but it may be worth specifically signposting Chapters 3, 4, 5 and 6, which contain more detailed discussions of some of the most important theories of law from both the natural law and positivist traditions, together with Chapter 9, which discusses some critical analyses of the nature and functions of law from an explicitly political perspective, and Chapter 11, which deals with the question of whether (and, if so, when) it is justifiable to use the law as a means of trying to compel individuals to obey moral precepts.

2.2 Natural law and positivist perspectives on morality and law

2.2.1 Introduction

The terms *natural law* and *positivism* each embrace a variety of different legal theories. Reduced to its simplest, the distinction between them is that natural law theories argue that the status of *law* depends not simply on the fact that it has been laid down in whatever way or ways are recognized by the legal system of which it is part, but also on some additional factor or factors external to that system. Positivist theories, on the other hand, argue that the status of *law* attaches to anything which has been laid down (or *posited*) as law in whatever way or ways is or are recognized by the legal system in question. The ways in which laws may be laid down may, of course, vary widely from one legal system to another, but will commonly include one (or more) of the following: judicial pronouncements, statutes, decrees, delegated legislation and treaty articles.

The distinction between the two types of theory is often expressed by saying that *natural law* theories are *normative*, while *positivist* theories are *analytical*. Nothing much need be said about the statement that some theories are analytical, since analysis is simply the process of breaking something down into its constituent parts. In other words, analytical theories seek to identify the ingredients, which, when they come together, result in something which we call *law*.

However, the meaning of the word *norm* and its derivative form *normative* may be worth considering a little more closely. Beyond the fact that the word *norm* comes from the Latin word *norma*, meaning a stonemason's set-square (which is, of course, a device for ensuring that things are as they ought to be) there lies the point that, in the vocabulary of philosophy, a norm is a *rule* or an *authoritative standard*. Another way of putting it is that a norm is an *ought* proposition, in the sense that it prescribes what *ought*, or *ought not*, to happen, as distinct from being merely an *is* proposition, which describes what actually *is*, or *is not*, the case, or what *does*, or *does not*, happen in fact.

In the context of legal theory, therefore, *natural law* theories may be labelled *normative*, because they deal with what law *ought* to be, while *positivist* theories may be labelled *analytical* because they deal with what law *is*. The validity of this distinction is, of course, in no way undermined by the commonplace observation that the results of a positivist analysis may be used as the basis of arguments for law reform.

In one sense, of course, law as a whole is inescapably a normative undertaking (since it tells people what they ought, or ought not, to do), even though the language in which laws are articulated does not always make this quality explicit. For example, a statutory provision which states 'It shall be an offence to do X' is normative because it is stating a rule (or an authoritative standard) as to how people ought to behave, even though the word *ought* does not appear within the statutory text.

However, it is essential to maintain in your mind a clear distinction between this kind of normative statement (which relates to the fact that a relevant legal text exists) and the kind which deals with what the law ought to be (which deals with what may broadly be termed moral matters).

It will be useful to consider the essence of both natural law and positivist theories before proceeding to a closer examination of each.

2.2.2   The essence of natural law

It is one thing to say that natural law theories are distinguished by their recourse to factors which are external to the positivist scheme of things; it is another to identify those factors. The short answer is that different natural lawyers have recourse to different external factors. However, this must be amplified by saying that all natural lawyers would probably agree that, because law may, in the final analysis, involve the coercive power of the state, the basis of the law should at least be moral, because otherwise the state will be a party to immoral conduct.

Some natural lawyers look to religious beliefs, while others are content to derive their moral foundation from observable facts and certain logical inferences which, they claim, may be drawn from them. The Stoic school of philosophy in ancient Greece, for example, taught that everything has its own nature, and that it is in the nature of humankind to be rational. Therefore, according to the Stoics, humankind ought to live according to reason, because to do otherwise would be contrary to nature. One aspect of this argument is that the criteria for assessing the validity of human laws can be identified by the exercise of human reason. Even those lawyers who are committed to a particular religious belief may express themselves in rationalistic terms. Thus St Thomas Aquinas (the pre-eminent 13th century Christian theologian whose theory we examine more closely in Chapter 3), together with certain other theorists within the natural law tradition, regards natural law as the 'dictate of right reason'.

By way of refinement to what has been said so far, however, it must be added that some natural law theories do not regard external factors as essential *constituents* of valid human laws, but merely as *criteria* for *evaluating* such laws. Friedmann distinguishes these *constitutive* and *evaluative* versions thus:

> 'The most important distinction would appear to be that between natural law as a higher law, which invalidates any inconsistent positive law, and natural law as an ideal to which positive law ought to conform without its legal validity being affected. Broadly speaking, ancient and medieval law theories are of the first type; modern law theories are of the second. This change coincides on the whole with the rise of the modern state and its claim to absolute sovereignty.' (*Legal Theory*, 5th edn, 1967, p. 96.)

2.2.3   The essence of positivism

H.L.A. Hart, himself a leading 20th century positivist, offers the following overview of positivism:

> 'It may help to identify five (there may be more) meanings of 'positivism' bandied about in contemporary jurisprudence:
>
> (1) the contention that laws are commands of human beings;
> (2) the contention that there is no necessary connection between law and morals or law as it is and law as it ought to be;
> (3) the contention that the analysis (or study of the meaning) of legal concepts is (a) worth pursuing and (b) to be distinguished from historical inquiries into the causes or origins of laws, from sociological inquiries into the relation of law and other social phenomena, and from the criticism or appraisal of law whether in terms of morals, social aims, 'functions', or otherwise;

(4) the contention that a legal system is a 'closed logical system' in which correct legal decisions can be deduced by logical means from predetermined rules without reference to social aims, policies, moral standards; and

(5) the contention that moral judgments cannot be established or defended, as statements of fact can, by rational argument, evidence, or proof ('noncognitivism' in ethics).' (*Positivism and the Separation of Law and Morals*, first published in (1958) 71 Harv LR 593 and reprinted in *Essays in Jurisprudence and Philosophy*, 1983, in which see p. 57, n. 25.)

Without seeking in any way to challenge Hart's list of possible meanings of *positivism*, the second (which because of its insistence on separating law and morals is often called the *separation thesis*) has been called 'the quintessence of legal positivism'. (Howard Davies and David Holdcroft, *Jurisprudence: Texts and Commentary*, 1991, p. 3.)

However, three points must be made about positivism if we are to avoid serious misunderstanding.

First, just as there is an internal subdivision within the field of natural law theory, so there has developed an internal subdivision within the field of positivist legal theory. The basis of the subdivision within positivist legal theory is, of course, necessarily different from that within natural law theory. More particularly, the categories are usually known as *strict* (or *strong* or *exclusive*) and *soft* (or *weak* or *inclusive*) positivism (with the *soft* version sometimes also being called *incorporationism*).

Strict positivism insists on observing the separation thesis at all times. In the words of one of its leading proponents:

'A jurisprudential theory is acceptable only if its tests for identifying the content of the law and determining its existence depend *exclusively* on the facts of human behaviour capable of being described in value-neutral terms, and applied without resort to moral argument.' (Emphasis added. Joseph Raz, *The Authority of Law*, 2nd edn, 2009, pp. 39–40.)

By way of contrast, soft positivism accepts the possibility of taking moral factors into account when identifying the law. Unfortunately, however, and even leaving aside the differing terminology which may be used to identify each category, that terminology is not always used consistently by all commentators. For example, W.J. Waluchow, one of the leading advocates of soft (or, as he calls it, *inclusive*) positivism, says:

'A distinguishing feature of inclusive positivism is its claim that standards of political morality, that is the morality we use to evaluate, justify and criticize social institutions and their activities and products, e.g. laws, can and do in various ways figure in attempts to determine the existence, *content and meaning* of valid law.' (Emphasis added. *Inclusive Legal Positivism*, 1994, p. 2.)

Another commentator puts essentially the same point in a slightly more cautious way by arguing that there are two versions of soft positivism, with one being limited to questions concerning the *existence* of valid law, while the other also extends to questions concerning its *content*. (See Eleni Mithrophanous, *Soft Positivism* (1997) 17 OJLS 620.)

But however this view is expressed, some people would regard it as something of an overstatement, since *all* positivists would accept that at least some moral factors, such as fairness and justice, *may* be taken into account when determining the *content* and *meaning* of law. For example, in relation to the *content* of the law, even strict positivists would accept that, in a case where the authorities are unclear, a judge who has to decide whether or not a particular legal doctrine exists may legitimately prefer a conclusion which produces a fair or just result to one which does not do so. Similarly, in relation to the *meaning* of the law, even strict positivists would accept that, in a case where a statute or a previous case may be read as having two alternative meanings, a judge may legitimately prefer a meaning which produces a fair or just result to one which does not do so.

A more limited statement of the essence of soft positivism is simply that, adopting the language in which Mithrophanous states the first of her versions of the doctrine, it 'allows that morality *can* figure in the determination of the *existence* of valid law'. (Emphasis added, *op. cit.*) It is by reference to this usage of the term that, for example, Hart accepts that his theory is a form of soft positivism. (*The Concept of Law*, 2nd edn, 1994, p. 250.)

Secondly, soft positivism's concession that moral factors *can* be relevant when identifying the existence of law must not be taken to be a wholesale surrender to the constitutive strand of the natural law tradition. In particular, even the softest of positivists would be likely to maintain the distinction between morals and law for the purpose of limiting to the moral sphere the power of those (such as religious leaders) whose moral authority has not been endorsed by any form of law-making.

Suppose, for example, that the predominant religion in a given society teaches that divorce is contrary to the law of the god which that religion serves, and is therefore immoral. If, as Friedmann suggests is typically the case with classical and mediaeval natural law theories (see p. 19), this moral teaching is allowed to invalidate any positive law which permits divorce, the effect is to allow believers in that religion to enforce their beliefs upon non-believers. If, on the other hand, law and morality are treated separately, adherents of the predominant religion may, of course, campaign against the introduction of divorce laws, or for their repeal where they already exist. However, the *validity* (as distinct from the *desirability*) of either new or existing laws will not be open to question.

Those who wish to remain untrammelled by other people's moral convictions will sympathize with Oliver Wendell Holmes' comment that

> 'the jurists who believe in natural law seem... to be in that naïve state of mind that accepts what has been familiar and accepted by them and their neighbours as something that must be accepted by all men everywhere.' (*Natural Law* (1918) 32 Harv LR 41.)

Thirdly, it is not merely of some importance but of fundamental importance to emphasize that even the strictest positivist separation of law and morals does not indicate any lack of concern about the morality of law, but merely an insistence that the two questions (*is it law?* and *is it good law?*) are essentially different from each other. (Moving beyond the field of law, it can scarcely be denied that many highly undesirable things undoubtedly exist, while many highly desirable ones do not.) However, without seeking to detract from what has already been said, the essential point of the positivist argument (at least in its strict form) is that allowing moral factors to enter into the identification of law will, when such factors are so open to dispute (see pp. 7–13), always introduce an unacceptable degree of uncertainty into a question which lies at the very heart of the legitimacy of the exercise of power by, or on behalf of, the state.

All in all, therefore, it may seem that anyone with any liberal leanings must regard the debate between natural lawyers and positivists as open-and-shut, with the latter being the clear winners. However, two points commonly arise in response to this reaction.

First, it is appropriate to recall (from p. 19) Friedmann's point that modern natural law theories tend to present themselves as serving merely to evaluate the law, rather than to constitute it. On this basis, such theories are really theories of justice rather than law; and few people would question the propriety of theorizing on the subject of justice. (Theories of justice are considered in Chapter 10.)

Secondly, and in the alternative, many people have a very deep-seated instinct according to which the law's reasonable claim to be obeyed means that measures which are morally abhorrent, such as many of the laws of Nazi Germany, ought not to be granted the status of law in the first place. This second point leads us from the question of the validity of, to the question of the duty of obedience to, law.

2.2.4 The duty of obedience to law: the example of the Nazi *grudge-informer* cases

Once we have decided whether something which is alleged to be a law does actually have that status, it is tempting to think that the answer to the next question – namely *must it be obeyed?* – follows automatically. In practice, however, the question of the limits of obedience to law can be very complex.

The starting point is to notice that there are, potentially at least, three questions, beginning with *is this provision law?* If the answer to this is *yes*, there remains the second question, namely, *is it good law* in the sense of being *just*, or *morally defensible?* If the answer to this second question is *no*, a third question arises, namely, *is there nevertheless a non-legal* (or *collateral*) *duty to comply with it?*

The answers which natural law theorists have given to this question provide one of the pervading issues of Chapters 3 and 6, but for the moment the question may be usefully considered in the context of what are generally known as the

Nazi grudge-informer cases, which arose from Nazi laws which criminalized criticism of the regime. (See H.O. Pappe, *On the Validity of Judicial Decisions in the Nazi Era* (1960) 23 MLR 260.)

In two cases, which were totally independent of each other, soldiers in the German army during the Second World War criticized the Nazi regime to their wives, who reported them to the authorities. Both men were convicted under laws enacted by the Nazi regime and were initially condemned to death, although both in fact survived. After the war, the men brought prosecutions (for unlawful deprivation of liberty, contrary to para. 239 of the German Criminal Code of 1871) against both their wives and the judges who had convicted and sentenced them.

In the first case, the Provincial Court of Appeal took the view that the relevant Nazi enactments were 'highly iniquitous laws which, especially because of their severe penalties... were considered to be terror laws by the great majority of the German people. However, they *cannot* be held to be statutes violating natural law'. (Original emphasis. *Op. cit.*, p. 263.) It follows that the judge of the military court should be acquitted since he had acted within his jurisdiction, but it did not follow that the wife should be acquitted. More particularly, she had been motivated by malice towards her husband and must have realized that informing the authorities 'was contrary to the sound conscience and sense of justice of all decent human beings'. (*Ibid.*) Although 'the decision is certainly not clearly reasoned... it is obvious that the court decidedly did not invalidate a [Nazi] statute... ' (*Ibid.*)

In passing, it may be observed that, quite apart from the question of the validity of the Nazi law, the decision looks rather odd to an English lawyer, who is accustomed to thinking of a defendant's *motive* – as distinct from *intention* – as being generally relevant only to the exercise of the discretion to prosecute and to the quantification of sentence, rather than to the substantive question of guilt.

In the second case, the Federal Supreme Court said that the question of the legality of a court decision must be answered uniformly for all those concerned. In other words, in a situation such as this, either both the judge and the wife, or neither of them, should be convicted. On the present facts, both should be convicted, because it was an essential element of the offence that the criticism must have been public; and it is not clear that an intra-marital communication satisfies this test. Moreover, even if there were an offence it would have been towards the bottom end of the scale of seriousness, which meant that the sentence was disproportionate. On this analysis, it follows that the wife was guilty because it was her participation which had brought the husband to court in the first place, while the judge was guilty because he had failed to exercise his judicial discretion properly.

The first of these two cases gave rise to an exchange between Hart and Lon L. Fuller. (See, respectively, *Postivism and the Separation of Law and Morals*, cited at p. 20, and *Positivism and Fidelity to Law: a Reply to Professor Hart* (1958) 71 Harv LR 630.) Unfortunately, the debate was based on an inaccurate account of the case contained in volume 64 of the *Harvard Law Review*. According to this account, the Provincial Court of Appeal held that the relevant Nazi enactments had not been truly law at all, whereas, as Pappe points out, this was not in fact what the court had said.

Proceeding on the basis of this account, however, Hart accepts that the wife had committed 'an outrageously immoral act'. Nevertheless, he argues that retrospective legislation should have been used, rather than achieving the same result through judicial means.

> 'Odious as retrospective criminal legislation and punishment may be, to have pursued it openly in this case would at least have had the merits of candour. It would have made plain that... a choice had to be made between two evils, that of leaving her unpunished and that of sacrificing a very precious principle of morality endorsed by most legal systems.' (*Op. cit.*, pp. 76–77.)

He concedes that such statutes are objectionable in principle, but argues that they do at least have the merit of making it obvious what price is being paid, in terms of compromising on principle, in order to attain the desired end.

On the other hand, Fuller sees the existence of a legal system as being a matter of degree, and therefore expresses himself in more cautious terms. We shall consider Fuller's version of natural law in Chapter 6, but for the moment it is sufficient to observe that he identifies the purpose of law as being the promotion of order. He goes on to argue that it is necessary to distinguish between societies which are characterized simply by order, and those which are characterized by good order. In this context, moral quality is an intrinsic element in the status as law. He develops the point thus:

> 'When we realize that order itself is something that must be worked for, it becomes apparent that the existence of a legal system, even a bad or evil legal system, is always a matter of degree. When we recognize this simple fact of everyday legal experience, it becomes impossible to dismiss the problems presented by the Nazi regime with a simple assertion: "Under the Nazis there was law, even if it was bad law." We have instead to inquire how much of a legal system survived the general debasement and perversion of all forms of social order that occurred under the Nazi rule.' (*Op. cit.*, p. 646.)

However, despite their differing analyses which reflect their positivist and natural law approaches respectively, at a purely practical level, Fuller agrees with Hart that retrospective legislation should have been enacted, although he justifies this course of conduct in somewhat different terms:

> 'My reason... is not that this is the most nearly lawful way of making unlawful what was once law. Rather I would see such a statute as a way of symbolizing a sharp break with the past, as a means of isolating a kind of cleanup operation from the normal functioning of the judicial process.' (*Op. cit.*, p. 661.)

The inaccuracy of the report on which Hart and Fuller based their exchange means that we must regard that exchange as being based on a hypothetical case rather than an actual one, but this technique is not uncommon in legal theory and certainly does not render the ensuing discussion any the less worthwhile.

It will be obvious that cases such as these seldom come before the English courts, but the Court of Appeal's decision in *Bucocke v Greater London Council* [1971] 2 All ER 254 does raise the question of the limits of the duty of obedience to law, albeit in a less emotive context.

Reduced to its simplest terms, the case raised the question of whether a Chief Fire Officer could lawfully issue an order requiring drivers of fire appliances to pass through red traffic lights (provided they observed certain precautions while doing so), when, as a matter of law, those drivers were bound by red traffic lights in the same way as all other motorists.

The Court of Appeal, led by Lord Denning MR, took the view that the order was lawful, and that therefore firefighters who refused to travel on appliances whose drivers were willing to 'shoot the lights' were properly subject to disciplinary proceedings.

The court accepted that no moral blame could be attached to a driver who, while exercising due caution, 'shot the lights', but was confident that in practice the matter could be dealt with by the police exercising the discretion not to prosecute, with the long-stop power of the court to order an absolute discharge if, for some reason, a prosecution were to be brought in circumstances where no moral blame attached to the driver. (Despite this conclusion, the court expressed the view that the law ought to be changed so that the drivers would not – even technically – be committing offences. This was effected by the Traffic Signs and General Directions Regulations, 1975.)

2.2.5   Are the natural law and positivist traditions mutually exclusive?

The final question for this part of this chapter is whether the natural law and positivist traditions are mutually exclusive. The best answer takes us back to Procrustean beds (see p. 6) and the view that rigid compartmentalization is more likely to hinder understanding than to promote it. More particularly, if the range of possible theories is seen as forming a continuous spectrum, with the most uncompromising version of constitutive natural law at one end and the hardest of hard positivism at the other, it will be clear that various intermediate positions are possible, through, for example, the evaluative versions of natural law and soft positivism.

Nevertheless, whatever the range of possible positions may be, the one which each individual adopts is likely to be essentially a matter of belief, and is therefore unlikely to be susceptible to change through rational argument. Barney Reynolds neatly catches this point:

'The age-old battle for supremacy between natural law and positivism is, at root, far from conceptual. Stripped of the differences invented by one, when interpreting the other, we are left with a conflict of background ideological and philosophical beliefs.... Natural law... involves the attempted imposition of values on others and often the hijacking of the coercive nature of law to achieve this.... Positivism also connotes beliefs, but in a different fashion. It is linked to a belief that law and non-legal normative values ought to be seen as being separate, perhaps for analytic purity and therefore for fundamental philosophical and/or ideological reasons, or for those fundamental reasons pure and simple.' (*Natural Law versus Positivism: The Fundamental Conflict* (1993) 13 OJLS 441.)

Or, as Oliver Wendell Holmes puts it even more succinctly, 'deep-seated preferences cannot be argued about – you cannot argue a man into liking a glass of beer'. (*Op. cit.*, p. 41.)

2.3 The dependence of morality on law

The second stage of the discussion of the relationship between morality and law involves the question of the extent (if any) to which morality depends on law.

At first sight, the answer to this question appears to be *not at all*, since moral precepts clearly originate from non-legal sources. However, Tony Honoré argues that

'in any complex society a viable morality must have a legal component. It is incomplete without law and cannot be taken seriously unless filled out by law. Some obligations can be spelled out only by law and in certain moral conflicts law plays a special role. So some laws at least relate to morality in two ways: they form part of it and at the same time are open to moral criticism.' (*The Dependence of Morality on Law* (1993) 13 OJLS 1.)

Honoré acknowledges that the term *morality* has 'rather uncertain limits' but makes it plain that, in the sense in which he is using it, it is

'concerned with conduct that has a significant impact on other people, and perhaps also animals, individually or collectively, and with the restraints on behaviour that we should accept because of this.... Moreover, since we live in groups and communities and belong to states and other political entities, the central core of morality is concerned with how to co-exist and co-operate with others.... The core of morality is, in a broad sense, political.'

Developing the point that morality is incomplete, Honoré takes the example of road traffic law. Cooperative morality of the kind with which he is dealing requires a shared code of conduct between road users as to which side of the road to drive on, who gives way to whom at junctions and so on. However, if this aspect of morality is to be viable, these matters must be determined in an authoritative and enforceable way and it is only the intervention of the law which makes this possible. Similarly, while cooperative morality requires people to contribute to the costs of maintaining the state and its essential services, without a system of tax law to identify appropriate rates of payment and provide practical means of collection and enforcement, the moral obligation to pay would be so incomplete as to be practically useless.

Turning to the role of law in relation to moral conflicts, Honoré takes abortion as an example. He accepts that some people would oppose abortion 'in all circumstances except to save a pregnant woman's life... because they are committed to the value of respecting human life'. On the other hand, there are those who 'treat the quality of human life as a competing value which can... override numbers or length of life'. There are further conflicts between 'those who see prospective life as of equal value to existing life and those who give priority to existing lives'. Similarly there are those 'who give great weight to the freedom to choose one's own way of life and those who recognize this value but give it a subordinate status'. Having expressed the view that 'moral reasoning by itself... cannot... resolve these issues', he concludes this part of his argument by saying 'the competing views are not irrational, but the differing values and ordering of value on which they rest cannot be reconciled'.

From observations such as those set out in the previous paragraph, Honoré proceeds to say that, since 'cooperative morality requires... a minimum moral consensus' and since the attempt 'to ensure or trying to ensure justice between moral communities... is something that only a political entity can do', it follows that 'if the state does not intervene, justice is not well served'. However, even where the state does intervene on this basis, Honoré concedes that 'laws do not usually rule on moral conflicts directly'. Instead 'legal intervention usually takes the form of prescribing or removing penalties, conditions or incentives which attach to behaviour (say abortion or selling drugs), or granting or withholding recognition from certain institutions (say, slavery or homosexual marriage)' and it is in this way that 'the official attitude to the conduct in dispute is obliquely conveyed'.

Reduced to its essence, therefore, Honoré's argument is that when law resolves moral conflicts, it is intervening 'as a determinant of justice'.

Having considered various perspectives on the nature of law and having identified some possible relationships between law and morality, we can now progress to consider in somewhat broader terms the topic of the functions of law.

2.4   The functions of law

2.4.1   What are the general functions of law?

If we ask ourselves what law *does*, rather than what law *is*, it becomes obvious that the short answer is that law does various things, such as regulating contractual relationships, providing a system of property rights and so on. Although it would be inappropriate to pursue such specifics here, some observations about the role of legal orders generally may be useful. (For the avoidance of confusion, it may be worth saying that, in this context, the phrase *legal orders* is used to mean *legal systems* rather than *legal commands*.)

Kelsen, whose *Pure Theory of Law* is considered more closely in Chapter 5, is particularly useful for this purpose.

'The living together of human beings is characterized by the setting up of institutions that regulate this living together. Such an institution is called an "order". The living together of individuals, in itself a biological phenomenon, becomes a social phenomenon by the very act of being regulated. Society is ordered living together, or, more accurately put, society is the ordering of the living together of individuals.

'The function of every social order is to bring about certain mutual behaviour of individuals; to induce them to certain positive or negative behaviour, to certain action or abstention from action. To the individual the order appears as a complex of rules that determine how the individual should conduct himself. These rules are called norms.' (Original emphasis. *The Law As A Specific Social Technique* (1941) 9 U Chi L Rev 75.)

He proceeds to identify the distinguishing characteristic of all legal orders, and to place them within the context of their moral and religious counterparts. More particularly, he says that in every age and in every society, the word 'law' is 'the expression of a concept with a socially highly significant meaning' (*op. cit.*, p. 79) because it refers to

'[that] specific social technique... which consists in bringing about the desired social conduct of men through threat of a measure of coercion which is to be applied in case of contrary conduct.' (*Ibid.*)

Kelsen goes on to say that this makes law notably different from constraints which are social or religious in character:

'Law, morality, and religion – all three forbid murder. But the law does this by providing that if a man commits murder, then another man, designated by the legal order, shall apply against the murderer a certain measure of coercion, prescribed by the legal order. Morality limits itself to requiring: thou shalt not kill.' (*Op. cit.*, p. 80.)

The distinguishing mark of the legal sanction is that it is

'an act of coercion which a person determined by the order directs, in a manner determined by the order, against the person responsible for conduct contrary to the order.' (*Ibid.*)

He concedes that religious norms are commonly associated with sanctions, but the fact that these sanctions issue from a 'superhuman authority' is crucial, because it renders their character transcendental rather than social. They may, of course, be more effective than legal sanctions, but only among believers. In any event, it is the social origins and organization of the sanctions, rather than their effectiveness, which concerns Kelsen.

On the evidence of this extract, you may be immediately tempted to accuse Kelsen of narrowness of vision, since his emphasis on *coercion* and *sanctions* may appear to limit what he has to say to only that part of the law which deals with criminal matters, but it is apparent from the whole of the article that Kelsen intends these key words to have wider meanings, so that, for example, the possibility of a defendant's property being seized in order to provide the money to satisfy a judgment for damages for breach of contract would be a coercive sanction within his scheme of things.

2.4.2 What are the specific functions of law?

Kelsen's approach was adopted and developed by the American legal theorist Robert S. Summers in *The Technique Element in Law* (see (1971) 59 Calif LR 733). Summers argues that 'different social functions are discharged in different societies in different degrees and by different techniques', and suggests the following as 'a useful, though inexhaustive, listing:

'reinforcement of the family;
promotion of human health and a healthful environment;
maintenance of community peace;
provision for redress of wrongs;
facilitation of exchange relationships;
recognition and ordering of property ownership;
preservation of basic freedoms;
protection of privacy;
surveillance of private and official law-making activities.' (*Ibid.*)

2.4.3 How does law perform its specific functions?

Summers proceeds to suggest a five-fold classification of legal techniques which the law uses to perform the functions which he identifies, namely the *grievance remedial* technique, the *penal* technique, the *administrative–regulatory* technique, the *public benefit conferral* technique, and the *private arranging* technique. Each technique requires closer examination.

The grievance remedial technique

The grievance remedial technique 'defines remediable grievances, specifies remedies, administers processes for resolving disputed claims to such remedies, and provides for enforcement of remedial awards.' (*Ibid.*)

This technique is typified by the mainstream areas of civil law, such as tort and contract, and the system through which civil justice is administered.

The penal technique

The penal technique prohibits certain kinds of antisocial conduct, much of which will also be prohibited by moral rules, as well as providing the machinery of law enforcement, from the police force, through the courts exercising criminal jurisdiction, to the prison service. In other words, we are talking about criminal law.

The administrative–regulatory technique

The distinguishing characteristic of the administrative–regulatory technique is that it tends to operate in relation to activities which are socially desirable (or, at least, are not intrinsically socially undesirable).

The law of town and country planning provides an obvious example of the administrative–regulatory technique, with the requirement that planning permission shall be obtained before land is developed, coupled with an extensive system of enforcement. Admittedly, in the case of planning law, as in the case of other administrative–regulatory regimes, enforcement may ultimately result in prosecution, but the fact that this technique and the penal technique may be used together does not mean that they are interchangeable. As Summers says

> 'The administrative-regulator need not wait until harm is done... [but]... will have various pre-sanction control devices in his arsenal, including licensing, cease-and-desist orders, warning letters, and inspection requirements ... [Furthermore] while the prospect of incurring moral disgrace for being convicted of a crime is one of the principal preventive mechanisms of the penal mode, it is not similarly significant in the regulatory.' (*Op. cit.*, pp. 738–739.)

The public benefit conferral technique

The public benefit conferral technique involves the governmental provision of services such as education, highways, social security, the health service and defence.

The private arranging technique

The private arranging technique reflects the fact that

> 'some affairs ... have to be left to private determination if they are to remain what they are. Marriage and parenthood are perhaps the best examples... the family is a private arrangement in essence and par excellence. Various private clubs and associations, religious and social, may be similarly classified.' (*Op. cit.*, p. 741.)

The private arranging technique and the administrative–regulatory technique may be regarded as opposite ends of a single spectrum, and which technique is applied to which field of law is largely a matter of political (but not necessarily *party* political) ideology. For example, at common law there is no rule against letting a tumbledown house, whereas successive Housing Acts have provided a variety of regimes under which local authorities may require the improvement, closure, or even demolition, of substandard housing.

2.4.4 The uses of Summers' analysis

The principal use of Summers' analysis for our purposes is simply that, by demonstrating the wide variety of ways in which law can perform its functions, it helps to develop an understanding of those functions. Clearly, however, it may be put to other uses, and in particular, it may help policy-makers to adopt the most appropriate technique for dealing with a specific problem.

For example, the American experience of Prohibition may be taken to show that the penal technique is inappropriate as a means of controlling alcohol consumption in a society in which alcohol has been commonplace. On the other hand, this objective may be achieved by public health education measures (conferral of public benefits technique), as well as the more obvious technique of a licensing regime (administrative–regulatory technique), with the proper (i.e. effective) use of the penal technique being limited to the long-stop function of dealing with breaches of the licensing laws, as well as with instances of anti-social drunkenness.

As the last example shows, it must not be supposed that only one technique may be used at a time. For evidence of an intermingling of techniques in English law, it is necessary to look no further than the availability of *punitive* (or *exemplary*) damages in certain types of civil cases, or the possibility of courts making compensation orders while exercising their criminal jurisdiction, both of which clearly mix the grievance remedial and punitive techniques.

Summers himself illustrates the possibility of all five techniques being brought to bear on a single problem, namely 'the broad social function of securing a safe and healthful environment' which includes taking steps to deal with 'the problem of "slaughter on the highways"'.

Translating Summers' analysis into contemporary English terms, the grievance remedial technique provides a mechanism through which those who suffer loss as a result of road traffic accidents may recover damages, while the penal technique provides a variety of road traffic offences such as driving without due care and attention and causing death by dangerous driving. In addition, the administrative–regulatory technique provides a system of driving tests and licences, while Ministry of Transport tests attempt to ensure a minimum standard of roadworthiness for certain vehicles, including cars which are more than three years old. Public benefits are conferred by minimum design standards for roads, as well as by advertising campaigns on road safety themes. Finally, private arrangements are commonplace in the form of membership of motoring organizations, the benefits of which include inspection on behalf of prospective purchasers to ensure the roadworthiness of second-hand vehicles.

Additionally, however, Summers' analysis may be used to illustrate the fact that the law commonly proceeds on the basis that everyone shares the same political values and that, therefore, these values need not be made explicit. For example, the phrase *reinforcement of the family* tells us nothing of what we mean by the word *family*. Presumably nobody would doubt that it would include a married couple, with or without children, and many people would simply assume that this is the sole meaning of the word for the purposes of the law. (Summers himself suggests as much by his comment on the private arranging technique which is quoted at p. 30.) But what of an unmarried couple living in a long-term, stable relationship? Or a same-sex couple? Are all worthy of equal respect in the eyes of the law? (For some practical examples of the same-sex problem, see the cases discussed at pp. 122–126.)

In more general terms, Chapter 9 shows that the law will often proceed on the basis of a variety of implicit assumptions, and that when these assumptions are made explicit, the nature and functions of the law as an instrument of political power are revealed.

2.5 Natural law and positivism in context: the Case of the Speluncean Explorers

Although *The Case of the Speluncean Explorers* may sound more like an episode from the professional life of Sherlock Holmes than an essay in legal theory, it is in fact the title of an article by Lon L. Fuller (whose own version of natural law theory we will consider in Chapter 6). Many generations of students have used this article to sharpen their perceptions of, among other things, the kind of material which has been introduced in the earlier part of this chapter.

The article (see (1949) 62 Harv LR 616) is plainly based on the case of *R v Dudley and Stephens* (1884) 14 QBD 273, in which three people adrift in an open boat on the high seas were reduced to such a state of starvation that the only means for any of them to survive was for one of them to be killed so that the others could eat his flesh. The killing and the eating having taken place, the survivors were rescued. At their trial for murder, the court rejected their defence of necessity and imposed mandatory death sentences. In due course, however, the sentences were commuted to six months' imprisonment.

From this basic idea, Fuller creates a scenario in the fictitious state of Newgarth, in the year 4300 CE, which is approximately as far in the future as we are from the ancient Greeks. The scenario is based on an accident in which five men were trapped by a landslide while exploring a cave. A major rescue operation ensued, involving substantial expenditure of both public and private money, as well as the loss of ten workmen's lives owing to another landslide during the rescue attempt. While trapped, the explorers were able to make radio contact with the outside world, as a result of which they were able to establish that their existing supplies of food would not be sufficient to enable them to survive until they could be rescued, but that if they killed and ate one of their number, they could do so. One of the men, W, suggested that they should throw dice in order to identify which of them should be killed. After his companions had agreed to this course of action, but before the dice were cast, W withdrew his agreement. The others nevertheless continued and, when it came to W's turn, the dice were cast on his behalf. He accepted the fairness of the throw, which, as it happened, went against him. His companions duly killed him and ate his flesh. The men survived long enough to be rescued.

The law of Newgarth provided that 'whoever shall wilfully take the life of another shall be punished by death' and accordingly the surviving explorers were subsequently charged with murder. The procedure at their trial was a little unusual because, at the instigation of the foreman who happened to be a lawyer, the jury found the facts but left it to the judge to decide whether, as a matter of law, the defendants were guilty. The judge decided that, as a matter of law, the men were indeed guilty and then passed mandatory death sentences. However, both the judge and the jury recommended that the Chief Executive of Newgarth should commute the sentences to six months' imprisonment.

While the Chief Executive's decision was awaited, the case came before the Supreme Court of Newgarth which was composed of Truepenny CJ together with Foster, Tatting, Keen and Handy JJ.

Chief Justice Truepenny (*op. cit.*, pp. 616–620), having approved of the procedure adopted by the trial court, and having also agreed that the 'principle of executive clemency' was 'admirably suited to mitigate the rigours of the law', was content to uphold the convictions.

Foster J began his judgment (*op. cit.*, pp. 620–626) by describing the Chief Justice's proposal as 'an expedient at once... sordid and... obvious'. He proceeded to characterize the attitude shared by both the trial court and the Chief Justice as amounting to an admission that the law itself (leaving aside to the possibility of executive clemency) could no longer pretend 'to incorporate justice'. After these preliminaries, he based the substance of his judgment on two alternative grounds.

First, he argued that the law is 'directed toward facilitating and improving men's co-existence and regulating with fairness and equity the relations of their life in common'. In a situation such as that which gave rise to the present case, however, it could no longer be assumed that the people involved could continue to live together and therefore 'the basic premises underlying our whole legal order have lost their meaning and force'. The consequence of this was that, in all the circumstances of the case, the men had been 'not in a "state of civil society" but in a "state of nature"', and therefore they had committed no crime.

The second limb of his judgment, which he advanced in case the first limb should be rejected, proceeded on the basis that 'every proposition of positive law... is to be interpreted reasonably in the light of its evident purpose'. Since deterrence is one of the main purposes of the criminal law and since nobody in the position in which the defendants had found themselves would use the criminal law as a guide to how they should behave, it followed that the law of murder was inapplicable.

This part of the judgment relies on an analogy with the law relating to self-defence. More particularly, although killing in self-defence is contrary to the plain words of the statute, the courts had long held that such killing is no crime because people whose lives are threatened will, if necessary, kill their assailants rather than allowing themselves to be killed, without weighing their conduct against the requirements of the criminal law. In other words, excusing those who kill in self-defence does not undermine the deterrent purpose of the criminal law.

Whichever limb of Foster J's judgment is preferred, the conclusion is the same, namely that the convictions must be quashed.

Tatting J (*op. cit.*, pp. 626–631) began by saying how he had been unable in the present case to maintain his usual distinction between emotional and intellectual responses, with only the latter being used as the basis of legal judgment. Although he was sympathetic to the defendants, he found Foster J's judgment 'shot through with inconsistencies and fallacies'. For example, when had the defendants entered 'the state of nature' – was it when the landslide occurred; when their hunger reached an undefined but overwhelming level; or when they agreed to throw the dice? Additionally, how can judges who are appointed by a state to administer the laws of that state decide to turn themselves into judges in a Court of Nature?

Additionally, pursuing the logic of Foster J's judgment, if W had resisted those who set out to kill him and had killed them instead, he would himself be a murderer. This startling consequence flows from his inability to rely on self-defence because, according to the Law of Nature, his assailants would have been acting lawfully.

Turning to the second limb of Foster J's judgment, Tatting J pointed out that deterrence is only one of the purposes of the criminal law, and that other purposes include the provision of 'an orderly outlet for the instinctive human demand for retribution' and the 'the rehabilitation of the wrongdoer'.

In any event, quite apart from any considerations based on deterrence, killing in self-defence may be justified on the basis that it is the result of an instinctive reaction and cannot therefore be said to be 'wilful'. This justification clearly had no application to the present facts, where the killing was carefully premeditated. And again, if near-starvation cannot justify the theft of a loaf of bread, how can it be said to justify killing a human being?

Even if the court could be certain that the situation which gave rise to the present case would never recur, 'the soundness of a principle [should] be tested by the conclusions it entails, without reference to the accidents of later litigational history'.

On the other hand, in addition to his natural sympathy for the defendants, Tatting J was influenced by 'the absurdity' of executing the defendants when other lives had been saved 'at the cost of the lives of ten heroic workmen'. While it would have been better if the defendants had been charged with some lesser offence or (if no appropriate lesser offence could be identified) not at all, the fact remained that a murder charge had been brought and a conviction had ensued.

Tatting J concluded his judgment by taking what he believed to be the unprecedented step of withdrawing from making any decision in the case.

Keen J began his judgment by a setting aside two questions. First, executive clemency was not a matter for the court all, although, if he were speaking as a private person, he would be in favour of a pardon for the defendants, on the ground that they had already suffered enough. Secondly, he also put aside consideration of such matters as 'right', 'wrong', 'wicked' and 'good'.

In his view, the problem confronting the court arose from 'a failure to distinguish the legal from the moral aspects of this case'. Failure to respect this distinction can lead not only to conflict between the legislature and the executive on the one hand and the judiciary on the other but also (as had historically been the case in Newgarth) to civil war. Under the present constitutional settlement, however, the supremacy of the legislature had been established and 'the principle that forbids the judicial revision of statutes has become a tacit premise underlying the whole of the legal and governmental order I am sworn to administer'.

Attacking Foster J's approach, Keen J (*op. cit.*, pp. 631–637) doubted whether the statute in question could truly be said to have any purpose, as distinct from being a reflection of 'a deeply held human conviction that murder is wrong and that something should be done to the man who commits it'.

In relation to the self-defence argument, the real question centred on the scope of the provision creating the offence, rather than on its purpose. When viewed in this way, the present case was clearly outwith the scope of self-defence because those who killed W were not in fear of their own lives at his hands.

While he acknowledged that his decision would not be popular, Keen J was firmly of the view that 'judicial dispensation does more harm in the long run than hard decisions'. Furthermore, the legal system would be better if previous judges had followed this precept. For example, if the statutory provision criminalizing murder had been strictly interpreted in earlier times, there would doubtless have been some legislative amendment which would have placed self-defence on 'an understandable and rational basis, instead of the hodgepodge of verbalisms and metaphysical distinctions that have emerged from the judicial and professorial treatment'.

Accordingly, Keen J was of the opinion that the convictions should be affirmed.

Handy J (*op. cit.*, pp. 637–644) began his judgment by commenting on the 'tortured ratiocinations to which this simple case has given rise', before characterizing the problem as 'a question of practical wisdom, to be exercised in a context, not of abstract theory, but of human realities'. Viewed in this way, the case became 'one of the easiest... that has ever been argued before this court'. More particularly 'government is a human affair, and... men are ruled, not by words on paper or by abstract theories, but by other men. They are ruled well when their rulers understand the feelings and conceptions of the masses. They are ruled badly when that understanding is lacking. Of all branches of the government, the judiciary in the most likely to lose its contact with the common man'.

He conceded the existence of 'a few fundamental rules of the game that must be accepted if the game is to go on at all'. For example, 'restraint on discretion and dispensation... is... essential' in relation to the laws governing elections and appointments to public office. Otherwise, however, judges should 'treat forms and abstract concepts as instruments'.

Noting that the present case had aroused a great deal of public comment, with approximately 90% of those expressing an opinion being in favour of pardons or token punishments, Handy J also noted that although both Tatting J and Truepenny CJ had expressed the view that the case would be best dealt with on the basis of commonsense (by the exercise of prosecutorial discretion or executive clemency respectively) neither was willing to proceed on a commonsense basis himself. The question before the court concerned 'the life or death of four men who have already suffered more torment and humiliation than most of us would endure in a thousand years' and it would be appropriate for the court to set aside their convictions.

Tatting J (*op. cit.*, pp. 644–645) having reaffirmed his decision to withdraw despite an invitation to reconsider, the court found itself equally divided. Since an appeal either succeeds or not, it followed that the appeals failed. In due course, no executive clemency being forthcoming, the sentences of death were carried out.

Although Fuller appends a postscript (*op. cit.*, p. 645) in which he insists that 'the case was constructed for the sole purpose of bringing to a common focus certain divergent philosophies of law and government' and that anyone 'who seeks to trace out contemporary resemblances... is engaged in a frolic of his own', he does concede that the philosophies which underpin the judgments 'presented men with live questions... in the days of Plato and Aristotle... [and]... perhaps will continue to do so when our era has had its say about them. If there is any element of prediction in the case, it does not go beyond a suggestion that the questions involved are among the permanent problems of the human race'.

Summary

▶ Legal theories are often classified into those which are based on natural law and those which are positivist, but some modern legal theorists view the subject in more explicitly political terms.

▶ The essence of natural law theories is that the identification of law involves some external factors beyond the workings of the political process which produces laws within a legal system. However, some natural law theories state that positive laws which are inconsistent with natural law are not truly laws (constitutive theories), while others argue merely that such laws are open to criticism (evaluative theories). However, even those who argue that positive laws may lack true validity may nevertheless concede that there can still be some non-legal duty to obey them.

▶ The essence of positivism is that the existence of laws does not depend upon morality, although those theories which may be classified as soft positivism do allow some limited overlap between the two categories.

▶ Extreme versions of natural law and positivism are best seen as opposite ends of a continuous spectrum, with the possibility of various intermediate positions.

▶ The adoption of a specific position within the natural law–positivist spectrum is likely to be the result of an individual's underlying ideological and philosophical beliefs.

Summary cont'd

▶ Laws perform many functions, most if not all of which are likely to reflect the political structure of the society which is served by those laws.

▶ Lon L. Fuller's fictional case of the *Speluncean Explorers* provides a useful vehicle for considering some of the conflicting views on the nature of law and its relationship with morality.

Further reading

Davies, Howard and Holdcroft, David, *Jurisprudence: Texts and Commentary*, 1991

Friedmann, W. *Legal Theory*, 5th edn, 1967

Fuller, Lon L., *Positivism and Fidelity to Law: a Reply to Professor Hart* (1958) 71 Harv LR 630

Fuller, Lon L., *The Case of the Speluncean Explorers* (1949) 62 Harv LR 616

Hart, H.L.A., *Positivism and the Separation of Law and Morals* (1958) 71 Harv LR 593, reprinted in *Essays in Jurisprudence and Philosophy*, 1983

Holmes, Oliver Wendell, *Natural Law* (1918) 32 Harv LR 40

Honoré, Tony, *The Dependence of Morality on Law* (1993) 13 OJLS 1

Kelsen, Hans, *The Law As A Specific Social Technique* (1941) 9 U Chi L Rev 75

Mithrophanous, Eleni, *Soft Positivism* (1997) 17 OJLS 620

Pappe, H.O., *On the Validity of Judicial Decisions in the Nazi Era* (1960) 23 MLR 260

Raz, Joseph, *The Authority of Law*, 2nd edn, 2009

Reynolds, Barney, *Natural Law versus Positivism: The Fundamental Conflict* (1993) 13 OJLS 441

Summers, Robert S., *The Technique Element in Law* (1971) 59 Calif LR 733

Waluchow, W.J., *Inclusive Legal Positivism*, 1994

Chapter 3

The natural law tradition

3.1 Introduction

This chapter explains the evolution of the natural law tradition from Ancient Greece to the 18th century and shows how some of the ideas underlying this tradition have been of enduring practical significance in terms of legal doctrine.

3.2 Ancient Greece

3.2.1 Introduction

From the perspective of legal theory, the Ancient Greeks constitute something of a conundrum. On the one hand,

> '[they were] the first people – at any rate, the first of whom Europe retains any consciousness – among whom reflective thought and habit became a habit of educated men... not confined to observation of the physical world and universe... but extending to man himself, his nature, and his place in the order of things, the character of human society, and the best way of governing it.' (Kelly, *A Short History of Western Legal Theory*, 1992, p. 1.)

On the other hand, they appear to have had little or no interest in the study of either law or legal theory as discrete disciplines, even to the point of having no names for law as an abstract concept or for *jurisprudence*:

> 'Such questions as the origin and basis of the state, the source of obligation in law, or the relation of law to some higher or more fundamental standard, were not discussed in monographs on those themes alone, or by theorists specializing in them.' (Kelly, *op. cit.*, p. 6.)

When seeking to understand the Greek view of law and legal theory, therefore, it is necessary to refer to sources drawn from other disciplines, including philosophy in general, politics and literature. (This is, of course, an early illustration of Friedmann's point, which is cited at p. 3.)

3.2.2 Plato (c. 429–347 BCE)

In order to locate Plato within the field of legal theory as a whole, we must notice both his theory of forms and his political philosophy.

Plato's own explanation of his theory of forms is based on an analogy with people confined to living in a cave, with their backs turned permanently towards the mouth of the cave. Furthermore, there is a fire between the cave-dwellers and the cave mouth, so that all the cave-dwellers can see are flickering shadows on the back wall of the cave. Knowing no better, they take these shadows to be reality, although, of course, reality actually lies in the wider, and daylit, world beyond the cave. According to this model of human knowledge, reliance on sense-perception leads people into error. On the other hand, such error could be avoided if people relied on reason instead. More particularly, Plato says that reason leads us to conclude that there is an *ideal* world outside the one which we experience through our senses. This other world is *ideal* in the very literal and specific sense that it consists of ideas, or forms, which are the archetypes of everything which we encounter in the world which we perceive through our senses. Thus, for example, if we perceive a black cat, there must be an ideal form of a cat and an ideal state of blackness. As Roger Scruton puts it:

'Plato... argued that the truth of the world is not revealed to ordinary sense-perception, but to reason alone; that truths of reason are necessary, eternal and (as we would now say) *a priori*; that through the cultivation of reason man can come to understand himself, God and the world as these things are in themselves, freed from the shadowy overcast of experience.' (*A Short History of Modern Philosophy*, 2nd edn, 1995, p. 13.)

Turning to Plato's political philosophy, the starting point is his conception of humankind as a political (or social) species, living within a tightly structured, hierarchical society, with the need to promote the common good of that society being paramount.

In more detail, there are three social classes, namely rulers, auxiliaries (which includes not only soldiers but also what in a modern state would probably be called 'the executive'), and the rest, including artisans, farmers and so on. (In some contexts, Plato treats the rulers and the auxiliaries as members of a single class which he calls 'guardians'.) The hierarchy is legitimated by a myth, which, in the course of time, all members of society will come to accept as being true, to the effect that all three classes are children of the earth, but that their make-up contains, respectively, gold, silver and either bronze or iron. Thus all owe common allegiance to their origins, while being clearly differentiated from each other. However, some social mobility is possible, because although children will normally resemble their parents 'occasionally a silver child will be born of golden parents, or a golden child of silver parents, and so on'. (*The Republic*, translated by H.D.P. Lee, 1955, p. 415.) More particularly, if the rulers find that 'one of their own children has bronze or iron in its make-up, they must harden their hearts, and degrade it to the ranks of the industrial and agricultural class where it properly belongs'. (*Ibid.*) Equally, if a child born to bronze or iron parents is found to have gold or silver in its nature, it is the duty of the rulers to promote it into their own ranks. However, there is no flexibility for those who are within their proper class, since 'interference by the three classes with each others' jobs, and interchange of jobs between them... does the greatest harm to our state'. (*Ibid.*) This is not only 'the worst of evils', but also (because 'the worst of evils for a state is injustice') 'gives us a definition of injustice. And conversely, when each of our three classes... does its own job... that... is justice and makes our city just'. (*Op. cit.*, p. 434.)

Moreover, the purpose of law is the benefit of the whole community, rather than of one particular class, and to this end it 'uses persuasion or force to unite all citizens and make them share together the benefits which each individually can confer on the community... to make each man a link in the unity of the whole'. (*Op. cit.*, pp. 519–520).

We will pick up the threads of Plato's ideas again when we come to St Augustine (see p. 46), but before doing so we must move forward a very few years and consider Aristotle's contribution to legal theory.

3.2.3 Aristotle's contribution to legal theory

Introduction

In his fifth book *Ethics* (or *Nichomachean Ethics*, to give the work its full title), which Kelly (*op. cit.*, p. 26) describes as 'the nearest thing to conscious legal theory in classical Greek literature', Aristotle (384–322 BCE) deals with the concept of justice. More particularly, following in a direct line from Plato's view of humankind as a political animal, Aristotle emphasizes that the subject matter of his discussion is *political justice*, by which he means that kind of justice which exists in order that people who share a common way of life are able to establish whatever state of affairs is necessary to enable them all to live as free and equal members of their society.

The central point is two-fold. First, justice cannot exist among people unless their relationships with each other are governed by law. Secondly, law exists only among people who have the capacity to be guilty of injustice. In short, it is the function of the law to distinguish between those who are just and those who are unjust.

By way of further explanation of what he means by *political justice*, Aristotle says that it has two forms, namely the *natural* and the *conventional*.

Justice is *natural* when it is universal and unaffected by human perception of what it is. By way of contrast, justice is *conventional* in those situations where it may take a variety of forms, and will be applied only after the appropriate form has been established. As examples, Aristotle takes the sum of money to be paid as ransom for a prisoner of war, or the requirement that a particular ritual requires the sacrifice of one goat rather than two sheep. Since these rules vary, their detailed content must be laid down individually. Aristotle concedes that some philosophers argue that all justice is conventional, since it is a matter of common observation that the requirements of justice are constantly changing, whereas things which are truly natural are universal. As an example of universality, he takes the proposition that fire burns in Greece in the same way as it does in Persia. (This example is less than happy, because it deals with a universal physical occurrence, rather than a moral precept, but the gist of the point is plain enough.) He also concedes that some things which appear to be natural may, on closer consideration, be found not to be so, but to be variable.

Aristotle takes a non-legal example in order to illustrate the point. Most people are right-handed, and therefore this may be regarded as the natural condition of humankind, but it is nevertheless possible for people to learn to use both hands equally. However, he insists that there will always be a real distinction between those requirements of justice which are natural and those which are merely legal and conventional, even though this distinction will not always be apparent in every case. In particular, a consequence of the fact that forms of government are variable from place to place is that human laws are also variable from place to place, but this does not alter the fact that there is only one natural form of government, namely, that which is best.

In passing, it may be noted that this view is counter to that expressed by Alexander Pope (some two thousand years later), in his *Essay on Man*, to the effect that the form of government is irrelevant to its quality:

For forms of government let fools contest;
Whate'er is best administer'd is best.

Distributive justice and corrective justice

Aristotle distinguishes between *distributive* and *corrective* justice on the basis that the former is concerned with the 'distribution of honour, money and other things' which a community divides among its members, while the latter is concerned with 'correcting any unfairness that may arise'. Two points arise.

First, Aristotle does not say that distributive justice necessarily requires distribution in equal shares (because it would be generally agreed that any distribution of benefits must take comparative merit into account). However, he does insist that it involves 'the expression of a proportion... and the unjust in this sense is a violation of proportion'.

Secondly, although corrective justice deals with the type of subject matter which routinely comes before the courts in both civil and criminal law, it would be a mistake simply to apply Aristotle's categorization to the contemporary English legal system in an uncritical manner. Some examples may be useful.

First, in a modern, complex state a court may have to decide whether to award damages to individuals who have been harmed by the way in which a public body has performed (or failed to perform) its functions. In practice, this decision may well turn to a large extent on the court's view of whether the burden should fall on individual claimants who have been harmed or on the general body of taxpayers who fund the public service. In this context, the court is likely to take into account the realities of insurance cover, as evidenced by *Stovin v Wise (Norfolk County Council, Third Party)* [1996] 3 All ER 801, which is discussed at p. 169. When viewed in this way, what initially appears to be a straightforward example of corrective justice may, on reflection, also be seen as an example of distributive justice.

Secondly, the concept of proportionality (which, of course, Aristotle places within the *distributive* category) is now also seen as an element within the *corrective* category. Take, for example, the leading statement of the distinction in English law between contractual penalties (which are unlawful) and liquidated damages (which are lawful):

> 'There is a presumption... that it is a penalty when "a single lump sum is made payable by way of compensation, on the occurrence of one or more or all of several events, some of which may occasion serious and others but trifling damage".' (Lord Dunedin, in *Dunlop Pneumatic Tyre Co Ltd v New Garage & Motor Co Ltd* [1914–15] All ER Rep 739, citing Lord Watson in *Elphinstone v Monkland Iron & Coal Co* (1886) 11 App Cas 342.)

Putting this in explicitly Aristotelian terms, a payment which is disproportionate to the loss suffered will be a penalty, and will therefore be unlawful.

Thirdly, in one of the leading cases in English public law, a local authority decided that none of its employees should work for less than a specified minimum wage, irrespective of the value of the work done and the prevailing state of the labour market. The House of Lords held that there was no proportionately causal relationship between the work and the money paid, and therefore the payments fell outwith the definition of 'wages' and were unlawful. (*Roberts v Hopwood* [1925] All ER Rep 24, which was, of course, decided long before the introduction of the current statutory regime of minimum wages.)

Quite apart from the common law's underlying acceptance of the doctrine of proportionality, the Human Rights Act 1998 (see p. 60) has created a need to respond explicitly to the case law of the European Court of Human Rights, which (as befits a court established within the mainstream of the European tradition) has always held the doctrine in high regard. In this context, it is useful to consider the following formulation of the questions which a court should ask itself, namely whether:

> '(i) the legislative objective is sufficiently important to justify limiting a fundamental right; (ii) the measures designed to meet the legislative objective are rationally connected to it; and (iii) the means used to impair the right or freedom are no more than is necessary to accomplish the objective.' (Lord Clyde, in the Privy Council case of *de Freitas v Permanent Secretary of Agriculture, Fisheries, Land and Housing* [1999] 1 AC 69.)

Finally, in the context of European Community (now Union) law (which is, of course, incorporated into English law by the European Communities Act 1972), the European Court of Justice has formulated the following approach:

> 'In order to establish whether a provision of Community law is consonant with the principle of proportionality it is necessary to establish, in the first place, whether the

means it employs to achieve its aim correspond to the importance of the aim and, in the second place, whether they are necessary for their achievement.' (*Fromançais SA v FORMA* [1983] ECR 395.)

Equity

According to Aristotle, it is in the nature of law that its formulation is generalized, while it is in the nature of human behaviour that its manifestations are individualized. It follows from this that, with no fault on the part of either the lawyers or the legislature, the law will inevitably contain loopholes, thus creating a need for some remedial mechanism which is capable of 'restoring the balance of justice when it has been tilted by the law'. The concept which Aristotle employs to fulfil this role is *equity*, which operates to adapt the law to individual circumstances and to produce the result that the legislature would have produced had it foreseen the circumstances of the individual case. Aristotle is careful to emphasize that his concept of equity is essentially practical:

> 'So while it is true that equity is just and in some circumstances better than justice, it is not better than absolute justice. All we can say is that it is better than the error which is generated by the unqualified language in which absolute justice must be stated.' (*Ethics*, bk 5, ch. 10. Translated by J.A.K. Thomson, 1953.)

Aristotle does not proceed to give examples of the way in which equity operates, but the fundamental idea that equity remedies imbalances which the law has created is, of course, the origin of the concept of equity in English law, which developed from the practice, adopted by the court of chancery, of giving relief in cases where injustice was caused by the application of the more rigid doctrines which had been developed by the courts of common law (see, for example, McLeod, *Legal Method*, 8th edn, 2011, pp. 24–28).

Moreover, although equity is an important part of the overall classification of English law, the underlying idea may be discerned even in contexts where the terminology itself is not used. For example, *Anisminic v Foreign Compensation Commission* [1969] 1 All ER 208 concerned the interpretation and application of the Foreign Compensation Act 1950. The Act created the Foreign Compensation Commission and gave it the task of determining claims for compensation made by British nationals against foreign governments. Section 4(4) of the Act provided that the Commission's determinations 'shall not be called into question in any court of law'. The House of Lords held that the function of the Commission was limited to identifying and applying the law, and did not extend to deciding what the law was. It followed from this that if the Commission had misinterpreted the law, it had done something which it had no power to do, or, putting the same idea more technically, it had exceeded the jurisdiction which Parliament had conferred upon it. Since this must mean that the apparent determination had no existence in law, the statutory immunity from challenge, which attached only to determinations, was irrelevant. Although this decision was made on constitutional grounds, it is clearly also open to justification on the Aristotelian basis that to uphold the Commission's immunity from challenge would be to allow a loophole in the legislation to frustrate the right of access to the courts.

The validity of human law

As we shall see throughout much of the remainder of this book, the question of what makes a law valid, and in particular the question of whether a human law may be invalid for want of consistency with some external standard, has exercised the minds of many legal theorists. However, Aristotle, in common with other Greek philosophers, does not address this question at all, although the dramatist Sophocles, in his version of the story of *Antigone*, does so in a classic manner.

The plot of *Antigone* springs from the story of Oedipus, King of Thebes, who is displaced into exile when his brother, Creon, takes the throne. When Oedipus dies, while still in exile, his son, Polynices, who considers himself to have a claim to the throne, attacks Thebes. In a battle with his brother, Eteocles, who is defending the city, each man kills the other. Eteocles' body receives proper burial rites, but Creon forbids the burial of Polynices' body, with the result that it is left outside the city, to be devoured by wild animals. This raises a particular problem for Polynices' sisters, because their religious convictions tell them that unless Polynices' body is buried, his soul cannot rest in peace, although even a nominal handful of earth thrown on the corpse will suffice. One of the sisters, Ismene, relying on the general duty of obedience to law, coupled with fear of the consequences of disobedience, refuses to do anything, but the other sister, Antigone, ignores the king's decree and leaves the city to scatter the token earth on the corpse. When she is subsequently asked whether she was aware of the decree, and if so, why she had disobeyed it, Sophocles puts the following words into her mouth:

> 'These laws were not ordained of Zeus,
> And she who sits enthroned with gods below,
> Justice, enacted not these human laws.
> Nor did I deem that thou, a mortal man,
> Couldst by a breath annul and override
> The immutable unwritten laws of heaven.
> They were not born today nor yesterday;
> They die not; and none knoweth whence they sprang.'
> (*Antigone*, 453–7. Translation cited in Kelly, *op. cit.*, p. 20.)

Having been entombed alive by way of punishment, Antigone commits suicide.

3.3 Rome

3.3.1 Introduction

In common with the case with the Greeks, the Romans did not regard legal theory as a discrete branch of study. However, where our knowledge of the Greek view comes from a range of philosophical and literary sources, our knowledge of the Roman view comes principally from one man, Marcus Tullius Cicero, a politician and practising lawyer.

3.3.2 Marcus Tullius Cicero (106–43 BCE)

An important preliminary point to notice is that Cicero's thought falls squarely within the Stoic tradition, a central part of which is that ethical questions are integrally related to the way the universe works. Briefly, Stoicism, which had originated in Greece with Zeno of Citium (335–263 BCE), but had subsequently become influential in Rome, teaches that there is an impersonal force of reason which is the fundamental guiding principle of the whole universe. This force may appear in the form of fate, providence or necessity, but it is also manifested in human reason. Furthermore, Stoicism involves a purposive view of nature, in the sense that everything has its appointed nature and end (fire burns, acorns grow into oak trees, and so on). Therefore the Stoic ideal requires that individuals should not only exercise their (distinctively human) reason, but should do so in such a way that they are in harmony with the wider order of things. (The fact that this requires individuals to accept whatever has been ordained for them explains the modern use of the word *stoical*.)

Turning to the specifically legal context, Cicero says that 'the most learned men', define law as 'the highest reason, inherent in nature which enjoins what ought to be done and forbids the opposite'. (*The Laws*, 1.18, translated by Niall Rudd, 1998.)

Proceeding to the relationship between law and justice, Cicero draws a distinction between what would now be called *positive law* and *natural law*.

> 'The origin of justice must be derived from law. For law is a force of nature, the intelligence and reason of a wise man, and the criterion of justice and injustice.... But in establishing what justice is, let us take as our point of departure that highest law which came into being countless centuries before any law was written down or any state was even founded.' (*Op. cit.*, 1.19.)

It follows, therefore, that there is a sense in which conduct can be unlawful, even in the absence of any relevant human law, because reason directs humankind towards doing right and away from doing wrong. Moreover, and crucially:

> 'That reason did not first become law when it was written down, but rather when it came into being. And it came into being at the same time as the divine mind. Therefore the authentic original law, whose function is to command and forbid, is the right reason of Jupiter, Lord of all.' (*Op. cit.*, 2.10.)

Cicero emphasizes the importance of natural law thus:

'Law in the proper sense is right reason in harmony with nature. It is spread through the whole human community, unchanging and eternal.... This law cannot be countermanded, nor can it be in any way amended, nor can it be totally rescinded... all peoples at all times will be embraced by a single and eternal and unchangeable law.... Whoever refuses to obey it will be turning his back on himself. Because he has denied his nature as a human being he will face the gravest penalties for this alone, even if he succeeds in avoiding all the other things that are regarded as punishments.' (*The Republic*, 3.33, translated by Rudd, 1998.)

On the question of *justice*, Cicero says:

'Most foolish of all is the belief that everything decreed by the institutions or laws of a particular country is just.... There is one, single, justice. It binds together human society and has been established by one, single, law. That law is right reason in commanding and forbidding. A man who does not acknowledge this law is unjust, whether it has been written down anywhere or not.' (*The Laws*, 1.42, translated by Rudd, 1998.)

In view of the fundamentally purposive nature of the Stoic philosophy, it is not surprising that Cicero develops his concept of the nature of human law and the reason for its bindingness thus:

'It is agreed, of course, that laws were devised to ensure the safety of citizens, the security of states, and the peaceful and happy lives of human beings; and those who first passed such enactments showed their communities that they meant to frame and enact measures which... would allow them to live happy and honourable lives.... From this it is reasonable to infer that those who framed harmful and unjust rules... acting in a way quite contrary to their claims and promises, introduced measures which were anything but laws.' (*Op. cit.*, 2.11.)

The view that rules which have the formal appearance of law may, on proper analysis be 'anything but laws' leads clearly – indeed, tautologically – to the conclusion that there can be no *legal* obligation to obey them, but leaves open the question of whether there is, or may be, a *moral* obligation to do so. This question is specifically addressed by St Thomas Aquinas, but before we consider his contribution to legal theory we must consider the work of St Augustine, which provides a crucial link between the pre-Christian and the Christian eras.

3.4 The Christian contribution

3.4.1 St Augustine (354–430)

The acceptance of Christianity as the religion of the Roman Empire in 312 was clearly capable of causing major conflicts between the old ideas and the new. From the point of view of legal theory, however, this problem was solved more or less at source by St Augustine, who was Bishop of Hippo, near Carthage in what is now Tunisia, who assimilated much of Plato's philosophy into the teaching of the church. (No such assimilation was possible in respect of Aristotle's philosophy, because at that time Aristotle's works were unknown in Christendom, emerging from the worlds of Judaism and Islam only in the 12th century of the Christian era.)

First, Augustine emphasizes the central importance of justice by asking, rhetorically, 'what are states without justice, but robber bands enlarged?'. (*The City of God*, 4, iv.) This attitude is also reflected in one of Augustine's most famous, but also most problematic, pronouncements, namely *lex injusta non est lex*, which may be translated literally as 'an unjust law is not a law'. (*On Free Will*, 1.5.33.) Although this sounds like a definitional point, making legal obligation co-terminous with justice, it may simply be an example of accuracy being sacrificed to brevity, with Augustine's true meaning being more accurately represented by para. 1.6.50 of the same work, which Anthony J. Lisska (while discussing St Thomas Aquinas) translates thus:

> 'In temporal [i.e. human] law, nothing is just nor legitimate which human beings do not derive from the eternal law.' (Aquinas's *Theory of Natural Law*, 1996, p. 269.)

If this version is preferred, it is only the justice, and not the existence, of human law which is in issue.

Secondly, in a way reminiscent of Plato's theory of forms (see p. 38), Augustine asserts that there must be an ideal law (or in other words, natural law) which he proceeds to identify with the law of the Judæo-Christian God.

3.4.2 St Thomas Aquinas (1225–1274)

The ideas of St Thomas Aquinas (which are sometimes labelled Thomism – pronounced *toamism* – by way of reference to his first name), have formed the basis of certain core aspects of the teaching of the Roman Catholic church for more than seven centuries. The central point of Aquinas's argument is that there are four types of law, namely the *eternal*, the *natural*, the *human* and the *divine* .

Aquinas explains the concept of *eternal law* as being 'a dictate of practical reason coming from a person who has the charge of a perfect community'. (*The Complete Theology*, Q91, A1, translated by Lisska, *op. cit.*, p. 263.) Furthermore, if it is accepted that the whole universe is governed by God (and, of course, Aquinas does accept this), it follows that the whole universe is governed by divine reason, which is beyond time, and therefore is the source of that law which may properly be called *eternal*.

By way of introduction to his definition of *natural law*, which is his second category, Aquinas argues (Q91, A2, *op. cit.*, p. 264) that everything which is subject to divine providence is therefore ruled by eternal law (or, to put it another way, 'participates in some way or another in the eternal law'), but that human beings, as rational creatures, participate more fully than any other part of creation, because 'each person has a natural inclination towards deriving its proper act and end'. (*Ibid.*)

However, the crucial distinction is that only God can know eternal law, whereas the fact that 'the natural law is nothing other than the participation of the eternal law in the rational creature or human being' (*ibid.*) means that anyone can know natural law. In support of this contention, in the same Article of the same Question (*op. cit.*, pp. 263–264), Aquinas cites Augustine's reliance on St Paul's Epistle to the Romans: 'it is not by hearing the law but by doing it that men will be justified before God' [and] 'Gentiles who do not possess the law' [may nevertheless] 'carry out its precepts by the light of nature'. (*New English Bible*, 1961, ch. 2, vv. 13–14.)

In short, therefore, Aquinas not only continues the pre-Christian tradition which establishes natural law as being discoverable by human reason, but confirms Augustine's absorption of the essence of that tradition into the teaching of the Roman Catholic church by placing both the source of that law, and the reason by means of which it is discovered, firmly within the context of Christian doctrine. In doing so, it will be obvious that he also places the church in a uniquely powerful position, since its religious teaching becomes inextricably involved with that most fundamental of all secular affairs, the validity of laws.

Thirdly, there is *human law*, which comes about because 'from the precepts of natural law... it is necessary that the human reason proceed towards making certain things more specific and determined' although it is essential that these human laws 'observe the conditions which pertain to the very idea of law itself'. (Q91, A3, *op. cit.*, pp. 264–265.) More particularly, human law is necessary because, as Aristotle says in his *Politics*, the power conferred by the faculty of reason means that a person who is 'perfect in virtue' may be 'the best of all animals', but by the same token, a 'person... separated from law and justice... is the worst of all animals'. (Q95, A1, *op. cit.*, p. 279.)

Aquinas deals finally with *divine law*, although in some ways this category comes hierarchically immediately below eternal law, since it is that part of eternal law which God has vouchsafed to humankind. According to Aquinas, the need for divine law is evidenced by Psalm 119, v. 33: 'Teach me, O Lord, the way of thy statutes; and I shall keep it unto the end'. (*Authorized Version*, 1611.) However, he develops the topic under four headings.

First, people are directed by laws. Human law and natural law will suffice in respect of those ends which can be comprehended by human reason, but there is an additional need for divine law because people are 'ordained to the ultimate well-being of eternal life' (Q95, A4, *op. cit.*, p. 265), and this is beyond the grasp of human reason.

Secondly, the fact that human judgments will vary means that human laws will vary, thus creating a need for divine law as an unequivocal yardstick of what ought, or ought not, to be done.

Thirdly, human law is limited to those things which the human mind can judge, which do not include 'the realm of interior acts or intentions'. (*Ibid.*) Therefore, there is a need for divine law.

Fourthly, as Augustine said, human law cannot deal with everything. Therefore, divine law is necessary 'so that no evil might go unprohibited or unpunished... [and] everything which is sinful might be prohibited'. (Q91, A4, *op. cit.*, p. 266.)

On the question of the validity of human law, Aquinas (Q95, A2, *ibid.*) cites Augustine's view that 'an unjust law is not a law' (see p. 47), and draws two consequences. First, a human law which 'is in disagreement with... natural law... will not be a law but a corruption of law'. (*Op. cit.*, p. 280.) Secondly, the force of a law depends on its justice. In this context Aquinas draws a distinction between two types of human law. One type is derived by way of a *conclusion from premises*, while the other is derived by way of *determination*. The first is 'similar to that used in the sciences, which produce demonstrative conclusions from the first principles'. (*Ibid.*) The second may be illustrated by considering the example of an architect who, when instructed to design a house, must particularize the activity by designing one house from the infinite range of possible houses which could be designed. Derivation by conclusion must, therefore, produce a single, correct answer, while derivation by determination may produce a range of possible, and legitimate, answers.

Taking the examples which Aquinas uses to put this distinction into a specifically legal context, the rule that one should not kill other people derives by way of conclusion from the principle (or premise) that one should not harm other people, while the nature and extent of the penalty to be imposed on someone who breaks the law is simply a determination, because only the need for, and not the nature of, punishment may be derived (by way of conclusion) from natural law. It follows that those provisions of human law which are derived by way of conclusion from natural law enjoy two sources of authority and therefore have dual force, while those derived merely by way of determination have only the force of human law.

On the question of the duty of obedience to human law, Aquinas (Q96, A4, *op. cit.*, p. 286) envisages two situations. First, laws may be contrary to *human* good. For example, they may be made for the benefit of the law-maker rather than the community; or they may be made for the benefit of the community but the law-maker may nevertheless exceed its powers, or make laws which impose unequal burdens on different members of the community. Such provisions are 'more like acts of violence than laws'. (*Ibid.*) It follows that they 'do not oblige in the matter of conscience', except perhaps where obedience will 'avoid scandal [by which Aquinas means something like *corrupting example*, rather than its modern meaning of *salacious gossip*] or disturbance' (*ibid.*), because in such cases, it can be proper for individuals to forego their rights.

Secondly, laws may be contrary to the *divine* good. Aquinas provides the example of a decree of a tyrant requiring acts of idolatry. Laws of this nature ought not to be observed in any way, because, in the words of St Peter, 'we must obey God rather than men'. (*Acts of the Apostles*, ch. 5, v. 29, *New English Bible*, 1961.)

3.5 The secularization of natural law

3.5.1 Introduction

As we have seen, the earliest formulations of natural law theory tended to link reason with some notion of a deity, and this view subsequently became consolidated into the specifically Roman Catholic version of Christian teaching. However, from the 16th century when, with the Reformation, northern Europe went its own way with the Protestant version (or versions) of Christianity, many people who wished to espouse the natural law position had to re-think the basis on which they could do so. The leading figure in this process was the Dutch Protestant, Hugo de Groot (more commonly known simply as Grotius).

3.5.2 Grotius (1583–1645)

Grotius's book, *On the Law of War and Peace*, was published in 1625 while he was working in Paris on behalf of the King of Sweden. However, the most important aspect of the contemporary context was the Thirty Years War, the destructive effects of which provided the motive for Grotius's work.

Writing within a culture which had emphatically rejected Roman Catholicism, and which was therefore profoundly unsympathetic to the Thomist version of natural law (discussed in the earlier part of this chapter), Grotius chose to emphasize reason as the source of natural law, with his starting point being – as had been Plato's – the social nature of humankind. However, Grotius notes that the essential human characteristic is not simply a desire to live in society, but a desire to live in a peaceful and well-ordered society. Thus right reason not only requires the maintenance of social order, but may also be said to be the source of all law properly so-called. Furthermore, and crucially, although he personally remained a committed believer, and therefore attributed to God both humankind's social nature and the existence of right reason, Grotius nevertheless asserted that the validity of his case would be undiminished even if God did not exist. In other words, the fact of right reason was all that was necessary. Thus, by delivering an account of natural law devoid of the taint of Popery, Grotius made it possible for people to subscribe to its tenets, irrespective of the nature, or even the existence, of their personal religious beliefs.

3.5.3 The transition to social contractarianism

The secularization of natural law not only ensured its survival into an age when the influence of the Roman Catholic church, and ultimately of Christianity as a whole, was in decline, but also provided a challenge: in the absence of divine authority, what is it that confers legitimacy on the authority of government and law? In order to answer this question, theorists returned to an idea whose origins are traceable to ancient Athens towards the end of both the 5th century BC and the war with Sparta, when the prevailing view was that 'submission to government and law, the fundamental civic duty, rests on a supposed original agreement to which the individual citizen remains by implication a party.' (Kelly, *op. cit.*, p. 14.)

It is to this idea of a 'supposed original agreement', more commonly termed the *social contract*, that we now turn in order to trace the next stage in the history of the idea of natural law, although in this context the focus of attention tends to be more on the idea of natural *rights* than on the wider concept of natural *law*.

3.5.4 The rise of social contractarianism

Thomas Hobbes (1588–1679)

Hobbes lived through the constitutional turmoil which characterized the greater part of the 17th century, although he died before that turmoil was finally resolved by the Glorious Revolution of 1688. It is, therefore, hardly surprising that his mind was much exercised by the threat of disorder and even anarchy, which caused him to write, in one of his most-quoted passages:

> 'Whatsoever... is consequent to a time of war, where every man is enemy to every other man, the same is consequent to the time wherein men live without other security than what their own strength and their own invention shall furnish them.... In such condition, there is no place for industry, because the fruit thereof is uncertain; and consequently no culture of the earth; no navigation, nor use of the commodities which may be imported by sea; no commodious building;... no arts; no letters; no society; and which is worst of all, continual fear and danger of violent death; and the life of man, solitary, poor, nasty, brutish and short.' (Modernized spelling and punctuation. *Leviathan*, 1651, ch. 13.)

The final few words of this passage are often quoted out of context, as if they represented Hobbes' view of the life of man generally. In context, of course, they describe the position only while in a state of nature (or, in Hobbes' words, when 'men live without other security than what their own strength and their own invention shall furnish them'). Two questions arise: what rights do individuals have in this state, and what may be done to moderate its unpleasant aspects? Hobbes gives the following reply:

> 'The right of nature, which writers commonly call *jus naturale*, is the liberty each man hath, to use his own power as he will himself, for the preservation of his own nature; that is to say, of his own life; and consequently, of doing anything which, in his own judgment and reason, he shall conceive to be the aptest means thereunto.
>
> 'By liberty is understood... the absence of external impediments...
>
> 'A law of nature... is a precept or general rule, found out by reason, by which a man is forbidden to do that which is destructive of his life, or taketh away the means of preserving the same...
>
> 'And because the condition of man... is a condition of war of every one against every one... it is a precept or general rule of reason, *that every man ought to endeavour peace as far as he has hope of obtaining it...*

'From this fundamental law of nature... is derived this second law: *that a man be willing, when others are so too, as far-forth as for peace and defence of himself he shall think it necessary, to lay down this right to all things; and be contented with so much liberty against other men as he would allow other men against himself.*' (Modernized spelling and punctuation; original emphasis; *op. cit.*, ch. 14.)

Hobbes then argues that individuals surrender their natural rights (or, more accurately, their natural liberties) by agreeing with each other to accept the jurisdiction of a sovereign. (*Liberties* is more accurate than *rights* because the latter generally indicates interests which are protected in some way, and the interests involved here are shared equally by all people. It follows that people cannot claim that their interests of this type should be individually protected, without infringing the corresponding interests of other people.) The sovereign, which may or may not be an individual, is not a party to this (notional) social contract, but an essential aspect of the status of sovereign is the power to issue commands which are enforceable against all members of society, whether or not they agreed to accept the sovereign's authority in the first place.

However, Hobbes is quite clear that individuals do not abandon their rights irrevocably, which raises the question of when they may reassert them. The answer to this is that they may do so only under extreme conditions. For example, Hobbes recognizes that in practice the sovereign may make oppressive laws, but takes the view that even oppressive government is almost certainly better than no government. More particularly, those who complain about such oppression should realize that

'the estate of Man can never be without some incommodity or other; and that the greatest that in any form of government can possibly happen to people in general, is scarce sensible in respect of the miseries... that accompany a civil war; or that dissolute condition of masterless men, without subjection to laws.' (Modernized spelling and punctuation. *Ibid.*)

But the duty of obedience is not necessarily endless:

'The obligation of subjects to the sovereign is understood to last as long as, and no longer than, the power lasteth by which he is able to protect them.' (*Ibid.*)

In other words, the benefits of having a government, even a bad government, outweigh the disadvantages, but if government fails to perform its fundamental obligation of maintaining order, the citizens who entered into the social contract will no longer be receiving the benefit which they contracted with each other that they should gain, and therefore their obligation to obey the government will terminate.

John Locke (1632–1704)

Where Hobbes' principal concern is with the threat of anarchy, which is ever-present in time of civil war, Locke's principal concern (in his *Two Treatises on*

Government, which were probably written between 1679 and 1683, but remained unpublished until 1690) is to limit the legitimate authority of government, and therefore to justify revolution where those limits are exceeded.

More particularly, Locke differs from Hobbes not only in seeing humankind as a far more social animal, but also in regarding individuals as possessing certain natural rights, especially rights in relation to property, and even more especially rights in relation to property which has increased in value as a result of the expenditure of labour upon it. These rights, being natural, exist even while the individuals who have them are in that state of existence which pre-dates human laws and legal systems. However, in the absence of government, the protection of these rights will be at best uncertain and at worst non-existent. The rational solution, therefore, lies in a social contract which will provide the necessary protection.

A further difference between Hobbes and Locke is that the latter emphasizes the fiduciary nature of governmental power, thus providing a broader basis than the former for justifying a change in the form of government. Locke's argument is that people cannot transfer to government any greater power than they themselves possess, and since no one can possess absolute and arbitrary power (because this would be inconsistent with other people's rights), it follows that government cannot do so either. The logical conclusion of this argument is, therefore, that if any government does lay claim to such power, it will necessarily be in breach of the trust which the people have displayed by conferring power upon it, with the consequence that they will be entitled to withdraw their acceptance of the government's legitimacy.

In short, therefore, where Hobbes saw the duty of obedience as terminating only in the event of non-government, Locke saw it as terminating in the event of the less extreme situation of merely bad government.

3.6　The logical attack on the natural law tradition

Although Aquinas has enjoyed unbroken influence within the Roman Catholic tradition, many of those outside that tradition have long argued that his views, and those of natural lawyers generally, involve the fundamental logical fallacy of seeking to derive an *ought* from an *is*.

The classic statement of this criticism is found in David Hume's *A Treatise of Human Nature*, 1739, Bk III, Pt i, sec. 1:

> 'I cannot forbear adding to these reasonings an observation, which may, perhaps, be found of some importance. In every system of morality, which I have hitherto met with, I have always remarked, that the author proceeds for some time in the ordinary way of reasoning, and establishes the being of God, or makes observations concerning human affairs; when of a sudden I am surprised to find that instead of the usual copulations of propositions, is and is not, I meet with no proposition that is not connected with an *ought*, or an *ought not*. This change is imperceptible; but is, however, of the last consequence. For as this *ought, ought not*, expresses some new relation or affirmation, it is necessary that it should be observed and explained;

and at the same time that a reason should be given, for what seems altogether inconceivable, how this new relation can be a deduction from others, which are entirely different from it. But as authors do not commonly use this precaution, I shall presume to recommend it to the readers; and am persuaded, that this small attention would subvert all the vulgar systems of morality, and let us see, that the distinction of vice and virtue is not founded merely on the relations of objects, nor is perceived by reason.' (Original emphasis; modernized spelling.)

The essence of the fallacy which Hume identifies is best conveyed by contrasting two examples of syllogistic reasoning. First,

All animals breed
Humankind is a species of animal
Therefore
Humankind breeds.

The logic of this is impeccable, and therefore, provided the premises are sound, the conclusion must be true. Contrast, however, the following:

All animals breed
Humankind is a species of animal
Therefore
Humankind ought to breed.

In this example, the premises are statements of fact, but the conclusion is a statement of moral value. Since the conclusion introduces a term which is not contained in the premises, it has not been logically validated. (As a matter of coincidence, of course, the conclusion may happen to be true, and where this is self-evidently the case, there may be a tendency to overlook the lack of logic which results in its formulation; but the lack of logic is nevertheless real.)

Hume's analysis clearly places a formidable obstacle in the way of natural law theory, although as we shall see in Chapter 6 it is possible to attempt a refutation. Whether that attempt is successful is a matter of individual judgment. For the moment we shall adjourn consideration of this question and conclude the present chapter with a consideration of the place of natural law and natural rights in English and European Community (now Union) law, before turning, in the next two chapters, to a discussion of the positivist tradition in legal theory. Before doing so, however, it is worth repeating the point that the positivist attack on the natural law tradition is not simply a matter of challenging the logic by which that tradition is presented, but also involves the fundamental proposition that it is objectionable in principle to define law in such a way as to include morality, since this may result in moral doctrine acquiring the force of law even within those areas of life which ought arguably to be matters of individual responsibility. (See the example of marriage and parenthood, which is given at p. 30.)

3.7 Natural law and natural rights in English and European Union law

3.7.1 Introduction

Although the word *right* is commonly used by lawyers in a wide variety of contexts, careful analysis reveals that what appears to be a single concept is, in reality, significantly more complex. A leading academic analysis of this complexity is contained in the work of the American theorist, W.N. Hohfeld, which appeared in (1913) 23 Yale LJ 16 and (1917) 27 Yale LJ 710, with an accessible explanation by A.L. Corbin following at (1919) 29 Yale LJ 163.

Hohfeld's analysis reveals a four-fold scheme. First, there are *rights in the strict sense* of the word, which may usefully be called *claim rights* in order to differentiate them from rights in the general sense, which is the subject matter of the analysis. The existence of a claim right in one person involves a corresponding (or *correlative*) duty in someone else. Hohfeld takes the example that one aspect of ownership of land is the claim right to exclude other people from entering upon it. In this situation, therefore, *A's claim right* means that *B has a correlative duty* to keep off the land.

Secondly, the word *right* may be used to indicate what may be seen, on closer examination, to be more accurately described as a *privilege* (or a *liberty* to use a term which is perhaps more appropriate), which means that other people lack the right to prevent the exercise of the privilege or liberty. Returning to the example of land ownership, if we say *A has the right to enter on her own land*, the *correlative* is that *B lacks the right* (or *has a no-right*, to use Hohfeld's hyphenated form) to prevent her from doing so.

Thirdly, the statement that *A has the right to do X* on her land means that she is immune from action taken by B to prevent her from doing it. Thus the word *right* may be used to indicate an *immunity*, the correlative to which is that someone else will have *no power* or *no ability*, or to put it in Hohfeld's terms will have a *disability*, in relation to whatever it may be.

Fourthly, if A makes a contractual offer to sell her land to B, the statement that B has a right to buy the land simply means that A is under a *liability* to sell it if B exercises his *power* to accept the offer. In Hohfeldian terms, a *right* may, therefore, be shown to be more accurately described as a *power*, in which case someone else will be under a correlative *liability*.

Although Hohfeld's analysis may seem purely academic, it has a practical value in sharpening your perception of what you are really discussing when you use the word *right*. Thus, for example, it underlines the point that Hobbes' version of natural rights is more accurately described as natural *liberties*, while Locke's version qualifies as dealing with *rights in the strict sense* of the term. Furthermore, although Hobbes' version is the cruder of the two, it may be seen to provide a more accurate basis for the common law's protection of *natural* (or what would now be more likely to be called *human* or *fundamental*) rights, which, as we shall shortly see, may be more accurately described as *liberties*. Finally, Hohfeld's analysis shows that *having a right* indicates a relationship between right-bearers and other people, rather than indicating a quasi-object which is owned in the same way as any actual object may be.

3.7.2 Natural law and natural rights in pre-revolutionary England

Before the Revolution of 1688, the English courts considered even Acts of Parliament to be subject to natural law, in the sense that they could not validly infringe natural rights. For example, in *Dr Bonham's Case* (1610) 8 Co Rep 114 the court said:

> 'And it appears in our books, that in many cases, the common law will control Acts of Parliament, and sometimes judge them to be utterly void: for when an Act of Parliament is *against common right and reason*, or repugnant, or impossible to be performed, the common law will control it, and adjudge such an Act to be void.' (Emphasis added.)

Similarly, but even more explicitly, in *Day v Savadge* (1614) Hob 85, the court said:

> 'An Act of Parliament, made against natural equity, as to make a man judge in his own case, is void in itself, for *jura naturae sunt immutabilia* [the laws of nature are unchangeable].'

The echoes of the classical tradition of natural law are unmistakeable.

3.7.3 Natural law and natural rights in the modern English legal system

Introduction

The major legal consequence of the Revolution is that Parliament is legislatively supreme. One consequence of this is that no court may hold an Act of Parliament to be void. For example, in *British Railways Board v Picken* [1974] 1 All ER 609, the House of Lords held that the courts must uphold an Act even in a case where it is alleged that Parliament has been misled by those at whose instance an Act has been passed. The task of investigating whether there has been an abuse of the internal procedures of Parliament is a matter exclusively within the jurisdiction of Parliament. Admittedly there appears to be an exception in cases such as *Factortame Ltd v Secretary of State for Transport (No 2)* [1991] 1 All ER 70, where the courts will disapply statutes which are contrary to European Union law, but in reality this is an application of (rather than a derogation from) the legislative supremacy of Parliament. (The question of the United Kingdom's membership of the European Union in relation to the legislative supremacy of Parliament is explored further at p. 93.)

Although the doctrine of the legislative supremacy of Parliament may be stated simply enough, two points must be made about its operation. First,

'The legally unlimited power of the legislature is not used to its limits, but is exercised in accordance with broad principles described in terms of constitutionalism, the rule of law and toleration of minority rights.' (Marshall, *Constitutional Conventions*, 1984, p. 201.)

Secondly, all legislation must be interpreted, even if, as a result of interpretation, it is said to have only one possible meaning. In this connection, it is worth noticing that the body of principle embodied in what are usually termed the *presumptions of statutory interpretation* reflects to a substantial extent the existence of a set of values existing beyond the legislative text. For example, the presumption against injustice may be illustrated by the case of *Coltman v Bibby Tankers Ltd* [1987] 3 All ER 1068, which involved s. 1(3) of the Employer's Liability (Defective Equipment) Act 1969. The section provided that 'equipment' 'includes any plant and machinery, vehicles, aircraft and clothing'. In the High Court, Sheen J held that a worker injured in a ship had a remedy under the Act even though the definition makes no mention of ships, because it would be unjust to differentiate between accidents in, say, aircraft and ships. A majority of the Court of Appeal reversed the decision, but Sheen J's conclusion was unanimously reinstated by the House of Lords, where Lord Oliver said:

'The purpose of the Act was manifestly to saddle the employer with liability for defective plant of every sort with which the employee is compelled to work in the course of his employment, and I can see no ground for excluding particular types of chattel merely on the ground of their size or the element on which they are designed to operate.'

The presumptions of statutory interpretation are normally used to decide which meaning will be held to prevail where various meanings are possible. However, in extreme cases they may even be held to embody some fundamental principle, or aspect of public policy, which requires, or at least empowers, the courts to refuse to implement specific statutory provisions altogether. Two examples will suffice to illustrate the point.

First, the case of *Re Sigsworth* [1934] All ER Rep 113 (which is also mentioned at pp. 83 and 117) was decided under s. 46 of the Administration of Estates Act 1925, which provides that on an intestacy the deceased's property 'shall be distributed' in accordance with the section. The court held that, despite the unequivocal words of the Act, the section did not apply where a son had murdered his mother, because otherwise he would inherit her property and this would contravene the fundamental principle of the common law which prevents people from profiting from their own wrongdoing.

Secondly, under s. 51(1) of the Adoption Act 1976, the Registrar-General was under a duty to give applicants who had been adopted certain information which would enable them to obtain certified copies of their birth certificates, which would in turn, of course, enable them to identify their natural mothers. This duty was stated to be subject to the satisfaction of certain conditions specified in the Act, but otherwise it was couched in absolute terms. In *R v Registrar-General ex parte Smith* [1991] 2 All ER 88, Smith had been adopted while he was still a baby. While serving life imprisonment for murder, he killed another prisoner, saying that he believed his victim to be his adoptive mother. He was convicted of manslaughter and sent to a secure mental hospital. He then applied to the Registrar-General under s. 51(1) of the 1976 Act. The Registrar-General took medical advice and refused to issue the information, fearing that Smith would do harm to his natural mother.

The Court of Appeal held that, as a rule of public policy, even when Parliament has enacted statutory duties in apparently absolute terms, there is a presumption that there was no intention either to enable people to benefit from serious crimes committed in the past, or to assist them to commit serious crimes in the future, and therefore refused Smith the relief which he sought.

It will be apparent that, in cases such as these, both *fundamental principle* and *public policy* are no more than circumlocutions for *natural law*.

(For further examples, and discussion, of the presumptions of statutory interpretation, see, for example, McLeod, *Legal Method*, 8th edn, 2011, pp. 267–282.)

The constitutional difficulty which prevents the courts from quashing statutes is, of course, absent in relation to delegated legislation, which may be quashed on a wide range of grounds, including breach of fundamental rights. For the present purposes, however, it is sufficient to notice only *R v Secretary of State for Social Security ex parte B and Another* [1996] 4 All ER 38, where the respondent made regulations under the Social Security (Contributions and Benefits) Act 1992, removing all entitlement to income-related benefits from certain categories of asylum-seekers. The effect of the regulations was that some people who would previously have been eligible for benefits while pursuing their claims to asylum under the rights conferred on them by the Immigration and Asylum Appeals Act 1993, would be reduced, in Simon Brown LJ's words, to 'a life so destitute that to my mind no civilized nation can tolerate it'. The Court of Appeal, by a majority, quashed the regulations.

Natural rights or natural liberties?

In the mid-18th century case of *Entick v Carrington* [1558–1774] All ER Rep 41, the validity of the King's warrant, which authorized the King's messengers to enter private property and seize goods without the consent of the occupier, was asserted on the basis that it was 'the only means of quieting clamours and sedition'. Rejecting this argument, in words which clearly echo Locke's view of both the importance of private property and the existence of natural rights, Lord Camden CJ said:

'The great end, for which men entered into society, was to secure their property. That *right* is preserved sacred and incommunicable in all instances, where it has not been taken away or abridged by some public law for the good of the whole.' (Emphasis added.)

Although Keir and Lawson, two of the most distinguished commentators of their generation on Constitutional law, describe *Entick v Carrington* as being 'perhaps the central case in English Constitutional law' (*Cases in Constitutional Law*, 5th edn, 1967), it is clear that, in many cases, the common law regards individual interests of this kind as being liberties rather than rights.

The case of *Malone v Metropolitan Police Commissioner (No 2)* [1979] 2 All ER 620 provides a leading example. Malone, who had been convicted of handling stolen goods, complained that the police had tapped his telephone during the investigation which led to his being charged. Holding that there had been no infringement of any right which Malone could legitimately claim, Sir Robert Megarry V-C said:

> 'I am not unduly troubled by the absence of English authority: there has to be a first time for everything, and if the principles of English law, and not least analogies from the existing rules, together with the requirements of justice and commonsense, pointed firmly to such a right existing, then I think the court should not be deterred from recognizing the right....
>
> 'One of the factors that must be relevant in such a case is the degree of particularity in the right that is claimed. The wider and more indefinite the right claimed, the greater the undesirability of holding that such a right exists.... *To create a right for one person, you have to impose a corresponding duty on another*.' (Emphasis added.)

Turning this decision round the other way, Malone's absence of a right meant that the police had a *liberty* to tap his telephone. (Admittedly, as a result of this case and of subsequent proceedings before the European Court of Human Rights, Parliament enacted the Interception of Communications Act 1985 in order to regulate, *inter alia*, telephone tapping, but the need for statutory intervention serves to emphasize the inability, or at least the unwillingness, of the common law to meet a perceived need.)

The European Convention on Human Rights and the Human Rights Act 1998

As we have just seen, English law has always had some capacity to protect fundamental rights and freedoms, but for centuries it did so on an *ad hoc* basis. Since the Second World War, however, many legal systems have moved towards systematic protection, in the form of international agreements. In the European context, the leading international instrument is the European Convention for the Protection of Human Rights and Fundamental Freedoms (commonly abbreviated to the European Convention on Human Rights, or simply the ECHR), which was agreed in 1950, came into force on 3 September 1953.

Although the United Kingdom ratified the ECHR in 1951, 15 years passed before it conceded the right of individuals to have access to the remedial mechanism established by the Convention. Furthermore, there was for many years a consensus between the Conservative and Labour parties that the Convention should not be incorporated into English law, with the result that litigants could not rely directly on its provisions in the English courts. Despite this, however, some judges managed to adopt an approach which gave some effect to the Convention, at least when deciding cases where statutes had been passed in the light of its terms.

For example, in *R v Parole Board ex parte Wilson* (1992) 4 Admin LR 525 the Parole Board had repeatedly refused to recommend the release of a prisoner, and to let him see the reports on himself which the Board had considered. The European Court of Human Rights had said that he should have the right to see the reports, and Parliament had responded obediently by including appropriate provisions in the Criminal Justice Act 1991. Although at the relevant time these provisions had not been brought into force, when the case reached the Court of Appeal Taylor LJ felt able to extend the common law in such a way as to give the prisoner the right which he claimed, since it would have been unfair to have made him wait until the 1991 provisions came into force.

Similarly, in *R v Secretary of State for the Home Department and Another ex parte Norney and Others* (1995) 7 Admin LR 861 the High Court was dealing with s. 34 of the Criminal Justice Act 1991, which had been enacted in order to bring English law into line with the requirements of the Convention. Under these circumstances, Dyson J, while dismissing an application for judicial review in the light of the case as a whole, did say that the court was entitled to have regard to the relevant provisions of the Convention.

Nevertheless, cases such as these notwithstanding, the English courts were clear that they should not go beyond the usual presumption of statutory interpretation which provides that, where possible, ambiguities should be resolved in a way which is consistent with international obligations. As Lord Bridge put it, in *R v Secretary of State for the Home Department ex parte Brind and Others* [1991] 1 All ER 720:

> 'When Parliament has been content for so long to leave those who complain that their Convention rights have been infringed to seek their remedy in Strasbourg, it would be surprising suddenly to find that the judiciary had, without Parliament's aid, the means to incorporate the Convention.'

The bi-party consensus on legislative inaction was broken in 1997 with the introduction into Parliament of the Bill which became the Human Rights Act 1998. However, even this measure falls short of simply incorporating the Convention into English law, preferring to define a new category of *Convention rights*, which are then given special status.

Section 1 of the Act defines *Convention rights* as:

> 'the rights and fundamental freedoms set out in –
>
> (a) articles 2 to 12 and 14 of the Convention, and
> (b) articles 1 to 3 of the First Protocol, and

(c) articles 1 and 2 of the Sixth Protocol,

as read with articles 16 to 18 of the Convention.'

One notable consequence of this definition is the exclusion of arts 1 and 13 (dealing respectively with the duty of the United Kingdom to secure to everyone within the United Kingdom the rights under the Convention, and the provision of effective national remedies). Furthermore, s. 1(2) provides that the operation of those articles to which the Act does apply may be subject to derogations and reservations.

Section 6 of the Act makes it unlawful for a public authority, excluding both Houses of Parliament but including 'any person certain of whose functions are functions of a public nature', to act in a way which is incompatible with Convention rights. Additionally, s. 3 creates a new principle of interpretation, which requires that

'so far as it is possible to do so, primary and subordinate legislation must be read and given effect in a way which is compatible with the Convention rights.'

The Act does not affect the validity of any primary legislation, nor of delegated legislation provided the parent Act under which it is made contains a provision to that effect. Any court, hearing any proceedings, may entertain an argument that Convention rights have been breached. Additionally, a court of at least the level of the High Court which finds a breach of Convention rights which cannot be resolved by interpretation may make a declaration of incompatibility with Convention rights (under s. 4), which may then result in the government taking action by way of a form of delegated legislation, which is known as a *remedial order*.

3.7.4 European Union law and the protection of fundamental rights

The role of the Court of Justice

At a relatively early stage in the life of the European Economic Community, the Court of Justice established that Community (now Union) law protects fundamental rights and freedoms.

For example, the case of *Stauder v City of Ulm* [1969] ECR 419 arose from the Community's plan to reduce surplus stocks of butter by selling it cheaply to certain groups within the population. One individual objected to the way in which the German authorities implemented the scheme, because he was required to disclose his name to the retailer of the butter, as a result of which the retailer would know that he was in receipt of certain welfare benefits.

The Court of Justice acknowledged that this infringed the principle of equality, and was therefore a breach of the individual's fundamental rights. (In the event, however, the Court of Justice avoided the problem by saying that the Commission's decision, which formed the basis of the scheme, should be interpreted so that such disclosure by individuals was not a precondition to their obtaining cheap butter.)

Similarly, in *Nold v Commission* [1974] 2 CMLR 338, a decision of the Commission allowed member states to control the supply of coal. The German authorities exercised this power to the disadvantage of a wholesaler of coal. In all the circumstances of the case, the Court of Justice concluded that the harm the wholesaler had suffered was the result of economic change, rather than the Commission's decision, but on the way to this conclusion it made the following observations:

'13. As the Court has already stated, fundamental rights form an integral part of the general principles of law, the observance of which it ensures.

'In safeguarding these rights, the Court is bound to draw inspiration from constitutional traditions common to the member states, and it cannot therefore uphold measures which are incompatible with fundamental rights recognized and protected by the constitutions of those states.

'Similarly, international treaties for the protection of human rights on which the member states have collaborated or of which they are signatories, can supply guidelines which should be followed within the framework of Community law. [But]

'14... Within the Community legal order... rights should, if necessary, be subject to certain limits justified by the overall objectives pursued by the Community, on condition that the substance of these rights is left untouched...'

The Joint Declaration of 5 April 1977

The commitment of the Court of Justice to the protection of fundamental rights and freedoms was endorsed at the political level by a Joint Declaration issued on 5 April 1977 by the Parliament, the Council of Ministers and the Commission, in the following terms:

'(1) The European Parliament, the Council and the Commission stress the prime importance they attach to the protection of fundamental rights, as derived in particular from the constitutions of the member states and the European Convention for the Protection of Human Rights and Fundamental Freedoms.

'In exercise of their powers and in pursuance of the aims of the European Communities they respect and will continue to respect these rights.'

The Treaty of Amsterdam 1997

Article 7 of the Treaty of Amsterdam developed a provision which had originated as art. F.2 of the Treaty on European Union, so that the European Union became not simply committed to respecting fundamental rights as guaranteed by the ECHR and as resulting from 'the constitutional traditions common to the member states, as general principles of Community Law', but also became committed to suspending certain of the rights (including voting rights) of a member state which is found to be in 'serious and persistent breach' of the principles of 'liberty, democracy, respect for human rights and fundamental freedoms, and the rule of law'.

The Treaty of Lisbon 2007

The broad purpose of the Treaty of Lisbon 2007, which came into force on 1 December 2009, was to reform the structure and functioning of the European Union. Its key provisions included converting the European Union (which had been created by the Maastricht Treaty 1992 as a purely political entity) into a body with legal personality; and dissolving the European Community. The Union's newly acquired legal status means that referring to European *Union* law (rather than European *Community* law) has finally become technically correct, as well as being almost universal. This change is further reflected by the change of the official title of the European Court of Justice from the *Court of Justice of the European Communities* to the *Court of Justice of the European Union*.

More particularly, the treaty provided for the European Union to become a party to the ECHR (which it had lacked the capacity to do while it was devoid of legal personality) as well as providing for the Charter of Fundamental Rights of the European Union to become part of European Union law. (The Charter, which was agreed by the Inter-Governmental Conference leading to the Treaty of Nice 2001, but was not included in that treaty, sets out the whole range of civil, political, economic and social rights which are enjoyed, under what is now Union law, by anyone who is resident in the Union, whether or not they are citizens of the Union.)

Summary

- The natural law tradition goes back to Ancient Greece.

- Plato says that the purpose of the law is the benefit of the whole community, to which end it uses persuasion or force to make each person part of the community as a whole.

- Aristotle classifies law into natural law, which is universal and unchanging, and *conventional law*, which varies from time to time and from place to place.

- Aristotle classifies justice into distributive justice, which approximates to what would now be called social justice, and corrective justice, which is concerned with correcting unfairness which arises when the law is broken.

- Greek theorists do not address the question of the validity of immoral law, but other members of their society do so, with Sophocles' *Antigone* providing a notable example.

- Ancient Rome, represented in this context particularly by the works of Cicero, provides the idea that law is the product of human reason, because everything has its own nature, and it is the nature of man to be rational. For Cicero, laws which are not for the benefit of the community are not truly laws.

Summary cont'd

▶ In the early Christian era, St Augustine provides an intellectual bridge between the pre-Christian and Christian eras. The true meaning of his proposition that 'an unjust law is not a law' has proved problematic.

▶ In the Middle Ages, St Thomas Aquinas develops a theory of natural law which continued the pre-Christian tradition of reason as the basis of law. This theory is still influential within the Roman Catholic church. For Aquinas there will usually, but not always, be no duty to obey positive law which contravenes natural law.

▶ After Aquinas, natural law theory begins to become secularized with the work of Grotius. Furthermore, with the work of Hobbes and Locke, the emphasis moves from *natural law* to *natural rights*.

▶ According to Hume, all natural law seeks to derive conclusions in the form of value judgments from proposition in the form of facts, and is therefore logically unsound.

▶ Fundamental rights are recognized and protected to some extent by both English and European Union law. The Human Rights Act 1998 raises the profile of the European Convention on Human Rights (ECHR) within English law, but does not incorporate the Convention into English Law. The Treaty of Lisbon 2007 confers legal personality on the European Union (EU) and provides for the EU to accede to the ECHR, and for the Charter of Fundamental Rights of the European Union to become part of European Union law.

Further reading

Aristotle, *Nichomachean Ethics*, translated by Thomson, J.A.K., 1953

Cicero, *The Laws*, translated by Rudd, Niall, 1998

Cicero, *The Republic*, translated by Rudd, Niall, 1998

Corbin, A.L., (1919) 29 Yale LJ 163

Grotius (de Groot, Hugo), *On the Law of War and Peace*, 1625

Hobbes, Thomas, *Leviathan*, 1651

Hohfeld, W.N. (1913) 23 Yale LJ 16 and (1917) 27 Yale LJ 710

Hume, David, *A Treatise of Human Nature*, 1739

Keir, D.L. and Lawson, F.H., *Cases in English Constitutional Law*, 5th edn, 1967

Kelly, J.M., *A Short History of Western Legal Theory*, 1992

Lisska, Anthony J., Aquinas's *Theory of Natural Law*, 1996

Locke, John, *Two Treatises on Government*, 1690

Marshall, Geoffrey, *Constitutional Conventions*, 1984

McLeod, Ian, *Legal Method*, 8th edn, 2011; 9th edn, 2013

Plato, *The Republic*, translated by Lee, H.D.P., 1955

Scruton, Roger, *A Short History of Modern Philosophy*, 2nd edn, 1995 (republished 2002)

Chapter 4

English analytical positivism

Introduction

This chapter identifies that part of legal theory which is known as analytical positivism, and considers the work of two of its leading English exponents, namely Austin and Hart. More particularly, it will show how the work of the latter remedies certain deficiencies in the work of the former.

The tradition of English analytical positivism may be traced back to the work of Jeremy Bentham (1748–1832). Although some of Bentham's work was published in his lifetime, the manuscript of his major work on legal theory was overlooked for more than a century, with its first publication occurring as late as 1945, under the title *The Limits of Jurisprudence Defined*, before appearing in definitive form in 1970 as *Of Laws in General*. There was, however, no such delay in the publication of the work of his follower, John Austin (1790–1852).

In 1826 Austin became the first Professor of Jurisprudence in the newly founded University of London, which subsequently became University College, London. (Before this time, access to university education was restricted to members of the Church of England, and University College was founded specifically to widen access to university education for people of other – or no – religious persuasions. This objective, together with the fact that it was – and indeed still is – based in Gower Street, not only explains why members of the college are commonly called 'the godless of Gower Street', but also made it a peculiarly appropriate environment for a positivist professor of law.) Austin's work, *The Province of Jurisprudence Determined*, which consisted of the text of six lectures which he had delivered in the college, was first published in 1832, but his version of what is known as the *command theory of law* continued to dominate the English teaching of jurisprudence well into the 20th century.

Finally, and by way of an aside, one reason why analytical positivism came to dominate English legal theory, is that 'late-nineteenth and twentieth century juristic thought evolved mainly within a university culture which emphasized rigorous inquiry and the systematization of knowledge'. (Neil Duxbury, *Why English Jurisprudence is Analytical*, in [2004] *Current Legal Problems*, 1.) Thus it is not surprising that the work of John Austin fell to be assessed by succeeding generations of scholars who were fundamentally sympathetic to (and therefore inclined to consolidate rather than challenge) his methodology, even if they eventually became disenchanted with his conclusions.

4.2 Austin's command theory of law

4.2.1 Introduction

As the title of his lectures (*The Province of Jurisprudence Determined*) indicates, Austin is concerned to identify the limits of the subject of jurisprudence. This necessarily involves eliminating a great deal of material which may in one way or another be said to be law, without being law for the present purposes. Austin begins with an unequivocal statement of his positivist position:

'The matter of jurisprudence is positive law: law, simply and strictly so called: or law set by political superiors to political inferiors.' (*The Province of Jurisprudence Determined*, 1832, p. 9.)

Further refinements are then introduced. First, the *political superior* must be a *sovereign*:

'If a determinate human superior, not in the habit of obedience to a like superior, receive habitual obedience from the bulk of a given society, that determinate superior is sovereign in that society, and the society (including the superior) is a society political and independent.' (*Op. cit.*, p. 194.)

The next stage is to explain the concept of *command*, which may be either 'direct or circuitous'. (*Op. cit.*, p. 134):

'The ideas or notions comprehended by the term command are the following. (1) A wish or desire conceived by a rational being, that another rational being shall do or forebear. (2) An evil to proceed from the former, and to be incurred by the latter, in case the latter not comply with the wish. (3) An expression or intimation of the wish by words or other signs.' (*Op. cit.*, p. 17.)

It will be apparent that, for these purposes, the idea of a *sanction* (i.e. the *evil* which is imposed in the event of non-compliance with the command) is inextricably involved in the idea of the command itself.

Finally, the status of law is reserved for a command which 'obliges *generally* to acts or forbearances of a class'. (Emphasis added.)

In summary, therefore, Austin's version of law requires a *command* which is both *express* and *general*, which is issued from a *sovereign* to a subject, and non-compliance with which results in the sovereign imposing a *sanction* on the subject. We must now consider each of these elements in more detail.

4.2.2 The nature of the command

The requirement that the command must be express may seem obvious enough, and is reflected in Lord Diplock's dictum that 'Parliament, under our constitution, is sovereign only in respect of what it expresses by the words used in the legislation it has passed'. (*Black-Clawson International Ltd v Papierwerke Waldhof-Aschaffenberg AG* [1975] 1 All ER 810.) Nevertheless, in practice it is by no means certain that Parliament has always expressed that which the courts hold to be the law, since interpretation will always be necessary, at which point factors other than the plain words of the statute (for example, the court's perception of the statutory purpose, or of judicial policy) may come into play.

The case of *Kammins Ballrooms Co Ltd v Zenith Investments Ltd* [1970] 2 All ER 871 provides a classic modern example of the way in which the purposive approach to interpretation may radically affect the meaning of an apparently clear, express legislative text. The facts arose under the scheme of security of tenure for business premises contained in Part II of the Landlord and Tenant Act 1954. Briefly, the statutory scheme requires that a tenant who wishes to retain the tenancy of premises on the expiry of the existing tenancy should ask the landlord to grant him a new one. If the landlord refuses to comply, the tenant can then apply to the court, where the matter will be resolved. In the context of this procedure, s. 29(3) of the Act provides that 'no application... shall be entertained unless it is made not less than two nor more than four months after... the making of the tenant's request for a new tenancy'. In *Kammins* the tenant's application to the court was made outside the statutory period, but the House of Lords held that this did not necessarily invalidate it. Lord Diplock acknowledged that:

> 'Semantics and the rules of syntax alone could never justify the conclusion that the words "No application... *shall* be entertained *unless*" meant that some applications should be entertained notwithstanding that neither of the conditions which follow the word "unless" was fulfilled.' (Original emphasis.)

Nevertheless, Lord Diplock pointed out that the purpose of the Act was to persuade landlords and tenants to proceed by agreement wherever possible, and that the time limit in question had been enacted for the protection of landlords. It followed that landlords should be allowed to waive compliance with the time limit if they so wished. (The fact that, in all the circumstances of the case, this particular landlord was held not to have waived compliance is irrelevant to the principle of interpretation.) It will be readily apparent that the law, *as formulated by the House of Lords*, did not rely on the express words contained in the statutory command.

The decision of the House of Lords in *Jones v Secretary of State for Social Services* [1972] 1 All ER 145 provides an example of the court's perception of judicial policy (in this case, in relation to the operation of the doctrine of binding precedent) being crucial to the outcome. The case was decided under a scheme of industrial injuries legislation which provided that claims for long-term benefit were determined in two stages and by two different tribunals. In the first place the question was whether an injury had been caused by an accident arising out of employment. If this question were answered in the affirmative, the second stage was to decide the extent of the disablement, and therefore the amount of benefit payable. The legislation stated that the answer to the first question was to be 'final'. In *Re Dowling* [1967] AC 725, the House of Lords had held that the tribunal determining the second question could not re-open consideration of the first question.

In *Jones*, on legislation which was substantially the same as that which was before the court in *Dowling*, the majority of a seven-member House of Lords decided to follow the earlier case. The relevance of the case in the present context is that even though four Law Lords held that, as a matter of statutory interpretation, *Dowling* had been wrongly decided, only three were willing to exercise their discretion to depart from that decision. Several reasons were given for the willingness to follow a case which had been wrongly decided, thereby consolidating the error, but for the present purposes the point is simply that the command (i.e. the relevant statutory provisions) required to be interpreted, and that different judges not only produced different interpretations, but also had different opinions about the effect of those interpretations on the final outcome of the case.

Once it is accepted that cases such as these show that in reality the courts may treat a statute, albeit one enacted by a legislatively supreme Parliament, as no more than a starting point when identifying and applying the law, the proposition that the express command of a sovereign is an essential element in law must be open to serious doubt.

Austin's requirement that a command must be *general* before it qualifies as a law may be thought to neglect the facts of legal life, because in practice all sorts of *individualized* commands clearly have legal effect. For example, orders of a court restraining a defendant from continuing to commit a trespass, or prohibiting the republication of a libel, are both clearly commands, backed by the sanction of imprisonment for contempt of court in the event of breach, and yet they are equally clearly individualized in the sense of being addressed to specific defendants. However, Austin would regard these as being merely applications of law to particular cases, rather than being law strictly so-called, and on this basis they provide no challenge to his theory.

4.2.3 The nature of the sovereign

The requirement that the sovereign must be human clearly excludes divine law from Austin's area of inquiry, but it would be unfair even for natural lawyers to lay this exclusion specifically at Austin's door by way of criticism, since it is a matter which is common to positivist theories generally. However, other aspects of Austin's concept of a sovereign are open to specific criticism.

The requirement that the sovereign shall 'not [be] in the habit of obedience to a like superior' may be reasonably accepted as a characteristic of sovereignty, while the proposition that the sovereign must 'receive habitual obedience from the bulk of a given society' may seem to be no more than a realistic acceptance that no legal system can expect to experience total compliance with its laws. However, this latter element does conceal a difficulty, since it is a commonplace observation that many laws are accorded habitual obedience even though the same cannot be said of the sovereign which enacted them, for the simple reason that that sovereign no longer exists. For example, the Offences Against the Person Act 1861 is unquestionably still law, despite the fact that no members of the Parliament which enacted it are still alive. Admittedly there are various ways in which it is possible to seek to avoid this objection.

For example, you may wish to argue that it is the *institution* Parliament, rather than a specific and transitory assemblage of parliamentarians, which is sovereign. While this contention obviously makes sense in general terms, and would no doubt satisfy most people, it must be said that according sovereignty to an *institution* fails to take account of Austin's requirement that the sovereign shall be *human*.

Alternatively, you may wish to argue that, at any given time, any current Parliament's failure to repeal earlier statutes may be taken to be tacit endorsement of them, and that therefore all unrepealed statutes must be taken to have the authority of every successive Parliament. This attempted defence of Austin, however, can fare no better than the previous one, because it fails to take account of his requirement that there must be an 'expression or intimation of the [sovereign's] wish by words or other signs', which clearly precludes the concept of an *implied* command.

Furthermore, Austin runs into difficulty during those periods when one Parliament has been dissolved and another has not yet been summoned. Who, then, is the sovereign? Austin's own analysis seeks to make this question irrelevant, by saying that, even when Parliament is sitting, the electorate is the true source of the House of Commons' contribution to the sovereignty of Parliament as a whole:

'Adopting the language of most of the writers who have treated of the British Constitution, I commonly suppose that the present parliament, or the parliament for the time being, is possessed of the sovereignty: or I commonly suppose that the king and the lords, with the members of the commons' house, form a tripartite body which is sovereign or supreme. But, speaking accurately, the members of the commons' house are merely trustees for the body by which they are elected and appointed: and, consequently, the sovereignty always resides in the king, and the peers, with the electoral body of the commons.' (*Op. cit.*, pp. 230–231.)

Once again, this seems more than a little strained, especially when it is remembered that part of the notion of sovereignty is habitual obedience by a political inferior to a political superior. Although admittedly Austin is not saying that the electorate *is* the sovereign, his analysis does seem to suggest that an essential element of sovereignty is that the electorate should be habitually obedient to itself; which is somewhat odd, to say the least.

4.2.4 The nature of the sanction

The need for a sanction fits the idea of criminal law quite well; or at least it did so at the time when Austin was writing, since the imposition of a sentence of imprisonment was the normal consequence of a conviction. (It would be churlish to criticize Austin for not taking account of alternative means of dealing with offenders, such as probation órders, which were not available in his day.) However, the general requirement of a sanction constitutes a serious weakness in Austin's theory, and did so even in his own day, since it appears to disqualify the whole field of civil law from his definition of *law*. The point may be illustrated most clearly by reference to areas of law which confer powers on people, such as the law relating to the making of wills and contracts.

Suppose I make a will but fail to observe the statutory requirements as to the witnessing of my signature. The consequence is that my will is a nullity, and therefore the beneficiaries I have named will not inherit. While Austin is content to describe nullity as a sanction, it is difficult to see how this can be said to fit the facts. Even if, in the abstract, it makes sense to speak of nullity as being a sanction, in this particular example I shall be dead before the consequences of the nullity occur, and therefore there is a degree of artificiality in saying that I am subject to a sanction.

Leaving aside the example of an improperly executed will, and taking a situation in which I am still alive at the relevant time, it may still be difficult to see nullity as a sanction. Suppose, for example, that I have a credit account with a bookmaker and that I place a bet on a horse. By virtue of the Gaming Act 1845, the contract is void; therefore if I lose before I pay the stake, and refuse to pay it thereafter, I cannot be sued. On any ordinary use of language, can I really be said to be subject to a sanction in this situation?

4.3   Hart's *Concept of Law*

4.3.1   Introduction

Despite its evident deficiencies, Austin's command theory of law dominated the field of English legal theory until well into the 20th century. The work which transformed English legal theory was H.L.A. Hart's *The Concept of Law*, first published in 1961, with a second edition appearing posthumously in 1994. (It is worth noticing that the second edition takes the rather unusual form of reproducing the first edition in practically identical terms, with the new part being confined to a postscript in which Hart responds to his critics.)

By way of an aside, it is interesting to note that although Hart had wanted to be a lawyer since before his student days (see Nicola Lacey, *A Life of H.L.A. Hart*, 2004, p. 40), while at Oxford he actually studied a combination of Greek, Latin, Ancient History and Philosophy. Then, having graduated 'with one of the top first class degrees of his year in spite of acute jaundice which left him bedridden for almost six weeks in the term preceding his final examinations' (*op. cit*, p. 25), Hart began to study Law with the aspiration of graduating after only one year's study. When it became clear, halfway through the year, that he would not obtain a First, he abandoned the project in favour of the easier option of proceeding directly to the first part of the Bar examinations. (*Ibid.*) However, his aspiration to acquire an academic (rather than only a professional) qualification in Law continued, and led him to prepare for the (postgraduate) degree of Bachelor of Civil Law at Oxford. On this occasion, though, he was hospitalized as the result of an accident, as a result of which he decided not to present himself for the examinations, which began only ten days after his discharge from hospital. (*Op. cit.*, p. 44.)

Having completed his Bar examinations, and after a period of successful practice at the Chancery Bar, followed by wartime service in MI5, a further twist to his career saw Hart obtaining a Fellowship in Philosophy at Oxford. From this vantage point, he moved to the Law Faculty on his election to the Chair of Jurisprudence in 1952. Thus Hart was distinctly unusual among those teaching and writing about jurisprudence, being not only an experienced and successful practitioner of Law, but also a professional philosopher.

Hart describes his book as 'an essay in analytical jurisprudence' which is intended to clarify 'the general framework of legal thought' rather than presenting a critique of law or legal policy. (*The Concept of Law*, 2nd edn, 1994, p. *v*.) Additionally, he says that the book is also 'an essay in descriptive sociology', by which he means that a great deal of light can be shed on social situations or relationships by examining the way in which we speak about them, and that although this will often depend on the social context, that dependence may well be left unstated.

Whatever labels are attached to it, one thing is clear about *The Concept of Law*: it makes no claim to offer a *definition* of law. Indeed, Hart rejects the attempt to provide a useful definition of *law* at all. He begins by identifying

'three recurrent issues: How does law differ from and how is it related to orders backed by threats? How does legal obligation differ from, and how is it related to, moral obligation? What are rules and to what extent is law an affair of rules?' (*Op. cit.*, p. 13.)

Having commented, *inter alia*, that 'definition... is primarily a matter of drawing lines or distinguishing between one kind of thing and another' (*ibid.*) Hart concludes that 'the history of attempts to provide concise definitions has shown' that 'nothing concise enough to be recognized as a definition' (*op. cit.*, p. 16) can prove satisfactory. Nevertheless, he says that bringing the three issues together 'has not been misguided; for... it is possible to isolate and characterize a central set of elements which form a common part of the answer to all three'. (*Ibid.*)

Hart proceeds to devote three chapters to a detailed, critical analysis of Austin's theory, but his conclusions (see *The Concept of Law*, 2nd edn, 1994, p. 79), may be summarized as follows. First, even the example of criminal law, which most clearly fits the idea of commands backed by sanctions, fails to fit Austin's theory fully, because it generally applies to those who enact it, as well as to others. Secondly, there are other types of law, such as those conferring powers on public bodies and those giving private persons the power to regulate their own legal relationships which cannot accurately be seen as commands backed by sanctions. Thirdly, some laws arise other than by way of express command. Finally, there is the problem of the continuity of law's validity, despite the limited life of the sovereign which enacts it.

Hart concludes that, after a study of Austin's theory, there is 'plainly need for a fresh start' and proceeds to locate 'the root cause of failure' in the fact that Austin's theory 'cannot... yield, *the idea of a rule*, without which we cannot hope to elucidate even the most elementary forms of law'. (Emphasis added. *Op. cit.*, p. 80.)

4.3.2 Law as a system of rules

There are several strands to Hart's argument that law consists of a system of rules, each of which needs to be understood individually before their joint effect may be properly appreciated. These strands may be summarized as the distinction between *personal habits* and *social rules*; the distinction between *being obliged* and *being under an obligation*; the distinction between the *external* and the *internal* aspects of rules; and the distinction between *primary* and *secondary* legal rules.

We shall consider each of these distinctions in turn.

The distinction between personal habits and social rules

Although it is obvious that certain personal habits are highly individual (such as always wearing a lucky charm for superstitious reasons), it is equally obvious that many are very widespread. Clearly, therefore, we must distinguish between widespread habits and social rules.

For example, as a matter of personal habit, I may invariably drink coffee after my dinner. Furthermore, the practice of after-dinner coffee drinking may be very widespread. Nevertheless those who prefer to drink tea, or not to drink anything, will not find themselves subjected to criticism by other members of society. In other words, although drinking coffee after dinner may be an example of convergent behaviour, when correctly analysed it is nothing more than *a large number of instances of individual behaviour*, and therefore cannot be called a rule.

By way of contrast, the convergent behaviour of standing up when the national anthem is played is more than simply a matter of personal taste, not only because most people conform, but also, and crucially, because those who do not do so are likely to incur the disapproval of other members of society. In other words, people feel themselves to be under an obligation to join in this example of convergent behaviour, and consequently it may be called a rule. In passing, it may be worth saying that although the existence of an obligation indicates the existence of a rule, Hart concedes that language is sometimes used in such a way that the converse does not necessarily apply. In other words, although we may speak of the *rules* of matters such as grammar and etiquette, and we may even express those rules in terms of what you *should or should not* do (for example, *always use a capital letter at the beginning of a sentence* or *don't put your elbows on the dining table*), it would not accord with the normal use of language to say that there is a *duty* to comply with such prescriptions and proscriptions. As Hart puts it:

> 'Rules are conceived and spoken of as imposing obligations when the general demand for conformity is insistent and the social pressure brought to bear upon those who deviate or threaten to deviate is great.' (*Op. cit.*, p. 86.)

It is clear, therefore, that Hart is using *rules* in a relatively strict sense. However, further insight may be gained by considering more closely his view of the nature of *obligation*, as clarified by the distinction between *being obliged* and *being under an obligation*.

The distinction between being obliged and being under an obligation

Although the phrases *being obliged* and *being under an obligation* to do something will commonly appear to be interchangeable, Hart argues (*op. cit.*, pp. 82 *et seq.*) that there is, in principle, an important distinction between them. He illustrates the distinction through the example of a gunman, A, who demands money from a victim, B. According to the ordinary use of language, we would say that B *is obliged* to hand over the money (because he fears the consequences if he does not do so), but we would not say that B is *under an obligation* (or *owes a duty*) to comply with A's demand. Hart develops the point by saying that we would not say that B is even *obliged* to comply with the demand if the harm which A threatens to inflict on B is merely trivial; or if the harm is serious but there are circumstances making it unlikely that A will actually inflict it.

Moreover, just as it is possible to *be obliged without being under an obligation*, so it is possible to *be under an obligation without being obliged*. For example, if the law requires that all able-bodied males within a specified age group shall undertake compulsory military service, we would say that X is *under an obligation* to undertake such service (provided, of course, that he is male, able-bodied and within the specified age group) even though, in fact, he has gone abroad, and will, therefore, never actually be obliged to perform his obligation.

Of course, in practice, the two situations will commonly overlap, so that, for example, someone who has been fined following conviction for an offence will be both obliged, and under an obligation, to pay the money. Nevertheless, this aspect of Hart's argument provides a useful insight into the distinction between commands which may be backed by nothing more than naked power and rules which create obligations.

The distinction between the external and internal aspects of rules

The third of Hart's distinctions which we must consider is that between the *external* and the *internal* aspects of rules.

As the expression suggests, the *external* aspect of a rule is apparent from the outside, so that, for example, systematic observation can be used to predict when an habitual after-dinner coffee-drinker will drink coffee. The *internal* aspect, on the other hand, is apparent only to those who are subject to the rule. Hart (*op. cit.*, p. 90) takes the example of a person who observes the way in which motorists respond to red traffic lights. Since it is an externally observable fact that most motorists stop at red traffic lights, it is reasonable to predict that any given motorist will do so. However, viewed internally (from the point of view of the motorist) the fact of a red traffic light is not simply evidence on which to base a prediction, but actually imposes an obligation (or a duty) to stop. This internal aspect of the rule may appear to be simply a feeling on the part of the person subject to it, but Hart rejects this analysis. More particularly, he argues:

> 'What is necessary is that there should be a critical reflective attitude to certain patterns of behaviour as a common standard, and that this should display itself in criticism (including self-criticism), demands for conformity, and in acknowledgments that such criticism and demands are justified, all of which find their characteristic expression in the normative terminology of "ought", "must", and "should", "right" and "wrong".' (*Op. cit.*, p. 57.)

Since there is nothing in the after-dinner coffee-drinking example which can be said to correspond to this internal element, it follows that that example of convergent behaviour remains at the level of a habit, rather than being elevated to the status of a rule.

The distinction between primary and secondary legal rules

We are now equipped to proceed to the core of Hart's theory, namely the distinction between *primary* and *secondary* legal rules, and the need for both to exist before there can be said to be a legal system.

Primary rules are those which impose obligations. Such rules may be either positive or negative, and would embrace both the rule which requires you to pay income tax and the rule which requires you to refrain from murder. However, it will be readily apparent that the idea of primary rules presents only a partial view of the law, since there will frequently be *uncertainty as to the content of the primary rules*, coupled with a need to *change* them from time to time, and a need to *resolve disputes* arising from the application of the rules in particular cases. It is to deal with these matters that Hart formulates the concept of *secondary rules*, which he classifies under three headings.

The first category of secondary rules deals with the problem of uncertainty. Here, Hart says, there must be a *rule of recognition*, so that actors within the legal system can recognize those rules which are law and distinguish them from those which are not.

> '[The rule of recognition operates] by reference to some general characteristic possessed by the primary rules. This may be the fact of their having been enacted

by a specific body, or their long customary practice, or their relation to judicial decisions.' (*Op. cit.*, p. 95.)

In the English system, therefore, the rule of recognition has at least two limbs: those things are law which are enacted by, or under the authority of, Parliament, as are the decisions of the courts which acquire authoritative status under the doctrine of binding precedent. It may be possible to formulate it in such a way that more limbs appear. For example, the rule of recognition may extend to laws emanating from the European Community (now the Union), and it may still be possible to regard custom as a source of English law. However, the first of these propositions stems directly from the European Communities Act 1972, while the second stems from a number of judicial decisions to this effect, and therefore the application of Occam's razor should leave the original formulation unadorned by any additions. (*Occam's razor* is the name given to the principle attributed to William of Occam, a 14th century Franciscan philosopher, which requires superfluous elements in any argument to be discarded. He is said to have dissected arguments as if he were taking a razor to them.) At this stage, therefore, it becomes plain why the obligation to stop at a red traffic light is law (because it is contained in the road traffic legislation), whereas the obligation to stand up when the national anthem is played is not (because there is no parliamentary or judicial authority that it is).

In passing, it may be worth commenting on the oddness of Hart's classifying the rule of recognition as being secondary, when common sense would seem to indicate that its being the very foundation of the legal system should make it primary, but we will introduce needless complication if we try to redefine his terms.

The second category of secondary rules, namely *rules of change*, has two dimensions. The first dimension deals with the need to change the primary rules, which, in the context of the English legal system, means overruling judicial decisions in order to terminate their status as binding precedents, and repealing or amending statutes. Obviously, therefore, these rules are intimately connected with the rule of recognition, because their application enables us to decide which of two apparently conflicting primary rules will prevail over the other. The second dimension of the rules of change is that they enable people to change the way in which the primary rules of obligation apply to their own personal situations, through such means as making contracts and wills 'and many other voluntarily created structures of rights and duties which typify life under law'. (*Op. cit.*, p. 96.)

The third category of secondary rules, which deals with the need to resolve disputes, consists of *rules of adjudication*, which not only confer upon public officials the power to determine legal disputes, but also govern the way in which that power is exercised and give special legal status to orders which are made in consequence of adjudication. (*Op. cit.*, pp. 96–97.)

It is, of course, the function of the rule of recognition to enable actors within the legal system to identify the other rules which make up that system as a whole. Therefore, while it may be stating the obvious to say that a rule must exist before the rule of recognition can be applied to it, it is essential to realize that those rules which satisfy the rule of recognition go beyond mere *de facto* existence and exist in the additional sense of having *legal validity*. Hart makes this point by way of comparison with the rule which requires Christian men to bare their heads when entering a church. The question of the validity of such a rule does not arise independently of its effectiveness. Therefore, if people were to stop complying with it, the rule would cease to exist, beyond which point it would make no sense to ask whether the rule was still valid. In the case of a law, on the other hand, mass disobedience of a rule (for example, of a speed limit) has no effect on the rule's validity. This quality of validity-irrespective-of-observance stems from the rule of recognition, which provides the criterion for granting or withholding the status of *law* from any given rule. More particularly, the rule of recognition itself 'exists only as a complex, but normally concordant, practice of the courts, officials and private persons in identifying the law by reference to certain criteria. Its existence is a matter of fact'. (*Op. cit.*, pp. 109–110.)

Two final points must be made about the rule of recognition. First, despite its factual nature, Hart specifically acknowledges that 'the rule of recognition may incorporate as criteria of legal validity conformity with moral principles or substantive values' and that therefore his theory is an example of soft positivism. (*Op. cit.*, p. 250. For the distinction between strict and soft positivism, see p. 20.)

Secondly, the proposition that the existence of the rule of recognition is a matter of fact creates a difficulty, since it is also, *ex hypothesi*, a matter of law. Hart responds to this by saying that 'the ultimate rule of recognition may be regarded from two points of view: one is expressed in the external statement of fact that the rule exists in the actual practice of the system; the other is expressed in the internal statements of validity made by those who use it in identifying law'. (*Op. cit.*, pp. 111–112.)

4.3.3 The *minimum content of natural law*

Although it will be apparent that Hart is first and foremost a positivist, he also identifies 'certain universally recognized principles of conduct which have a basis in elementary truths concerning human beings, their natural environment and aims' and which, he says, may be said to constitute 'the core of good sense' in, and therefore 'the minimum content' of, natural law. (*Op. cit.*, pp. 192–194). This notion is based on nothing more sophisticated or obscure than the assumption that humankind collectively, and the individuals who constitute the species, wish to survive, and simply consists of the 'rules of conduct which any social organization must contain if it is to be viable'.

In developing this aspect of his theory, Hart relies on five things which he terms 'generalizations' or 'truisms'. These are that while human beings are *vulnerable to each other*, they are nevertheless *approximately equal in their powers*, and are commonly motivated by *limited altruism*, with *limitations* also being evident in their *resources*, their *understanding* and their *strength of will*. It follows from these that there must be rules restricting violence. The facts of *vulnerability* and *approximate equality* and the *limited nature of altruism* require

'a system of mutual forebearance and compromise which is the base of both legal and moral obligation.' (*Op. cit.*, p. 195.)

More particularly, the fact of *limited resources* requires some

'minimum form of the institution of property (though not necessarily individual property), and the distinctive kind of rule which requires respect for it.' (*Ibid.*)

Finally, the facts of *limited understanding and strength of will* result in everyone being

'tempted from time to time to prefer their own immediate interests and, in the absence of a special organization for their detection and punishment, many would succumb to the temptation.' (*Op. cit.*, p. 197.)

Hart's mention of punishment may appear to take us back to Austin's command theory, in which the role of sanctions is, of course, basic. However, it is both clear and unsurprising that Hart does not intend this reversion to the theory which his own theory is intended to supplant. More particularly, Hart explains that

'"sanctions" are... required not as the normal motive for obedience, but as a guarantee that those who would voluntarily obey shall not be sacrificed to those who would not. To obey, without this, would be to risk going to the wall. Given this standing danger, what reason demands is *voluntary* co-operation in a coercive system.' (Original emphasis. *Op. cit.*, pp. 197–198.)

Despite Hart's use of the phrase *natural law*, it can be argued that this part of his theory simply deals with certain aspects of law which are essential to the functioning of society. Therefore, since no moral quality can attach to that which is truly essential, it is difficult to avoid the conclusion that Hart's use of the phrase *natural law* is merely an attempt to establish that his subject matter has a moral status which closer consideration reveals to be not only spurious but also fundamentally inappropriate.

Oliver Wendell Holmes, writing more than thirty years before Hart, sees the point clearly, even if he expresses it circumspectly:

'No doubt it is true that, so far as we can see ahead, some arrangements and the rudiments of familiar institutions seem to be necessary elements in any society that may spring from our own and that would seem to us to be civilized – some form of permanent association between the sexes – some residue of property individually owned – some mode of binding oneself to specified future conduct – at the bottom of all some protection for the person. But... the question remains as to the *ought* of natural law.' (*Natural Law* (1918) 32 Harv LR 40, at p. 41.)

4.3.4 When the rules run out

From time to time, it is inevitable that questions will arise to which the law has no ready answer. This clearly poses a difficulty for the judges who have to decide cases in which such questions arise, because the court must always provide an answer. Judges may protest the difficulty of their function, but they are not allowed to refuse to adjudicate on the issues which are placed before them. (A ruling that the court has no jurisdiction to deal with a particular matter may appear to be an exception, but it is not truly so, since the ruling as to lack of jurisdiction is itself a ruling on a matter of law.)

Hart acknowledges that this situation will arise, and takes the example of a legal prohibition on the use of vehicles in a park. Taking some examples, not of all of which Hart himself uses, the prohibition clearly includes motor cars, but what of a toy car which is electrically propelled; and if size is thought to be of the essence, how large can the toy be without falling foul of the prohibition? Similarly, what about bicycles; and children's push chairs; and wheelchairs; and roller-skates?

Hart's conclusion is that the judge has a discretion, which means that 'even though it may not be arbitrary or irrational, [the decision] is in effect a choice. [The judge] chooses to add to a line of cases a new case because of resemblances which can reasonably be defended as both legally relevant and sufficiently close'. (*Op. cit.*, p. 127.)

In making this choice, the judge will be using the fact that language is *open-textured*. This quality of language contrasts with systems such as, for example, mathematics and music, whose symbols have precise and universally recognized meanings.

More particularly, Hart maintains that the meaning of any given word will be made up of a *core* and a *penumbra*. The word *penumbra* is borrowed from the terminology which is used to describe the different densities of the shadows which occur during eclipses. The *penumbra* refers to the semi-shadow area which surrounds the deep shadow (or *umbra*) at the centre of the eclipse. Etymologically, *penumbra* derives from the Latin meaning *almost shadow*, but in the present context its meaning is more accessibly conveyed by the vernacular phrase *grey area*, within which there will be substantial scope for uncertainty. While it would be churlish to criticize Hart for using terminology which, when seen in its original context, could cause confusion by suggesting that the deepest shadow creates the greatest clarity, his use of the idea of the core is open to criticism on another ground. The problem is that Hart seems to assume that a word will have a single core meaning, whereas many cases giving rise to difficulties of interpretation in practice arise from a number of possible meanings, with no intrinsic indication of how they should be ranked.

(For Hart's discussion of the core and penumbral meanings, see *Positivism and the Separation of, Law and Morals* (1958) 71 Harv LR 593, reprinted in *Essays in Jurisprudence and Philosophy*, 1983, in which see p. 49.)

To take a straightforward, non-legal example, if I see a poster in a shop window saying *Last Week – Everything Half-Price*, it would be perverse to think that it refers to a sale which expired at the end of the previous, or *most recent*, week: it plainly means *Final Week – Everything Half-Price*. On the other hand, if I ask you to *name the last king of England*, you will almost certainly interpret my question as referring to the *most recent* (rather than the *final*) king, and therefore you will say *George VI*. Of course, if you were to understand my question as referring to the *final* king of England, you would perfectly properly reply that the question is currently unanswerable because there may well be many more kings still to come. However, it is very unlikely that you would put this interpretation on my question.

The point of this example is simply that neither *most recent* nor *final* is *the core* meaning of *last*, with the other being relegated to being part of the *penumbral* range of possible meanings; nor are they both penumbral. In other words, Hart's terminology tends to conceal the fact that, even at the heart of a word, courts must frequently choose between two or more meanings, all of which rank equally as possibilities unless and until contextual factors are taken into account.

As we shall see in Chapter 7, the conclusion that judges, faced with hard cases, make the law by exercising discretion is one of the main grounds on which Dworkin attacks Hart's theory; but we will adjourn our examination of this topic until we have considered both another version of positivism (namely that expounded by the Austrian theorist Hans Kelsen) and the revival of interest in the natural law tradition arising after the Second World War.

Summary

▶ In the 19th century, Austin's *command theory* defines law as a *command* from a *sovereign* backed by a *sanction*. Each of these elements is problematic.

▶ In the 20th century, Hart's *concept of law* analyses law into *primary rules* and *secondary rules*, with the legal system being the product of the union of both categories. The key to the validity of law lies in the *rule of recognition*, which is one of the secondary rules.

▶ Hart emphasizes the open texture of language and relies on the (not wholly convincing) concepts of core and penumbral meanings.

▶ When the rules run out, judges must, according to Hart, exercise their discretion.

Further reading

Austin, John, *The Province of Jurisprudence Determined*, 1832

Bentham, Jeremy, *The Limits of Jurisprudence Defined*, 1945, republished as *Of Laws in General*, 1970

Duxbury, Neil, *Why English Jurisprudence is Analytical* [2004] Current Legal Problems 1

Hart, H.L.A., *Positivism and the Separation of Law and Morals* (1958) 71 Harv LR 593, reprinted in *Essays in Jurisprudence and Philosophy*, 1983

Hart, H.L.A., *The Concept of Law*, 2nd edn, 1994

Holmes, Oliver Wendell, *Natural Law* (1918) 32 Harv LR 40

Lacey, Nicola, *A Life of H.L.A. Hart*, 2004.

Chapter 5

Kelsen's hierarchy of norms

5.1 Introduction

Having considered the English tradition of positivism in the form of both Austin's command theory and Hart's concept of law as a system of rules, it is appropriate to discuss what Harris terms 'the most famous contribution to legal philosophy of our century'. (*Legal Philosophies*, 2nd edn, 1997, p. 65.) This is the *pure theory of law*, expounded by Hans Kelsen (1881–1973), an Austrian who settled in America.

5.2 The nature and elements of the pure theory of law

5.2.1 The nature of the pure theory of law

The pure theory of law is wholly positivist, making none of the concessions to the natural law tradition which, as we saw at p. 76, Hart calls 'the core of good sense' in the doctrine of Natural Law. Originally published in 1943, it is intended to be a general theory of law, rather than being rooted in a particular legal system, and 'its exclusive purpose is to know and to describe its object'. (*The Pure Theory of Law*, translated by Max Knight, 1970, p. 1.) The theory's purity lies in the fact that it 'only describes the law and attempts to eliminate from the object of this description everything that is not strictly law'. (*Ibid.*)

5.2.2 The coercive nature of law

Having seen that sanctions are central to Austin's view of law, and that for Hart they guarantee 'that those who would voluntarily obey shall not be sacrificed to those who would not' (see p. 77), you will not be surprised to discover that they also loom large in Kelsen's scheme of things. The distinguishing mark of Kelsen's theory, however, is that it presents the imposition of sanctions (or coercion) as the result of the existence of a hierarchy of norms.

One preliminary problem is that the use of the word *norm* creates something of a difficulty for those with English as their first language (Kelsen wrote originally in German) because, as we saw at p. 18, normative language expresses *ought* propositions. The difficulty for a *pure* theory of law lies in distinguishing rigorously between *legal* oughts and *moral* oughts.

For example, I might say 'you ought not to commit murder'. Whether this statement is offered as a matter of law or morality, it is unexceptionable, not to say trite, and therefore it is easy to overlook the fact that the words themselves do not make it clear which type of statement it is. However, if we substitute some other word (such as *required*) for the word *ought* (so that the statement becomes 'you are required not to commit murder'), the moral nature of the original version can clearly be contrasted with the legal nature of the reformulated one. The difference between the two versions will, of course, prompt the question of what it means to be 'required' not to do (or to do) something. Kelsen's answer to this is that a breach of a requirement will result in coercion being applied to the transgressor, leading to 'the forcible deprivation of life, freedom, economic and other values'. (*Op. cit.*, p. 35.)

By way of example, the norm which prohibits murder is derived from another norm which requires a judge to impose coercion (which in this context means *pass sentence*) upon those who are convicted of murder. For Kelsen, therefore, the *requirements* of the law are directed *not at individuals* but *at the officials who operate the system.*

Before developing the idea of deriving one norm from another, it is worth commenting that Kelsen's emphasis on coercion may be criticized as being unrealistic, in the sense that the vast majority of matters handled by lawyers in professional practice never involve any kind of coercion. Even if it is conceded that in practically all cases coercion exists as a longstop, we are still left with those exceptional cases in which there is no coercion.

A good example arises in the field of public law, where Parliament may impose 'target duties', such as the Secretary of State for Education's duty, under s. 10 of the Education Act 1996, 'to promote the education of the people of England and Wales'. The intrinsic imprecision of this duty inevitably renders it unenforceable by the courts. Even if it is seen as nothing more than a statement of the political belief that it is better to have an educated population than an uneducated one, it is difficult to see how a statutory provision, expressed in plain and unexceptionable terms, is not a statement of law.

Returning to the proposition that one norm is derived from another, we come immediately to the central element of Kelsen's theory: the idea of a *hierarchy of norms*.

5.2.3   The hierarchy of norms

Since Kelsen, as a pure positivist, insists that morality must play no part in identifying law, he must clearly look elsewhere for the distinctive factor which provides law with that legitimacy which makes it law, and thus marks it out from other social rules. His solution is that the factor which legitimizes any normative statement which has the character of law will form part of a hierarchy of other norms, all of which – except one – will also be laws.

For example, the factor which gives legal status to the judge's order that a convicted murderer shall be imprisoned for life is the statutory provision which provides that life imprisonment shall be the sentence for murder. But, of course, this leaves the question: whence does the statute derive *its* validity? The answer is that, in the English legal system, Parliament is legislatively supreme, which means quite simply that the law is whatever Parliament says it is. (For the moment, it will simplify matters if we ignore the possibility that European Community law (which is now European Union Law) may be relevant, although we will return to this topic in due course.)

So the next question is: whence does the statement that Parliament is legislatively supreme derive *its* validity? The answer is that the legislative supremacy of Parliament is a constitutional doctrine which was established by the Glorious Revolution of 1688. It is at this point that Kelsen's hierarchy runs out, because there is nothing which, *as a matter of law*, can validate the constitution except the fact that *it is, and is accepted by the judges as being*, the constitution.

The point at which the hierarchy runs out requires closer examination, but before turning to this topic it is worth noting that we could have pursued the hierarchy in the other direction. For example, if our murderer had sued the governor of the prison in which he was incarcerated, alleging false imprisonment, the governor's reply would have been that the detention had been legally validated by the judge's sentence. Pursuing the hierarchy of norms in this direction constitutes what Kelsen terms *concretization*, since each step involves the formulation of a norm which is more precise and concrete (and thus less general and abstract) than the previous one.

Similarly, if our murderer had been *prima facie* entitled to inherit his victim's property in accordance with the law of intestacy, but the victim's personal representatives had nonetheless distributed the estate to the victim's other relatives, the murderer would be unable to sue for the return of 'his' property because there is a principle of common law that wrongdoers should not benefit from their wrongdoing. (See *Re Sigsworth* [1934] All ER Rep 113, which is also discussed at pp. 57 and 117.) In other words, the personal representatives' distribution of the property would be legally validated by a principle of common law, which would have become relevant as a result of the murderer's conviction.

At each stage, therefore, and depending on the direction in which the inquiry is pursued, each norm either validates the succeeding norm or derives its validity from the preceding norm. However, there must be an end to this process, irrespective of the direction in which the inquiry is pursued. At one end this will occur when the most specific norm is reached. Here we have simply arrived at the sort of law which is grist to the mill for practitioners. At the other end, the process will run out when the most general norm is reached. Kelsen deals with this situation by postulating a basic norm, or *grundnorm*, to use the German term which has become a loanword in English.

We must now consider the nature of the *grundnorm*.

5.3 The nature of the *grundnorm*

5.3.1 Introduction

To begin with a terminological point which may confuse those approaching Kelsen for the first time, the use of the term *basic norm*, or *groundnorm* (if a minor liberty with the German word may be permitted in order to emphasize the present point), seems to suggest that we are talking about something *on top of which* other things are constructed and on which they rest just as a building rests on its foundations. However, Kelsen himself speaks of the *grundnorm* as being 'at the top of the pyramid of norms', thus creating an image of something which is not only very precise rather than very general, but also something which is supported, rather than something which provides support. Nevertheless, despite Kelsen's own image of the *grundnorm*, it may be more helpful to think of the *grundnorm* as some form of bedrock, from which a pyramid of increasingly specific norms ascends, although it is important to emphasize that this is not actually how Kelsen himself modelled his theory.

Kelsen describes the *grundnorm* as 'the basic norm that constitutes the unity in the multitude of norms by representing the reason for the validity of all norms that belong to this order'. (*Op. cit.*, p. 195.) He goes on to formulate its content thus:

> 'Coercive acts ought to be performed under the conditions and in the manner which the historically first constitution, and the norms created according to it, prescribe.' (In short: One ought to behave as the constitution prescribes.) (*Op. cit.*, p. 201.)

As the revolution cases show, when Kelsen refers to 'the historically first constitution' he does not mean, literally, the first ever constitution of the state in question, but merely the root of legitimacy in the current constitutional order. For example, 'the historically first' English constitution would be the settlement which followed the Revolution of 1688, while in a former colony it would be the independence constitution, unless there had been an intervening episode of revolutionary discontinuity.

Before developing Kelsen's view of constitutions and their legitimacy, it is important to emphasize the key point that, as a matter of logic, the *grundnorm* cannot have been posited in the same way as any other norm of the legal order is posited, since if it was it would have to be validated by a higher norm; and if such validation could be identified, the norm with which we started must be located within the hierarchy, and therefore could not be the *grundnorm*. In short, the *grundnorm* is *presupposed as a matter of logical necessity*, rather than being posited as a matter of law. However, Kelsen emphasizes that the *logically necessary* nature of the *grundnorm* stems entirely from its *function*.

'It is not necessary to presuppose the basic norm... [but]... only *if* we presuppose it can we consider a coercive order which is by and large effective as a system of *objectively valid* norms. Consequently, the foundation of the objective validity of the legal norms is conditional, conditioned by the basic presupposition of the norm.' (Original emphasis. *Professor Stone and the Pure Theory of Law* (1965) 17 Stan LR 1143.)

He then develops his argument further by drawing a crucial distinction between 'the constitution in a *legal-logical* sense and the constitution in a *positive legal* sense'. Since the former cannot be 'a form of positive law... but a norm *presupposed in juristic thinking*' there is a sense in which it may be called 'metalegal'. However, there is also a sense in which it may be called 'legal', provided that 'by this term we understand everything which has legally relevant functions...' (*Op. cit.*, p. 1141.)

Joseph Raz explains the difference between the nature of ultimate legal rules and other legal rules by taking the example of the English proposition that statutes bind the courts.

'That the English courts hold themselves bound to apply statutes is not the reason why they ought to do so. The rule that they should apply statutes is such a reason. The practice is no more than proof... that the rule is a legal rule. It is neither a ground for the validity of the rule nor for the action it prescribes. It is this fact which establishes the character of the rule as an ultimate *legal* rule. The fact that a rule is an ultimate legal rule means no more than that there is no legal ground, no legal justification for its validity. It does not imply that there is no ground or justification for the rule, only that if such ground exists it is not a legal one.' (Original emphasis. *The Authority of Law*, 2nd edn, 2009, pp. 68–69.)

Reduced to its simplest, therefore, the *grundnorm* is nothing more nor less than a starting point which is logically necessary in order to validate the content of the legal system. This involves the constitution in a *legal-logical* sense, but this apparently simple proposition may be the source of confusion because lawyers are more accustomed to thinking in terms of those rules of law which Kelsen labels as being the constitution in a *positive legal* sense.

The use of the word 'constitution' in two distinct senses raises the question of their interrelationship. In general terms, perhaps the most illuminating context within which to discuss this question is that of changing the *grundnorm*. More particularly, the question of change may usefully be viewed under three sub-headings, namely, revolutionary regimes and their impact on the legal systems of the states in which they arise; the granting of independence to former colonies; and membership of the European Community. Even more particularly, the discussion under the second and third sub-headings will deal specifically with the British constitution, and the problems arising from its traditional assertion of the legislative supremacy of Parliament.

5.3.2   Changing the *grundnorm*

Generally

All lawyers are familiar with the idea that law changes, and all legal systems – with the well-known exception of that maintained by the Medes and the Persians in biblical times, which 'changeth not' (Daniel, ch. 6, v. 8) – must have their mechanisms to enable those changes to take place. (Indeed, as we have seen, Hart characterizes rules of change as one of the essential elements in any developed legal system.) However, this tells us nothing of the situation which arises when there is a revolutionary change in the basis of the legal system itself.

The grundnorm in a revolutionary context

In the 1950s and 1960s, the courts of Pakistan, Uganda and Southern Rhodesia (now Zimbabwe) all considered the relevance of Kelsen's theory to the situation in which judges who had been appointed under an old regime had to deal with laws enacted by a revolutionary regime. In practical terms, the question was whether the new laws should be enforced. In all three countries the courts answered this question in the affirmative, having quoted the following passage from Kelsen's *General Theory of Law and State*:

> '(D) Change of the Basic Norm: It is just the phenomenon of revolution which clearly shows the significance of the Basic Norm. Suppose that a group of individuals attempt to seize power by force, in order to remove the legitimate government in a hitherto monarchic state, and to introduce a republican form of government. If they succeed, if the old order ceases, and the new order begins to be efficacious, because the individuals whose behaviour the new order regulates actually behave, by and large, in conformity with the new order, then this order is considered as a valid legal order. It is now according to this new order that the actual behaviour of individuals is interpreted as legal or illegal. But this means that a new basic norm is presupposed. It is no longer the norm according to which the old monarchical constitution is valid, but a norm according to which the new republican constitution is valid, a norm endowing the revolutionary government with legal authority. If the revolutionaries fail, if the order they have tried to establish remains inefficacious, then, on the other hand, their undertaking is interpreted, not as a legal, a law-creating, act as the establishment of a constitution, but as an illegal act, as the crime of treason, and this according to the old monarchic constitution and its specific basic norm... It cannot be maintained that, legally, men have to behave in conformity with a certain norm, if the total legal order of which that norm is an integral part, has lost its efficacy. The principle of legitimacy is restricted by the principle of effectiveness.'

Two Southern Rhodesian cases are particularly instructive. The background to both cases was the unilateral declaration of independence (i.e., in legal terms, an act of rebellion against the Crown) made by the white supremacist government of the colony, as it then was. The legally visible form of this declaration of independence was a constitution, promulgated in 1965, which purported to replace the colonial constitution of 1961. Inevitably, the Southern Rhodesian courts had to decide what status, if any, they would accord to the 'laws' enacted by the new regime.

In *Madzimbamuto v Lardner-Burke* (1968) 2 SA 284, the Appeal Court discussed the concepts of *de facto* and *de jure* government (i.e. government *in fact* and government *as of right*). The court acknowledged that those concepts were more commonly encountered in international law than in municipal law, but declined to hold that they were completely irrelevant in the latter arena. Beadle CJ dealt with the matter thus:

> 'Recognition either express or implied by the United Kingdom would, of course, be well nigh decisive; but the lack of recognition in itself cannot be decisive because political recognition is often based on pure political expediency quite unrelated to the real factual position.... It was seven years after the success of the Russian Revolution before Britain recognized the government of the Soviet Union, and it was seventeen years after before the United States of America did so....
>
> 'It cannot therefore be assumed that the ultimate success of the present revolution must necessarily depend on some express or implied acquiescence by Great Britain or on recognition of the present Government by other states. At what particular stage it can be said that the revolution has succeeded must depend entirely on the particular circumstances obtaining at that particular time.'

The importance of approaching the matter at a particular time was emphasized by the fact that the court agreed to take judicial notice of the facts as they were at the date when the appeal was heard, rather than at the date of delivery of the decision at first instance. On those facts, the court proceeded to hold that, as far as the internal affairs of Rhodesia were concerned, the new government was the *de facto* government, because it was effectively in control of the country and seemed likely to continue to be so. It followed that the new government could do those things which it could have done had it been functioning under the authority of the 1961 constitution. However, it would not attain full *de jure* status until the court was able to say that the government was likely – and not merely *seemed* likely – to continue to be in effective control of the country, which Beadle CJ conceded is 'a difference purely of the degree of certainty with which the future can be predicted'.

Less than eight months later, Beadle CJ returned to the matter in *R v Ndhlovu* (1968) 4 SA 515. Even after such a short passage of time, he held that the revolution had become successful, 'because it is impossible to foresee any circumstance which will, in the foreseeable future, be likely to enable the British government to regain control [of Rhodesia]'. He went on to emphasize that:

> 'Acceptance of a situation and responsibility for that situation are two entirely different concepts. And so it is with the 1961 Constitution. That Constitution, in Rhodesia to-day, is no more. The Judges, by taking cognisance of the fact that this is so, cannot justly be accused of being in any way responsible for the change, nor can it be implied that by accepting the fact of the change they approved of it. The change is not a matter of their making.'

He dealt thus with the position of a court which, having been appointed under the old constitution, is required to adjudicate upon the new one:

'If a 1961 Constitution court, embarking on the factual enquiry which the Board [i.e. the Judicial Committee of the Privy Council] did, came to the conclusion that the 1961 Constitution had been annulled because of the efficacy of the change, it would have to decline further jurisdiction as a 1961 Constitution court, because in Taney CJ's words it would have ceased to exist as a court. If after arriving at the conclusion that the change had been effective the court nevertheless continued to sit and adjudicate on the matter before it, it could only do so as a court different from a court sitting under the 1961 Constitution. Its character would have undergone a transmogrification, as it were. There are recent precedents for making this transmogrification. For example, Sir Udo Udoma, CJ, in *Uganda v The Commissioner of Prisons*, 1966 EA 514, and Sir Muhammed Munir, CJ, in *The State v Dosso*, 1958 (2) PSCR 180, commenced their sittings in these cases as Judges appointed and sitting under the original constitutions of Uganda and Pakistan and as such enquired into the status of the new revolutionary governments. When, however, they continued to sit after they had found as a fact that as a result of successful revolutions the old constitutions had been effectively overthrown and replaced by new constitutions they, by continuing to sit, accepted the new constitutions, and when they held that the new constitutions were *de jure* constitutions they gave these decisions as Judges sitting under the new constitutions and not as Judges sitting under the old. By continuing to sit after they found the old constitutions had disappeared they sat as Judges in a new situation and as the new situation was that the new constitutions were the *de jure* constitutions they sat as Judges under those constitutions.'

This judgment makes it plain that both Kelsen's requirement of efficacy, and its application in practice, go one stage beyond the old doggerel, according to which

Treason doth never prosper. What the reason?
If it prosper, none dare call it treason.

More particularly, Kelsen's point is that a regime which comes into being under treasonable circumstances may subsequently provide effective government. When this happens, the political fact of subsequent success means that the regime has shed its treasonable character and has actually become legitimate, rather than merely being merely able to rely on its critics' lack of daring.

The cases which cited Kelsen generated a substantial body of academic legal discussion, the most useful summary and criticism of which is contained in *When and Why Does the Grundnorm Change?* (Harris, (1971) 29 CLJ 103.) One particular problem which is worth emphasizing is the potential for entering into a circular argument through the answer which a court gives to the question of whether 'the new order [is] efficacious, because the individuals whose behaviour [it] regulates actually behave, by and large, in conformity with [it]'. The danger is, of course, that the answer may become self-validating, in the sense that a judicial decision in favour of the new order is likely to enhance the efficacy of that order. However, Harris argues that this is not necessarily true, because 'it depends on the relative importance of [the judge's] decision as against other present and future elements in the efficacy of the revolutionary norms. If a judge believes that the success of the revolution may turn on what decision he gives in a case before him, then clearly he cannot decide as to the efficacy of the change without first making a political choice whether or not to join the revolution. If he believes, however, that whatever he decides, the revolution is likely to succeed (if need be, by his dismissal and the appointment of an acquiescent judge), then his decision that the revolution will be efficacious is not necessarily politically motivated.' (*Op. cit.*, p. 122.)

Since the *efficacy* of the new order is clearly of central significance, it is worth noting that Kelsen himself emphasized the importance of distinguishing the *validity* of a norm from its *effectiveness*. Essentially, the distinction is that *validity* involves an *ought* proposition, while *effectiveness* involves an *is* proposition:

'A legal norm becomes valid before it becomes effective, that is, before it is applied and obeyed... The basic norm can only establish a law-making authority whose norms are, by and large, observed so that social life broadly conforms to the legal order based on the hypothetical norm.' (*General Theory of Law and State*, p. 437.)

However, Harris (*op. cit.*, pp. 120–121) takes issue with Kelsen's own version, on the basis that the *by and large* test needs to be refined because it will commonly be impossible to know whether the sanction is applied more often than not. (How many motorists exceed the speed limit without being detected?) Furthermore, Harris points out that if, as Kelsen says, 'Law is observed by that behaviour to whose opposite is attached the coercive act of the sanction' it follows that 'laws which prohibit the performing of acts which most people do not in any case perform (such as laws against witchcraft) must always be generally "obeyed"...'.

Harris concludes that the *by and large* test should be reformulated so that it provides: 'a norm is to be judged effective if the official acts of application of sanctions bear a socially significant ratio to the recorded acts of disobedience'.

Important though the efficacy of the legal order is within Kelsen's theory, it is also important never to forget the key idea of the hierarchy of norms. The essential point is that while the efficacy of the legal order is a *necessary* condition to the validity of individual norms, it is not a *sufficient* condition, because it remains necessary for each norm to be validated by a higher norm. The most straightforward example within the English legal system may be found in the field of Public Law. It is, of course, basic that the doctrine of *ultra vires* means that a measure which purports to be a piece of delegated legislation will be void if it is outwith the scope of the statute which authorizes it (or, in Kelsenian terms, if it is not validated by the statute). Wherever this situation arises, the efficacy of the system as a whole will be nothing to the point.

Finally, it may be tempting to argue that Kelsen's reliance on efficacy involves taking account of the socio-political facts of life, and that therefore the pure theory loses its purity. However,

'This paradox is, however, more apparent than real. The *grundnorm* is the assumption of the validity of the constitution and not its particular identity. The relation of the *grundnorm* to the criterion of 'effectiveness' is simply the point at which Kelsen's hypothetical hierarchy of norms attaches to reality. Once it has been determined, through the test of effectiveness, what constitution is being assumed to be valid in a given State, the Kelsenian analysis begins to be applied to the actual substance of a real legal system. *The point of contact is vitally important but it is essentially extrinsic to the pure theory itself.*' (Emphasis added. *Textbook on Jurisprudence*, McCoubrey and White, 4th edn, 2008, ed. Penner, p. 49.)

5.4 The *grundnorm* of the British constitution

5.4.1 Introduction

There can be no doubt that the Glorious Revolution of 1688 established the legislative supremacy (or sovereignty) of Parliament, which remained practically unquestioned for almost three centuries, and that the success of the Revolution was a political fact which the existing judges accepted. (It is irrelevant for the present purposes that the existing judges' acceptance of the new order may have been significantly influenced by their realization that non-acceptance would result in their removal and the appointment of new judges who would be sympathetic to the new legal order.)

But what is the status of the legislative supremacy of Parliament? At one level, Munro says 'the concept of parliamentary sovereignty is only indicative of the legal relationship between the legislature and the courts, nothing less but nothing more'. (*Studies in Constitutional Law*, 2nd edn, 1999, p. 134.) Useful though this insight is, it is also worth considering Wade's analysis:

'The rule [that the courts obey Acts of Parliament]... is above the reach of statute... because it is itself the source of the authority of statute. This puts it in a class by itself among rules of common law, and the apparent paradox that it is unalterable by Parliament turns out to be a truism. The rule of judicial obedience is in one sense a rule of common law, but in another sense – which applies to no other rule of common law – it is the ultimate *political* fact upon which the whole system of legislation hangs. Legislation owes its authority to the rule: the rule does not owe its authority to legislation. To say that Parliament can change the rule, merely because it can change any other rule, is to put the cart before the horse...' (Original emphasis. Wade, *The Basis of Legal Sovereignty* [1955] CLJ 172, at pp. 187–188.)

Furthermore

'[The rule] is unique in being unchangeable by Parliament – it is changed by revolution, not by legislation; it lies in the keeping of the courts, and no act of Parliament can take it from them.' (*Op. cit.* at p. 189.)

It is clear that Wade's insistence on the distinction between *political* facts and *legal* facts (and his conclusion that although the doctrine of the legislative supremacy of Parliament is at the heart of British constitutional law, there is a sense in which it is not part of that – or indeed any – area of law), reflects Kelsen's distinction between *metalegal* and *legal* norms (see p. 85).

In practical terms, the English courts have had to consider the nature of the legislative supremacy of Parliament in two main contexts, namely the independence of former colonies and the impact of European Community (now Union) law on English law. These will now be considered in turn.

5.4.2 The changing *grundnorm* in relation to former colonies

In *Manuel v Attorney-General* [1983] 3 All ER 822, Sir Robert Megarry, speaking of the situation of a former colony which obtains independence, said:

> 'Plainly once statute granted independence to a country, the repeal of the statute will not make the country dependent once more; what is done is done.... But if Parliament then passes an Act applying to such a country, I cannot see why that Act should not be in the same position as an Act applying to what has always been a foreign country, namely an Act which the English courts will recognize and apply, but one which the other country will in all probability ignore.... Perhaps I may add this. I have grave doubts about the theory of the transfer of sovereignty as affecting the competence of Parliament. In my view, it is a fundamental of the English constitution that Parliament is supreme. As a matter of law the courts of England recognize Parliament as being omnipotent in all save the power to destroy its own omnipotence. Under the authority of Parliament the courts of a territory may be released from the duty to obey Parliament, but that does not trench on the acceptance by English courts of all that Parliament does. Nor must validity in law be confused with practical enforceability.'

To anyone other than an English lawyer brought up on the continuing version of the doctrine of the supremacy of Parliament, it would seem to be self-evidently absurd to say that Parliament can legislate in respect of a former colony which it has previously released from the duty of obedience to Acts of Parliament. Yet Megarry gives no indication that this proposition is anything other than self-evidently correct.

A Kelsenian analysis of this situation would take account of the fact that the grant of independence is not merely a legal act but also a political one, and would conclude that its fundamental nature produces a change in the *grundnorm* of both legal systems. The impact on the legal system of the former colony is clear, as Megarry acknowledged when, with more than a hint of understatement, he said that its courts would 'in all probability ignore' subsequent English legislation. However, the extent to which he is in thrall to the traditional theory of the supremacy of Parliament prevented him from taking the final, and logically necessary, step of acknowledging that Parliament has no power to enact such legislation.

The impact of colonial independence on the English legal system may be less obvious, but if the territorial extent of a constitution is regarded as being an integral part of that constitution, it follows that a reduction in that extent involves a revision of the constitution, and may therefore be said to involve a change in the *grundnorm*.

The proposition that Parliament can continue to pass Acts (in the sense of going through the relevant legislative procedures which produce a piece of paper bearing all the hallmarks of an Act) relating to a former colony, when such Acts would possess no substance in the eyes of the courts of the former colony, brings to mind the exchange which Shakespeare puts into the mouths of Owen Glendower and Harry Hotspur:

Glendower: I can call spirits from the vasty deep.
Hotspur: Why, so can I, or so can any man;
          But will they come when you do call for them?
(*King Henry IV Part I*, Act III, Sc. 1)

Perhaps the best summary of the position results from reformulating Wade's comment (see p. 90) that

'the rule of judicial obedience is... the ultimate *political* fact upon which the whole system of legislation hangs (original emphasis),'

so that it reads

'the rule of judicial obedience *reflects* the ultimate *political* fact that Parliament is supreme over the Executive, and that no one is supreme over Parliament.'

The importance of this reformulation is that, once legal doctrines are seen as *reflecting* political facts (rather than as *being* those facts), it follows that changed political facts may create a need for changed legal doctrines. For example, if the doctrine of legislative supremacy reflects the political fact of obedience to Parliament, it follows that the new-found non-obedience of a former colony is simply a reflection of the new political fact that the former colony has moved outwith the ambit of the doctrine. In other words, and adopting Megarry's language in *Manuel*, the transition to independence involves the 'transfer of sovereignty' and is therefore a changed political fact. Once the essence of the situation is seen as being political, with the legal dimension being merely consequential, it follows that there is no basis for Megarry's 'grave doubts about the theory of the transfer of sovereignty as affecting the competence of Parliament'.

It also follows that there is an element of overstatement in Wade's conclusion (see p. 90) that the rule that Parliament is legislatively supreme cannot be changed by Act of Parliament, because the proposition that the doctrine cannot be changed (*sc.* simply) by Act of Parliament does not mean that it cannot be changed by an Act of Parliament which is passed in order to reflect changed political facts.

A Kelsenian analysis is also instructive in terms of the United Kingdom's membership of the European Communities.

5.4.3 The changing *grundnorm* in relation to membership of the European Communities and the European Union

As far as English law is concerned, the European Communities Act 1972 is the basis of the United Kingdom's membership of the European Union and, previously, the European Communities, but in political terms the statute was preceded by a decision to accede to the treaties which constituted the communities. (It is a fundamental consequence of the legislative supremacy of Parliament that treaties do not take effect in domestic law unless incorporated by statute.) Section 2(1) of the 1972 Act provides:

'All... rights, powers, liabilities, obligations and restrictions from time to time created or arising by or under the Treaties, and all such remedies and procedures from time to time provided for by or under the Treaties, as in accordance with the Treaties are without further enactment to be given legal effect or used in the United Kingdom shall be recognized and available in law, and be enforced, allowed and followed accordingly; and the expression 'enforceable Community right' and similar expressions shall be read as referring to one to which this subsection applies.'

This provision is reinforced by s. 2(4) of the Act:

'Any enactment passed or to be passed... shall be construed and have effect subject to the foregoing provisions of this section.'

Briefly, therefore, the effect of these provisions is to incorporate what is now European Union law into the English legal system. Consequently, it is essential to note that as far as Union law is concerned, any conflict between Union law and the law of a member state must be resolved in favour of Union law. As the European Court of Justice said, in *van Gend en Loos* [1963] CMLR 105:

'The Community constitutes a new legal order... for whose benefit the states have limited their sovereign rights.'

Similarly, in *Costa v ENEL* [1964] CMLR 425, the Court of Justice said:

'The reception within the laws of each member State, of provisions having a Community source, and more particularly of the terms and of the spirit of the Treaty, has as a corollary the impossibility, for the member State, to give preference to a unilateral and *subsequent* measure against a legal order accepted by them on the basis of reciprocity...

'The transfer, by member States, from their national orders in favour of the Community order of the rights and obligations arising from the Treaty, carries with it a clear limitation of their sovereign right upon which a *subsequent* unilateral law, incompatible with the aims of the Community, cannot prevail.' (Emphasis added.)

Additionally, it is clear from *Internationale Handelsgessellschaft mbH* [1974] 2 CMLR 540, that Community (now Union) law prevails over even the most fundamental constitutional doctrines of member states. In the context of the British constitution, the legislative supremacy of Parliament is, of course, a fundamental doctrine, therefore the combined effect of the 1972 Act and the established case law of the Community (now Union) legal system appears to be that Parliament is no longer supreme to the extent that it is no longer competent to legislate contrary to Community (now Union) law.

By way of an aside, the only alternative possibility is to mount a rearguard action by arguing that there is now

'a rule of interpretation to the effect that Parliament is presumed not to intend statutes to override EEC law. On this view inconsistencies between United Kingdom statutes and EEC law would be resolved in favour of the latter unless "Parliament clearly and expressly states in a future Act that it is to override Community law".' (Craig, *Sovereignty of the United Kingdom Parliament after Factortame* (1991) 11 YBEL 221.)

However, it is difficult to the point of impossibility to maintain this argument in the face of both the case law of the Court of Justice on the supremacy of Community law (as it then was) and the House of Lords' acceptance of this supremacy. In the words of Lord Bridge:

'Some public comments on the decision of the Court of Justice, affirming the jurisdiction of the courts of member States to override national legislation if necessary to enable interim relief to be granted in protection of rights under Community law, have suggested that this was a novel and dangerous invasion by a Community institution of the sovereignty of the United Kingdom Parliament. But such comments are based on a misconception. If the supremacy within the European Community of Community law over the national law of member States was not always inherent in the EEC Treaty, it was certainly well established in the jurisprudence of the Court of Justice long before the United Kingdom joined the Community. Thus, whatever limitation of its sovereignty Parliament accepted when it enacted the European Communities Act 1972 was entirely voluntary. *Under the terms of the 1972 Act it has always been clear that it was the duty of a United Kingdom court, when delivering final judgment, to override any rule of national law found to be in conflict with any directly enforceable rule of Community law.* Similarly, when decisions of the Court of Justice have exposed areas of United Kingdom law which failed to implement Council Directives, Parliament has always loyally accepted the obligation to make appropriate and prompt amendments. Thus there is nothing in any way novel in according supremacy to rules of Community law.' (*Factortame Ltd v Secretary of State for Transport* (No 2) [1991] 1 All ER 70. Emphasis added.)

Since the treaty did not take effect in domestic law until it was incorporated by statute, it follows that the enactment of the 1972 Act can be seen as a legal response to the political fact that the government had agreed to the United Kingdom becoming a member of the European Communities. In other words, the enactment of the 1972 Act is evidence that the old legal order had changed to the extent that that aspect of the *grundnorm* of the British Constitution which deals with the legislative supremacy of Parliament had to be revised in such a way as to recognize that Parliament can no longer effectively legislate contrary to Community law. If this view is accepted, there is no need to accept Wade's conclusion, in *Sovereignty – Revolution or Evolution?* (1996) 112 LQR 568, that 'the prudential course may be to follow the example of the House of Lords [in *Factortame*] and turn a blind eye to constitutional theory altogether', since a Kelsenian reading of the position is quite capable of accommodating the consequences of membership of the Community (as it then was) and the Union (as it now is).

5.5 Kelsen's *grundnorm* and Hart's rule of recognition

Before leaving Kelsen, there remains one piece of unfinished business, namely how does the *grundnorm* differ from Hart's *rule of recognition*? Hart himself makes the following points.

First, the *grundnorm* is a matter of *logical necessity* whose validity has to be pre-supposed (see p. 84). The rule of recognition, on the other hand, is a matter of *fact*, which is identifiable from

> 'the actual practice of the courts and officials of the system when identifying the law which they are to apply... [and therefore]... no question concerning... [its]... validity or invalidity... as distinct from the factual question of its existence can arise.' (H.L.A. Hart, *The Concept of Law*, 2nd edn, 1994, p. 293.)

Secondly, the *grundnorm* 'has in a sense always the same content; for it is, in all legal systems, simply the rule that the constitution... ought to be obeyed'. (*Ibid*.) However,

> 'if... the constitution is accepted and actually exists... it seems a needless duplication to suggest that there is a further rule to the effect that the constitution... [is]... to be obeyed.' (*Ibid*.)

So, in the context of the British Constitution, 'it is mystifying to speak of a rule' which requires obedience to the rule that Parliament is legislatively supreme'. (*Ibid*.)

Thirdly, although Kelsen's view is that 'it is logically impossible to regard a particular rule of law as valid and at the same time to accept, as morally binding, a moral rule forbidding the behaviour required by the legal rule', Hart insists that 'no such consequences follow from the account of legal validity given in this book [i.e. *The Concept of Law*]'. (*Ibid*.)

Summary

- Kelsen's *pure theory of law* presents law as a hierarchy of norms.
- The validity of the hierarchy as a whole depends on the *grundnorm* or basic norm.

Summary cont'd

▶ The *grundnorm* performs the same function as Hart's rule of recognition, but the former is a matter of logical necessity while the latter is a matter of fact.

▶ The nature of the *grundnorm*, and the way in which it changes, shed light on the problems which arise in the context of both the independence of former colonies and the United Kingdom's membership of the European Community (which is now the European Union).

Further reading

Craig, P.P., *Sovereignty of the United Kingdom Parliament after Factortame* (1991) 11 YBEL 221

Harris, J.W., *When and Why Does the Grundnorm Change?* (1971) 29 CLJ 103

Harris, J.W., *Legal Philosophies*, 2nd edn, 1997

Hart, H.L.A., *The Concept of Law*, 2nd edn, 1994

Kelsen, Hans, *General Theory of Law and State*, 1945

Kelsen, Hans, *The Pure Theory of Law*, translated by Knight, Max, 1970

Kelsen, Hans, *Professor Stone and the Pure Theory of Law* (1965) 17 Stan LR 1128

McCoubrey, Hilaire and White, Nigel D., *Textbook on Jurisprudence*, 4th edn, 2008, ed. Penner, J.E.

Munro, Colin A., *Studies in Constitutional Law*, 2nd edn, 1999

Raz, Joseph, *The Authority of Law*, 2nd edn, 2009

Wade, H.W.R., *Sovereignty – Revolution or Evolution?* (1996) 112 LQR 568

Wade, H.W.R., *The Basis of Legal Sovereignty* [1955] CLJ 172

Chapter 6

The revival of natural law: Fuller and Finnis

6.1 Introduction

Although Hume's argument about the impossibility of deriving an *ought* from an *is* (see Chapter 3) is 'for many jurists... a knock-down argument against all forms of natural law thinking', in reality 'it merely deprives natural lawyers of that most revered of philosophic weapons, the deductive syllogism'. (Harris, *Legal Philosophies*, 2nd edn, 1997, pp. 12, 13.) The possibility remains, therefore, of seeking alternative forms of rational support for the idea of natural law, and as the scale of the Nazi atrocities committed before and during the Second World War became known, the desire to do so revived. In the event, two major, and quite distinct, theoretical expositions emerged. The earlier was contained in a set of lectures given by Lon L. Fuller, an American professor of law, in 1963 before being revised and published the following year as *The Morality of Law*. (The edition currently available was published in 1969, and contains a reply to some of the criticisms which followed the original version.) The later is John Finnis's *Natural Law and Natural Rights*, which was first published in 1980, with a second edition appearing in 2011. The second edition takes the form of a reprint of the first edition with the addition of a Postscript containing amplifications, clarifications, corrections and extensive cross-references to the author's other writing in the meantime. Page references given here apply equally to both editions unless they are stated to apply to the second edition.

We will now consider Fuller and Finnis in turn.

6.2 Fuller's *The Morality of Law*

6.2.1 Introduction

For Lon L. Fuller (1902–78) the starting point is that 'law has to do with the governance of human conduct by rules'. (*The Morality of Law*, revised edn, 1969, p. 53.) Although this appears to coincide with Hart's position (see Chapter 4), beyond this point there are fundamental differences between the two. In particular, where Hart places the emphasis on what is meant by a rule (and how those rules which are law are to be identified, and then how they combine into a legal system), Fuller concentrates on what is required to make the law work. His solution is that a legal system, properly so-called, must embody what he calls, interchangeably, an 'inner morality', 'an internal morality', 'the principles of legality', or 'procedural natural law'.

Since morality is clearly central to Fuller's enterprise, it is essential to consider how he clarifies the way in which he uses the term. In particular, he distinguishes between the morality of *duty*, which prescribes or proscribes conduct (as the case may be), and the morality of *aspiration*, which is concerned with 'our efforts to make the best use of our short lives'. (*Op. cit.*, p. 17.) Fuller develops the distinction by saying

> '[there is] an ascending scale, starting at the bottom with the conditions obviously essential to social life and ending at the top with the loftiest strivings toward human excellence. The lower rungs of this scale represent the morality of duty; its higher reaches the morality of aspiration. Separating the two is a fluctuating line of division, difficult to locate precisely, yet vitally important.' (*Op. cit.*, p. 27.)

It is with the morality of aspiration that his theory is concerned.

6.2.2   The elements of Fuller's *inner morality* of law

Introduction

The criteria which Fuller argues must be satisfied in order for something which can truly be called a legal system to exist are generality, promulgation, non-retroactivity, clarity, non-contradiction, not requiring the impossible, constancy through time and, finally, congruence between official action and the declared rule.

It will be helpful to look at each of these criteria in turn, and to consider the extent to which each is satisfied by the English legal system.

Generality

The criterion of generality amounts to nothing more than there shall be a rule. However, this is not without difficulty. Although generality is clearly an almost universal characteristic of those rules which may properly be called law (as it will also commonly be a characteristic of all sorts of other rules), it is also clear that an enactment which is unquestionably law may fail to satisfy this criterion. For an example from the English legal system, it is necessary to go no further than a personal Act of Parliament permitting two named individuals to marry each other despite the fact that they are within the prohibited degrees.

Promulgation

The requirement that laws shall be promulgated (or, to use a more common word, *published*) is clearly reasonable, since people cannot be expected to comply with rules of which they are unaware. However, in practice this requirement may overlap with the next one, namely non-retroactivity.

Non-retroactivity

Fuller acknowledges that retroactive legislation may be acceptable, as, for example, where it remedies official errors. However, it is unacceptable where it deprives people of their rights. (See, for example, the War Damage Act 1965, which reversed, retroactively, the decision of the House of Lords in *Burmah Oil v Lord Advocate* [1964] 2 All ER 348.)

Three points about retroactivity in English law may be made. First, where a statute is ambiguous, there is a presumption against retroactivity:

> 'The true principle is that Parliament is presumed not to have intended to alter the law applicable to past events and transactions in a manner which is unfair to those concerned in them, unless a contrary intention appears... it may well be a matter of degree – the greater the unfairness, the more it is to be expected that Parliament will make it clear if that is intended.' (*Secretary of State for Social Services v Tunnicliffe* [1991] 2 All ER 712, approved by the House of Lords in *L'Office Cherifien des Phosphates and Another v Yamashita-Shinnihon Steamship Co Ltd: The Boucraa* [1994] 1 All ER 20.)

Secondly, the provision currently contained in s. 4 of the Interpretation Act 1978 provides that a statute that makes no provision for its own coming into force shall come into force at the beginning of the day on which it receives the Royal Assent. (Such Acts are rare, but they clearly have at least a marginally retroactive effect.) Thirdly, the doctrine of binding precedent has traditionally operated in a retroactive way (although there may now be limits to this – see *Re Spectrum Plus Ltd, National Westminster Bank plc v Spectrum Plus Ltd* [2005] UKHL 41, [2005] 4 All ER 209).

Clarity

While no one can reasonably doubt the desirability of compliance with the criterion of clarity, there is an uncomfortably large number of instances in which such compliance is lacking. These may arise either because the judicial authorities are not clear, or because a statute has been drafted obscurely. To take a single, albeit extreme, instance of the latter category, in *Bismag Ltd v Amblins (Chemists) Ltd* [1940] Ch 667, MacKinnon LJ said, of s. 4 of the Trade Marks Act 1938:

> 'In the course of three days hearing of this case I have, I suppose, heard s. 4... read, or have read it for myself, dozen if not hundreds of times. Despite this iteration I must confess that, reading it through once again, I have very little notion of what the section is intended to convey, and particularly the sentence of two hundred and fifty three words, as I make them, which constitutes subs. (1). I doubt if the entire statute book could be successfully searched for a sentence of equal length which is of more fuliginous obscurity.'

Non-contradiction

The criterion of non-contradiction requires consistency within the law. When confronted with inconsistencies in statute law, the English courts generally resolve the conflict by applying the maxim *posteriora derogant prioribus* (or, in other words, the later derogates from – i.e. prevails over – the earlier).

Where a later Act makes no reference to, but is inconsistent with, an earlier, the later will prevail, although in this context the *posteriora* maxim takes the form of the doctrine of implied repeal. (See, for example, *Ellen Street Estates Ltd v Minister of Health* [1934] All ER Rep 385.) However, this is subject to an exception where the later statute is inconsistent with a provision of European Community law, which, as we saw at p. 93, was incorporated into English law by the European Communities Act 1972. Under these circumstances, Community (now Union) law will prevail and the court will disapply the English statute (*R v Secretary of State for Transport ex parte Factortame Ltd* [1991] 3 All ER 769).

Not requiring the impossible

It is obviously a desirable feature of any legal system that the law should not require people to do that which is impossible, although Fuller concedes that this topic requires careful consideration, and does not, for example, necessarily prohibit the imposition of strict liability even in criminal law, where this would result in potential defendants taking extra care to avoid the prohibited conduct. The leading statement of principle in English law is contained in *Gammon (Hong Kong) Ltd v Attorney-General for Hong Kong* [1984] 2 All ER 503, where the issue was whether it was an offence of strict liability to contravene the Hong Kong equivalent of the English Building Regulations, which prescribe standards aimed at ensuring the quality and safety of buildings. Holding that contravention was an offence of strict liability, the Privy Council said:

> '(1) There is a presumption of law that [intention] is required before a person can be guilty of a criminal offence; (2) the presumption is particularly strong where the offence is "truly criminal" in character; (3) the presumption applies to statutory offences, and can be displaced only if this is clearly or by necessary implication the effect of the statute; (4) the only situation in which the presumption can be displaced is where the statute is concerned with an issue of social concern, and public safety is such an issue; (5) even where a statute is concerned with such an issue, the presumption of [intention] stands unless it can also be shown that the creation of strict liability will be effective to promote the objects of the statute by encouraging greater vigilance to prevent the commission of the prohibited act.'

Constancy through time

Fuller accepts, of course, that the requirement that the law should be constant through time cannot be absolute, since laws must respond to the changing needs of changing times. However, the criterion of constancy through time does require that the law should not change so rapidly that people encounter real difficulty in identifying their legal position. This is hardly a problem in the English context, where a more common criticism is that the law changes too slowly, but a good example of the related problem of balancing the competing demands of certainty and flexibility may be found in the debate over the extent to which the House of Lords should have been – and the Supreme Court now should be – bound by its own decisions. From 1966 until its replacement by the Supreme Court in 2009, the Appellate Committee of the House of Lords followed the principles set out in the *Practice Statement (Judicial Precedent)* [1966] 3 All ER 77 and the case law which developed under it. The Supreme Court now takes the same approach. (See *Austin v Southwark London Borough Council* [2010] UKSC 28, [2010] 4 All ER 16.)

Congruence between official action and the declared rule

Having characterized congruence between official action and the declared rule as 'the most complex' of all the elements of the internal morality of law, Fuller goes on to identify the ways in which it may be 'destroyed or impaired', namely:

> 'mistaken interpretation, inaccessibility of the law, lack of insight into what is required to maintain the integrity of the legal system, bribery, prejudice, indifference, stupidity, and the drive towards personal power.' (*Op. cit.*, p. 81)

He then points out that in the American legal system (although in passing it may be said that the same is equally true of its English counterpart) the judiciary is the agency which carries the principal responsibility for ensuring that such incongruences do not arise, or are dealt with when they do. Thus the discharge of this responsibility is not only undertaken by those with experience of such matters, but is also open to public scrutiny. Furthermore, it has the advantage of 'dramatizing the integrity of law' (*ibid.*). On the other hand, it has disadvantages in that it relies on potential litigants being willing and financially able to commence and pursue proceedings, and 'it has proved relatively ineffective in controlling lawless conduct by the police'. (*Op. cit.*, pp. 81–82.)

6.2.3 Fuller's place in the natural law tradition

Fuller asks whether the principles which he formulates 'represent some variety of natural law' and responds that 'the answer is an emphatic, though qualified, yes'. (*Op. cit.*, p. 96.) More particularly, he goes on to distinguish his theory from those which purport to identify the morally acceptable content of individual laws (which he calls *substantive* natural law theories), preferring to apply the *procedural* label to his own theory. He summarizes his position thus:

> 'A total failure in any one of these eight directions does not simply result in a bad system of law; it results in something that is not properly called a legal system at all, except perhaps in the Pickwickian sense in which a void contract can still be said to be one kind of contract. Certainly, there can be no rational ground for asserting that a man can have a moral obligation to obey a legal rule that does not exist or is kept secret from him, or that came into existence after he had acted, or was unintelligible, or was contradicted by another rule of the same system, or

commanded the impossible, or changed every minute. It may not be impossible for a man to obey a rule that is disregarded by those charged with its administration, but at some point obedience becomes futile – as futile, in fact, as casting a vote that will never be counted.' (*Op. cit.*, p. 39.)

However, the total failure in respect of even one criterion is very seldom going to be encountered. The more realistic, though still mercifully rare, situation will be one where 'there is a general and drastic deterioration in legality, such as occurred in Germany under Hitler', with many laws being unpromulgated or retroactive, where instances of non-congruence between official action and the declared rule were frequent, and, overall, the 'principal object of government' became to 'frighten [people] into impotence'. (*Op. cit.*, p. 40.) This sort of situation presents individuals with peculiarly difficult problems which only they can solve for themselves, but 'one thing is... clear. A mere respect for constituted authority must not be confused with fidelity to law'. This last comment plainly reflects the same attitude of mind as that which prompted Lord Camden CJ's classic rejection of the argument that submission to governmental conduct may be evidence of the legality of that conduct: 'I answer that there has been a submission of... poverty to power and the terror of punishment'. (See *Entick v Carrington* [1588–1774] All ER Rep 41, which is also discussed at p. 58.)

Fuller rejects Hart's view (which is considered at p. 76) that the basis of all human conduct is the wish to survive. By way of explanation he not only recalls Aquinas's view that a captain who wishes to preserve his ship at all costs will never put to sea, even though this decision denies the purpose for which the ship was built, but also develops the point:

'I doubt if most of us would regard as desirable survival into a kind of vegetable existence in which we could make no meaningful contact with other human beings.

'Communication is something more than a means of staying alive. It is a way of being alive. It is through communication that we inherit the achievements of past human effort. The possibility of communication can reconcile us to the thought of death by assuring us that what we achieve will enrich the lives of those to come.' (*Op. cit.*, p. 186.)

This leads him to recognize the

'one central indisputable principle of what may be called substantive natural law – Natural Law with capital letters – ... [namely]... the injunction: Open up, maintain and preserve the integrity of the channels of communication by which men convey to one another what they perceive, feel and desire.' (*Ibid.*)

Three broad-brush criticisms are commonly made of Fuller's version of natural law. First, being avowedly procedural, it fails to address the important issue of the moral content of law. Secondly, since it is only a total failure in respect of any one or more of his criteria which results in the non-existence of a legal system, a partial failure (and as we have seen in the context of the English legal system, these are by no means unknown) will not have such a devastating effect, it seems that Fuller is committed to the idea that the existence (or non-existence) of a legal system may be relative rather than absolute. Thirdly, his criteria do not genuinely embody moral principles at all, coming down, as they do, to little more than saying that a legal system should do its job well.

It may well be that Fuller is really providing a theory of the rule of law, rather than a full-blown theory of law. However, the identification of the most appropriate label will seem to be of much greater importance to those whose minds are preoccupied with Procrustean beds (see p. 6) than to those who are interested in the insights which legal theory can offer the world of practical law. Whatever label is applied, Fuller provides a theory which, while avoiding the necessity of any appeal to a higher system of law, identifies the kind of practices which, if sufficiently widespread and unchecked, are likely to lead to the ascendancy of tyranny and the demise of the liberal ideal of law.

6.3 Finnis's *Natural Law and Natural Rights*

6.3.1 Introduction

Two preliminary points may usefully be made before considering the substance of Finnis's theory.

First, he argues that Hume falls into error when he asserts that 'the distinction of vice and virtue is not... perceived by reason' (see p. 54), preferring Aquinas's view, discussed generally at pp. 47–49, that 'the first principles of natural law', which are those identifying good and evil, 'are *per se nota* (self-evident) and indemonstrable'. He develops his argument thus:

> '[The first principles of natural law] are *not inferred or derived from anything*... When discerning what is good... intelligence is operating in a different way, yielding a different logic, from when it is discerning what is the case (historically, scientifically, or metaphysically); but there is no good reason for asserting that the latter operations of intelligence are more rational than the former...
>
> 'The basic forms of good grasped by practical understanding are what is good for human beings with the nature they have.... [and this]... begins not by understanding this nature from the outside... but by experiencing one's nature, so to speak, from the inside... But again, *there is no process of inference*... by a simple act of *non-inferential understanding* one grasps that the object of the inclination one experiences is an instance of a general form of good.' (Emphasis added. Finnis, *Natural Law and Natural Rights*, 1980 and 2011, pp. 33–34. For the citation of this book see p. 97.)

When referring to the principles of natural law as being *self-evident*, Finnis does not mean that they are obvious in the sense that everybody will accept them automatically, but merely that their truth is evident without the need for, or even the possibility of, proof by reasoned argument. As Boyle puts it:

> 'What defines a proposition as... [self-evident]... is that it is a necessary truth in which the connection between the terms is immediate, unmediated by the middle term of a demonstrative syllogism. So... there is no absurdity in saying that a

proposition is self-evident, that is, known through itself, and that some people do not see that it is self-evident.... Aquinas' standard example of such a proposition is that angels are not in a place. This proposition is self-evident, but will be known to be such only to those wise enough to have the concept of an angel as an immaterial being.' (*Natural Law and the Ethics of Traditions*, in Robert P. George (ed.), *Natural Law Theory*, 1992, p. 23.)

The difficulty with examples such as the immateriality of an angel is that those people for whom an angel is an entirely imaginary being will regard any statement about the nature of an angel as falling within the same category as a statement about, for example, the nature of a unicorn. In other words, such people will regard the idea of *self-evidence* as being nothing more than dressing up a belief in order to give its subject-matter the appearance of reality. They are also likely to observe that there are many propositions whose truth cannot be demonstrated for the very simple reason that they are not true. The fact that others (like Boyle) regard self-evidence as a manifestation of wisdom will leave them entirely unmoved. Speaking as a sceptic about the whole enterprise of natural law, Oliver Wendell Holmes states the difference between the two positions thus:

'To those who agree with me I am uttering commonplaces and to those who disagree I am ignoring the necessary foundations of thought.' (*Natural Law* (1918) 32 Harv LR 40, at p. 42.)

Or, as Reynolds puts it, 'we are left with a conflict of background ideological and philosophical beliefs'. (See p. 25.)

Giving Finnis the benefit of the last word on self-evidence, speaking of the good of knowledge (see p. 105) he says (*op. cit.*, pp. 64–65) 'the good of knowledge is self-evident, obvious. It cannot be demonstrated, but equally it needs no demonstration'.

However, putting aside arguments about the idea of self-evidence, and proceeding in Finnis's own terms, it is worth emphasizing that Finnis is going beyond the essentially negative point that he regards Hume's objection to natural law as misconceived, and is seeking to argue that the principles of right and wrong are rational.

Secondly, Finnis indicates the ways in which he uses the basic terminology of *law* and *natural law*. More particularly, he uses the term *law* to mean *positive law*, while he uses the term *natural law* to mean the basic principles which he says indicate 'the basic forms of human flourishing as goods to be pursued and realized' together with a methodology of 'practical reasonableness'. Practical reasonableness enables a distinction to be drawn between sound and unsound reasoning, which leads not only to criteria for distinguishing between those acts which are morally right and those which are morally wrong, but also to the formulation of moral standards which may be applied generally.

It is important to clarify at the outset, as precisely as possible, what Finnis is (and is not) saying. More particularly, he rejects the traditional view that natural law validates positive law, so that positive law which is incompatible with natural law is not truly law at all (indeed, he even disputes that this is the traditional view), preferring the view that natural law provides a means for assessing the merit or demerit of positive law. In other words, Finnis's view is that natural law is evaluative, rather than constitutive, of positive law.

At a practical level, this means that natural law impinges on positive law by restricting the *rational* freedom of choice of both legislators and those judges who function within systems which allow them a degree of creativity in decision-making. Those legislators and judges may, of course, choose to act irrationally, in the sense of acting counter to natural law. However, if they do so, they create law which is merely bad (in the sense of being wrong and therefore undesirable, and in respect of which there may be a supervening moral obligation justifying disobedience) but whose status as law is not open to question.

Finnis then proceeds to explain more fully what he means by both 'the basic forms of human flourishing as goods to be pursued and realized' and the 'basic methodological requirements of practical reasonableness (itself one of the basic forms of human flourishing)'. Before considering these basic human goods individually, however, it may be helpful to emphasize that Finnis uses the phrase *practical reasonableness* in two senses.

The first sense of the phrase is relatively narrow, amounting to only one of the human goods, while the second is much wider, amounting to the whole methodology of reasoning, which endows the human goods with moral force.

We now turn to a consideration of the human goods, or basic forms of human flourishing.

6.3.2   The human goods or basic forms of human flourishing

Introduction

Finnis identifies seven *human goods* or *basic forms of human flourishing*. These are *life, knowledge, play, aesthetic experience, sociability (friendship), practical reasonableness* and *'religion'*. We will consider each of these in turn.

Life

The 'first basic value, corresponding to the drive for self-preservation, is the value of life'. This 'signifies every aspect of the vitality... which puts a human being in good shape for self-determination'. (*Op. cit.*, pp. 86–87.) (But for alternative views, see pp. 221, 223–225, below.)

At p. 447 (second edition), emphasizing a point he originally made at p. 86, Finnis says that the good of life includes procreation, which is among the factors which lead him also to consider marriage as a good.

Knowledge

Finnis identifies the kind of knowledge he is discussing as 'speculative knowledge', using the term, in order 'to distinguish knowledge as sought for its own sake from knowledge as sought only instrumentally, i.e. as useful in the pursuit of some other objective'. (*Op. cit.*, p. 59.)

For Finnis, of course, the status of knowledge as a basic human good is, as with all the other basic human goods, self-evident and underived, but in the case of knowledge there is the additional point that to deny the goodness of knowledge would be 'operationally self-refuting' (*op. cit.*, p. 74) because if knowledge were truly not a good, at least the knowledge of that worthlessness would be a good. Whether this argument can be sustained is, of course, another matter, as the following two points will show.

First, many people would argue that a great deal of knowledge is fairly obviously neutral, with the question of whether or not it is a good being entirely dependent on how it is used. For example, knowledge which confers the ability to unleash nuclear power may be a good when applied to generating electricity cheaply, and yet be an evil when applied to creating weapons of mass destruction (although it may be argued, on environmental grounds, that even nuclear power stations are not goods).

Secondly, it is possible to argue that those who maintain, as Finnis does, that denying the goodness of knowledge is operationally self-refuting are falling into a variant of the same trap. More particularly, the self-refuting argument can be sustained only if the proposition is that *all* knowledge is a good. In other words, Finnis is again ignoring the possibility of knowledge being intrinsically neutral, with its goodness (or otherwise) arising only at the instrumental stage, namely the stage at which it is applied. If a supporter of Finnis replies that this argument misses the point because what is really at issue is the value of the knowledge *as a form of human flourishing*, there are two answers. The first is that Finnis himself distinguishes between speculative and instrumental knowledge, which shows that he considers that the type of knowledge can be relevant. The second is that the kind of person whose head is full of, say, statistics drawn from an extensive knowledge of the history of Test cricket (or anything else which, in the great scheme of human experience cannot reasonably be ranked above the category of trivia) would often be regarded as a sad case, rather than as a truly flourishing human being.

Play

Finnis comments (*op. cit.*, p. 87) that doing things purely for their own sake is a universal element within human culture. At pp. 447–448 (second edition), Finnis acknowledges that his original, brief treatment of *play* 'fails to articulate what is implied in it' and concludes that 'excellence-in-performance', for its own sake, whether in 'work' or 'play' would be a 'more adequate and accurate characterization of the good in question'.

Aesthetic experience

Although aesthetic experience is an integral part of many forms of play, Finnis distinguishes between the two on the basis that 'aesthetic experience, unlike play, need not involve an action of one's own'. (*Ibid.*)

Sociability (friendship)

In order to make his point that sociability is a human good, Finnis poses the rhetorical question: 'To be in a relationship of friendship with at least one other person is a fundamental form of good, is it not?' (*Op. cit.*, p. 88.)

Practical reasonableness

Practical reasonableness as a basic good means being able to use one's own intelligence when making decisions which affect one's life. (*Ibid.*)

'Religion'

Although Finnis is a convinced Roman Catholic, and therefore clearly believes in God as an uncaused cause, the quotation marks which he places around the word *religion* indicate that he is using the word in an extended sense, which, for the present purposes may be stretched to the point of including agnosticism and even atheism. His argument is that it is unreasonable to deny the importance of thinking about the fundamental questions of the origin, nature and purpose of the cosmos and the place of humanity within it, whatever answers may be forthcoming.

Two final points may be made to conclude this account of Finnis's basic human goods. First, he concedes that there are many other things which some people would wish to see included (he suggests, for example, courage, generosity, moderation and gentleness), but concludes that these are qualities which help in the pursuit of the basic goods rather than themselves being those goods. Secondly, although the basic human goods are all equally fundamental, and therefore cannot be hierarchically ranked against each other, individuals may differ as to which ones they choose to emphasize within their own lifestyles, and even a single individual may attach varying importances to them at different times. Thus, for example, a scholar may pursue knowledge at the expense of sociability, but this will be a matter of temperament rather than the result of ascribing a higher intrinsic value to one than to the other. By way of another example, someone in immediate peril of drowning may attach prime importance to the value of life, although for most people, most of the time, life is seen as being merely a precondition to the ability to pursue one or more of the other basic goods.

A revised list of basic human goods

In the second edition, Finnis comments (at p. 448) on the fact that he has reconsidered the list of basic human goods in a number of essays since the publication of the first edition. He then presents the following as his preferred version, 'where at last marriage gets its due'.

'(1) *knowledge* (including aesthetic appreciation) of reality; (2) *skilful performance*, in work and play, for its own sake; (3) *bodily life* and the components of its fullness, viz. health, vigour, and safety; (4) *friendship* or harmony and association between persons in its various forms and strengths; (5) the sexual association of a man and a woman which, though it essentially involves both friendship between the partners and the procreation and education of children by them, seems to have a point and shared benefit that is not reducible either to friendship or to life-in-its-transmission and therefore… should be acknowledged to be a distinct human good, call it *marriage*; (6) the good of harmony between one's feelings and one's judgments (inner integrity), and between one's judgments and one's behaviour (authenticity), which we can call *practical reasonableness*; (7) *harmony* with the widest reaches and most *ultimate source* of all reality, including meaning and value.'

Finnis identifies two ways in which this version of the list improves on the original one, namely that it understands *aesthetic appreciation* as a form of *knowledge* and it recognizes that *artistic creation* falls within the category of *work and play* because it involves 'mastery of materials for its own sake'. (*Ibid.*)

6.3.3 The requirements of practical reasonableness

Introduction

Identifying basic human goods is useful, but those goods have no moral force in themselves: this vital characteristic flows from the requirements of practical reasonableness.

More particularly, Finnis identifies nine requirements of *practical reasonableness*, namely *a coherent plan of life; no arbitrary preferences among values; no arbitrary preferences amongst persons; detachment and commitment; the (limited) relevance of consequences: efficiency within reason; respect for every basic value in every act; the requirements of the common good; and following one's conscience.* These requirements produce moral values, because 'reasonableness both *is* a basic aspect of human well-being and *concerns* one's participation in all the (other) basic aspects of human well-being'. (Original emphasis. *Op. cit.*, pp. 102–103.) We will now consider each of the requirements in turn.

A coherent plan of life

The requirement of a coherent plan of life means that, given the shortness of life and the need to make choices, those choices should be self-consistent. In other words, one should not simply live for the moment. (*Op. cit.*, pp. 103–105.)

No arbitrary preferences among values

Since arbitrariness is clearly inconsistent with reasonableness, it is not surprising that Finnis specifically proscribes it, as both this and the next requirement show. More particularly, the requirement of no arbitrary preferences among values acknowledges that a coherent plan of life must involve paying more attention to some basic goods and less to others, but insists that such choices must be rational in the sense of 'being on the basis of one's assessment of one's capacities, circumstances, and even of one's tastes'. Even more specifically, such choices will be unreasonable if they are based on a devaluation of any of the basic goods, or on an over-valuation of secondary goods, such as wealth or pleasure. (*Op. cit.*, pp. 105–106.)

No arbitrary preferences among persons

Just as reasonableness requires an absence of arbitrary preferences amongst values, so it involves an absence of arbitrary preferences among persons. While Finnis acknowledges a 'reasonable scope for self-preference', he insists that this requirement proscribes 'selfishness, special pleading, double standards, hypocrisy, indifference to the good of others whom one could easily help ("passing by on the other side"), and all the other manifold forms of egoistic and group bias'. (*Op. cit.*, pp. 106–107.)

Detachment and commitment

Placing 'detachment' and 'commitment' together under one heading, although he plainly regards them as two requirements, Finnis argues for a middle way between being so detached that one never really becomes involved in anything, and being so committed to an activity or a project that its failure would lead one to conclude that life had become pointless. (*Op. cit.*, pp. 109–110.)

The (limited) relevance of consequences: efficiency within reason

The requirement of efficiency within reason recognizes that there are many contexts in which it is reasonable to assess the consequences of alternative courses of action. For example, it is reasonable to give priority to the good of humans over that of animals, and to prefer human goods which are basic, such as life itself, to those which are merely instrumental, such as property. Nevertheless, the basic goods cannot be measured, and therefore any attempt to quantify them as part of a decision-making process is irrational. (*Op. cit.*, pp. 111–118.)

Respect for every basic value in every act

The requirement of respect for every basic value in every act is clearly and closely related to the previous requirement, and is the basis of the inviolability of fundamental human rights. More particularly, since the basic goods cannot be quantified, any action which is based on the premise that one such good is worth less than another must be irrational and is therefore proscribed. (*Op. cit.*, pp. 118–125.)

The requirements of the common good

The eighth requirement of practical reasonableness deals with promoting the common good of the community as a whole, with particular reference to enabling everyone to participate as fully as possible in the basic goods. (*Op. cit.*, pp. 125.)

Following one's conscience

Although a requirement of following one's conscience may sound capable of justifying anything which is subjectively attractive, it is clear that what Finnis means by this requirement is that one should act reasonably in all things, while accepting that even the exercise of a well-informed, honest and rational conscience will not always produce an answer which can be characterized as being right. As Finnis puts it, this requirement recognizes '[the] dignity of even the mistaken conscience'. (*Op. cit.*, pp. 125–126.)

6.3.4 The role of the requirements of practical reasonableness in creating moral obligations

You will recall that Finnis does not claim that, in themselves, the basic human goods create moral obligations, but that these arose only from the application of the principles of practical reasonableness. Finnis presents his argument in a form which is essentially syllogistic:

- all the requirements of practical reasonableness are really aspects of one fundamental human good (or form of human flourishing), namely freedom and reason;
- in any given context, each of the requirements of practical reason can be best satisfied by doing (or refraining from doing) something;
- therefore that 'something' ought (or ought not) to be done.

This formulation may prompt the criticism that the premises are statements of fact while the conclusion is a statement of value, so that the old trap of deriving an *ought* from an *is* opens up once again. However, closer analysis shows that although the premises are expressed in factual terms, they are essentially statements of value. Therefore, when properly understood, Finnis is merely deriving an *ought* from an *ought*, and, of course, there can be no logical objection to this. On the other hand, this kind of argument does raise another difficulty, namely the problem of establishing the truth of the premises in the first place, since, unlike matters of fact, matters of value cannot be established by empirical evidence.

As we have seen (at pp. 103–104), Finnis replies to this objection by relying on what he calls *self-evidence*. However, this is by no means universally accepted, and in particular, Weinreb (*Natural Law and Justice*, 1987) argues that the idea that reflection on the human condition can yield self-evident moral principles which are usable in real situations is simply wrong.

6.3.5 The extent of the duty to obey the law

When asking whether there is a duty to obey unjust laws, Finnis points out that there are four senses in which the question may be asked.

First, the question may simply mean: 'Will non-compliance with the law make me liable to a sanction?'. In practice, of course, the answer to this question is so obvious that the question itself is unlikely to arise. (This question may, of course, be asked in the spirit of 'Will I get away with it?', but since the justice or injustice of the law is irrelevant in this situation it is hardly surprising that Finnis does not mention it.)

Secondly, the question may mean: 'Given that this law is unjust, can I fail to comply with it and then persuade the court that it ought to be changed?'. The answer to this question depends upon the principles of precedent and interpretation which operate within the legal system in question.

Thirdly, the question may mean: 'Given that this law is unjust, but the courts will nevertheless enforce it, does the fact that the legal system is, on the whole, just, mean that I have a moral obligation to obey even this law?' Or, putting it more briefly and in Finnis' words, can it be said that 'an unjust law creates a moral obligation *in the way* that just law *of itself* does?' (Original emphasis. *Op. cit.*, p. 359.) Finnis, explicitly following the classical view, replies that such laws lack moral authority, and therefore give rise to no moral obligation of obedience, although of course his starting point (see p. 108) means that he does not deny such provisions their status as laws.

This leaves only the fourth sense in which the question of whether there is a duty to obey unjust laws may be understood, namely whether there may be a collateral moral obligation of obedience (or, in other words, an obligation originating elsewhere than in the legal status of the provision in question). Finnis replies that such an obligation may exist, where the result of disobedience would be to weaken the law as a whole, but the extent of obedience will be limited to that which is necessary to avoid the legal system as a whole becoming ineffective. The extent of such obedience will vary from one situation to another, but in the case of judges and other officials, it may be that full, or practically full, compliance will be required. Finnis characterizes this kind of duty obedience as 'in an important sense extra-legal'. (*Op. cit.*, p. 362.) Furthermore, despite whatever obedience may be given to such laws, the legislature will remain under an obligation to repeal or amend the law in such a way as to remove its injustice.

6.3.6   Finnis's place in the natural law tradition

There can be no doubt that Finnis has reasserted the claim of the natural law tradition to be worthy of close examination. Ultimately, however, whether that examination results in anything more than a recurrence of Humean scepticism is a matter for individual conclusion.

Summary

▶ After the Second World War, there was a revival of interest in natural law.

▶ Fuller's theory, largely contained in his book *The Morality of Law*, purports to provide a set of criteria for identifying the existence of legal systems. Whether the criteria do genuinely relate to the existence of legal systems may be open to debate, and they may more accurately be seen as providing a theory of the rule of law. However, irrespective of the label which is attached to it, Fuller's theory usefully emphasizes many aspects of the operation of legal systems which should be subjected to constant and critical scrutiny.

▶ Finnis's theory, largely contained in his book *Natural Law and Natural Rights*, locates the foundation of natural law in certain *basic human goods*, together with the *requirements of practical reasonableness*.

Further reading

Boyle, Joseph, *Natural Law and the Ethics of Traditions in Natural Law Theory*, 1992, George, Robert P, (ed.)

Finnis, John, *Natural Law and Natural Rights*, 2nd edn, 2011

Fuller, Lon L., *The Morality of Law*, revised edn, 1969

Harris, J.W., *Legal Philosophies*, 2nd edn, 1997

Holmes, Oliver Wendell, *Natural Law* (1918) 32 Harv LR 40

McLeod, Ian, *Legal Method*, 8th edn, 2011; 9th edn, 2013

Weinreb, Lloyd L., *Natural Law and Justice*, 1987

Chapter 7

Policies, principles, rights, interpretation and value: Dworkin's theory of law

7.1 Introduction

You will recall from the end of Chapter 4 that Ronald Dworkin (b. 1931), an American working in both England and America, is one of the most significant critics of Hart's concept of law. We will consider Dworkin's theory in three main stages, namely the inadequacy of viewing law as a system of rules, the importance of individual rights, and the idea that law is essentially an *interpretative* (although he prefers the American usage *interpretive*) process, before concluding with an overview of his view of the relationship between morality and law. However, by way of introduction, three matters may usefully be emphasized.

First, the stages of our consideration do not constitute self-contained topics: an understanding of each one will inform our understanding of the others. Secondly, Dworkin's theory is based on a liberal political position, which emphasizes the central importance of individual rights, and, in particular, the proposition that there should be equality between individuals. However, this proposition conceals an ambiguity, because it can be argued either that a government, when proceeding on the basis of equality, must leave it to individuals to identify what they consider to be the elements of a good life, or that a government cannot leave this to individuals because, before it can begin to think in terms of equality, it must first decide what it thinks human beings ought to be.

It is within the first of these answers that Dworkin locates the liberal response, which he calls 'the right to moral independence' (*A Matter of Principle*, 1986, p. 353), and on the basis of which he develops his theory.

The third point, which will emerge from the remainder of this chapter, is that by concentrating on what the courts should do – and to a significant extent what they actually do – it may seem that Dworkin is really offering a *theory of adjudication*, rather than a *theory of law*. As Harris puts it:

'Discovery of law in all cases requires "constructive interpretation", that is the morally soundest statements about the rights of citizens which will fit the legal materials. Law does not consist of the prescriptions which the authorities have laid down; it consists of the best politics which will fit such prescriptions. Law is not something we give information about. It is something we argue about.' (*Legal Philosophies*, 2nd edn, 1997, p. 188.)

Although Dworkin himself acknowledges that many people have seen his theory as being limited to adjudication, he argues that his theory goes beyond the field of adjudication and that it truly is a theory of law. (See *Justice in Robes*, 2006, generally and pp. 1–35 in particular, and *Justice for Hedgehogs*, 2011, generally.)

The only introductory matter which remains to be mentioned is that, as an explanatory device, Dworkin invents a super-human judge (whom he calls Hercules), whose idealized thought-processes he uses as a vehicle for illustrating his theory. It is important to understand that Dworkin's account of Hercules J is not intended to present a realistic portrait (nor even a caricature) of a judge. Its intention is, rather, to present a hypothetical model to represent an idealised judge, who can be expected to be 'wide-ranging and imaginative in his search for coherence with fundamental principle' (*Law's Empire*, 1986, p. 220). Moreover, Hercules J is 'more reflective and self-conscious than any real judge need be, or, given the press of work, could be'. (*Op. cit.*, p. 265.) Dworkin constructs Hercules J in order to explain how judges should decide *hard cases* – by which he means cases that have to be decided in the absence of clear answers provided by either statute or precedent.

7.2   The inadequacy of seeing law as a system of rules

Hart's view of a legal system as the union of primary and secondary rules raises the question of what happens where the court has no relevant rules available to it. As we saw in Chapter 4, Hart's answer to this is that the court must make a new rule by using its discretion. In reply to this, however, Dworkin, who labels such situations *hard cases*, makes two objections.

First, this is undemocratic. Secondly, law made in this way is retroactive because 'the losing party will be punished not because he violated some duty he had, but rather a new duty created after the event'. (*Taking Rights Seriously*, 1977, p. 84.) Since these conclusions flow incontrovertibly from the premise that judges make law, Dworkin's aim, initially at any rate, is to demonstrate the falsity of that premise.

For many years, a key element in Dworkin's argument was that there would always be one right answer to any legal problem, and therefore it was conceptually impossible for judges to make law. In other words, even in cases where there is no relevant statute or judicial precedent, judges merely *identify* and *state* the law, rather than *making* it. In any specific case, the judges may or may not succeed in getting it right, but cases where they get it wrong must not be allowed to distract attention from the fact that there was a *right answer*, which they failed to identify. Many people think that, in a common law system at least, this *right answer thesis* is unsustainable and that judges plainly do make law. Such people may well pray in aid the words of John Austin, who refers to

'the childish fiction employed by our judges that judiciary or common law is not made by them, but is a miraculous something, made by nobody, existing, I suppose, from eternity, and merely declared from time to time by the judges.' (*Jurisprudence*, 5th edn, 1885, ii, p. 655.)

Similarly, they may recall Lord Edmund-Davies's comment:

> 'But, like it or not, the fact remains that judges will continue to make law as long as our present system of determining disputes remains.... The simple and certain fact is that judges inevitably act as legislators.' (*Judicial Activism* [1975] *Current Legal Problems*, p. 1.)

At one time, Dworkin seemed to be having second thoughts about his *right answer* thesis, describing the argument as 'a waste of important energy and resource' and saying that it is better 'to take up instead how the decisions that in any case will be made should be made, and which of the answers that will in any case be thought right or best or true or soundest really are'. (*Pragmatism, Right Answers and True Banality*, in Brint and Weaver (eds), *Pragmatism in Law and Society*, 1991, p. 365.) However, he later put the matter beyond doubt:

> 'Some critics... suggest that I have changed my mind about the character and importance of the one-right-answer claim. For better or for worse, I have not.' (*Justice in Robes*, 2006, p. 266, n. 3.)

We now turn to the elements of Dworkin's theory, namely *policies*, *principles* and *rights*, along with *integrity*, *justification* and *fit*; and, especially in *Justice for Hedgehogs* (2011), *ethics*, *morality* and *value*.

7.3 Policies, principles and rights

7.3.1 Introduction

Dworkin places great emphasis on what he calls *standards*, which exist independently of the rules which positivists regard as the totality of law. More particularly, these standards fall into two categories, namely *policies* and *principles*.

> 'I call a "policy" that kind of standard that sets out a goal to be reached, generally an improvement in some economic, political or social feature of the community (though some goals are negative, in that they stipulate that some present feature is to be protected from adverse change). I call a "principle" a standard that is to be observed, not because it will advance or serve an economic, political or social situation deemed desirable, but because it is a requirement of justice or fairness or some other dimension of reality.' (*Is Law a System of Rules?* in *The Philosophy of Law*, 1977, p. 43.)

7.3.2 Policies

The concept of *policy* may be illustrated by the example of a governmental decision to subsidize farmers who agree not to grow a particular crop which is currently in overproduction. This violates nobody's rights, and certainly does not entitle other farmers to claim that they should be entitled to receive subsidies in return for not growing other crops for which there is a ready market:

'Decisions in pursuit of these strategies, judged one by one, are matters of policy, not principle; they must be tested by asking whether they advance the overall goal, not whether they give each citizen what he is entitled to have as an individual....

'Most working political theories also recognize, however, distinct individual rights as trumps over these decisions of policy, rights that government *is* required to respect case by case, decision by decision. These may be grand political rights like the right of each citizen to have his vote counted as equal to any other citizen's, or not to be denied freedom of speech or conscience even when violating these rights would contribute to the general welfare. Or rights drawn more directly from personal morality, like the right to be compensated for injuries caused by another's carelessness.' (Original emphasis. *Law's Empire*, 1986, p. 223.)

Of course, in practice, policies may conflict with each other, in which case judges must choose between them. For example, in the United States Supreme Court case of *Tennessee Valley Authority v Hill* 437 US 153 (1973) the argument came down to whether the Endangered Species Act should be given a meaning which would result in the waste of substantial public funds. More particularly, the question was whether the court should order that the construction of a $100 million dam, which was almost completed, should be stopped because it would destroy the only habitat of the snail darter, which Dworkin describes (*op. cit.*, p. 21) as 'a three inch fish of no particular beauty or biological interest or general ecological importance'. The majority of the court held that this was the correct result, because there was no indication that the plain words of the Act were not to be applied. On the other hand, a minority of two judges held that this result could only properly be achieved if there was evidence that Congress had intended it. If this decision is seen in Dworkinian terms, it can be said that there were two competing policies, namely conserving endangered species and obtaining value for public money.

The proposition that the court must choose between conflicting policies may be no more than a statement of the obvious, but where the conflict is between *policies* and *rights*, Dworkin argues that unless the context is wholly exceptional (such as wartime, when policies derived from the collective goal of national survival may prevail over rights, because otherwise the system which enables principled decisions to be made may itself cease to exist) the rights must always prevail, and therefore there is effectively no choice to be made. However, before considering Dworkinian rights more closely, we must first consider his concept of *principles*.

7.3.3 Principles

The nature and role of *principles* may be illustrated by the case where a testator makes a valid will in favour of a beneficiary, who then proceeds to murder him.

The beneficiary will not be allowed to inherit under the will, because there is a principle which prevents people from benefiting from their own wrongdoing. (Dworkin cites the American case of *Riggs v Palmer* 115 NY 506 (1889), but the English case of *Re Sigsworth* [1934] All ER Rep 113 – see pp. 57 and 83 – is an essentially similar example of the same reasoning, albeit the succession in this case was intestate rather than testate.)

For Dworkin, the crucial difference between rules and principles is that rules function in 'all-or-nothing' manner, in the sense that if two rules conflict, one of them must either be invalid, or at least be capable of being formulated as being an exception to the other. Principles, on the other hand, have the quality of *weight* or *importance*, in the sense of being considerations 'which officials must take into account... as... inclining in one direction or another.... When principles intersect... one who must resolve the conflict has to take into account the relative weight of each'. (*Is Law a System of Rules?* in *The Philosophy of Law*, 1977, p. 47.)

Dworkin concedes, as of course he must, that the weight of a principle cannot be calculated to a nicety, and that opinions as to weight may be controversial. But he nevertheless insists that 'it is an integral part of the concept of a principle... that it makes sense to ask how important or how weighty it is'. (*Ibid.*) Moreover, his perception of the nature of principles leads Dworkin to a specific criticism of Hart's theory, namely the inability (as Dworkin sees it) of the rule of recognition to deal with principles, because it would be impossible to 'devise any formula for testing how much and what kind of institutional support is necessary to make a principle a legal principle, still less fix its weight at a particular order of magnitude'. More particularly,

'[Identifying principles involves] grappling with a whole set of shifting, developing and interacting standards (themselves principles rather than rules) about institutional responsibility, statutory interpretation, the persuasive force of various sorts of precedent, the relation of all these to contemporary moral practices, and hosts of other such standards.' (*Taking Rights Seriously*, 1977, p. 36.)

Two points arise here. First, there is no doubt that the judges have always been familiar with the idea that certain types of proposition have weight, rather than simply being either right or wrong. Thus, for example, at one of the most basic levels of legal method ,when commenting on the nature of the so-called *rules* of statutory interpretation, Lord Reid said:

'They are not rules in the ordinary sense of having some binding force.... They are aids to construction: presumptions or pointers. Not infrequently one "rule" points in one direction, another in a different direction. In each case we must look at all relevant circumstances and decide as a matter of judgment what weight to attach to any particular "rule".' (*Maunsell v Olins* [1975] 1 All ER 16.)

When expressed in Dworkinian terms, therefore, what were at one time commonly called the *rules* of interpretation can be, and now commonly are, more accurately described as *principles* of interpretation.

Secondly, Hart acknowledges that he originally said far too little about adjudication and legal reasoning generally, and about propositions of the kind that Dworkin calls legal principles in particular (see *The Concept of Law*, 2nd edn, 1994, p. 259), but goes on to say:

'I see no reason to accept... [the] sharp contrast between legal principles and legal rules, or the view that if a valid rule is applicable to a given case it must, unlike a principle, always determine the outcome of the case. There is no reason why a legal system should not recognize that a valid rule determines the result in cases to which it is applicable, except where another rule, judged to be more important, is also applicable to the same case. So a rule which is defeated in competition with a more important rule in a given case may, like a principle, survive to determine the outcome in other cases where it is judged to be more important than another competing rule.' (*Op. cit.*, pp. 261–262.)

Characterizing the idea that 'a legal system consists of all-or-nothing rules and non-conclusive principles' as displaying 'incoherence', Hart continues by saying that

'this may be cured if we admit that the distinction is a matter of degree. Certainly a reasonable contrast can be made between near-conclusive rules, the satisfaction of whose conditions of application suffices to determine the legal result except in a few instances (where its provisions may conflict with another rule judged of greater importance) and generally non-conclusive principles which merely point towards a decision but may very frequently fail to determine it.

'I certainly think that arguments from such non-conclusive principles are an important feature of adjudication and legal reasoning, and that it should be marked by an appropriate terminology. Much credit is due to Dworkin for having shown and illustrated their importance and their role in legal reasoning, and certainly it was a serious mistake on my part not to have stressed their non-conclusive force. But I certainly did not intend in my use of the word "rule" to claim that legal systems comprise only "all-or-nothing" or near-conclusive rules.' (*Op. cit.*, pp. 262–263.)

However, there is something to be said for preserving the distinction between *rules* and *principles* as two distinct concepts, even though both may enter into any specific decision-making process. Kelly puts it thus:

'Of course, it could be said that the notion of a rule can be given a wide meaning, so as to embrace the principle-based qualifications to which it may, in a particular case, turn out to be subject, and that Dworkin's distinction is more verbal than substantial. On the other hand, there *is* a real difference – akin to that between a legal and a moral precept – between a rule in the narrow sense and a principle (or policy): rules are felt to be amenable to deliberate change or repeal, say, by legislation, whereas what is meant by a principle is something we do not think of as susceptible to deliberate alteration. Its relative weight in society may change over time, in the way, for example, that the principle that people should be free to make what bargains they choose has been eroded in the light of new social perceptions, and this change will be reflected in judicial as well as in legislative responses. But at any particular time a body of principles will be thought of as underlying, or transcending, a body of rules, and inherently possessing a stability which rules do not enjoy.' (Original emphasis. *A Short History of Western Legal Theory*, 1992, p. 409.)

Furthermore, Hart responds to Dworkin's argument that the rule of recognition cannot cope with principles by saying that at least some principles are capable of coming within the scope of the rule's operation, citing as an example the principle against deriving profit from one's own wrongdoing, which has been recognized by the courts in a variety of contexts.

7.3.4 Rights

As we have seen, Dworkin emphasizes the importance which he attaches to rights (or, more accurately, to *individual* rights) by using the image of rights as trumps. In other words, in any given case and in the absence of wholly exceptional considerations (see p. 116), arguments based on rights will defeat arguments based on any other interests:

> 'Individual rights are political trumps held by individuals. Individuals have rights when, for some reason, a collective goal is not a sufficient justification for denying them what they wish, as individuals, to have or to do, or not a sufficient justification for imposing some loss or injury upon them. That characterization of a right is, of course, formal in the sense that it does not indicate what rights people have or guarantee, indeed, that they have any. But it does not suppose that rights have some special metaphysical character, and the theory defended in these essays therefore departs from older theories of rights that do rely on that supposition.' (*Taking Rights Seriously*, 1977, p. xi.)

The final link in the chain is that judicial decisions which apply those principles, and uphold rights, are better than those which do not, because they will mean that the legal system is displaying what Dworkin calls 'the virtue of political integrity'. (*Law's Empire*, 1986, p. 166.) He goes on to analyse the idea of *political integrity* into two categories, namely 'the principle of integrity in legislation, which asks those who create law by legislation to keep that law coherent in principle' and 'the principle of integrity in adjudication [which] asks those responsible for deciding what the law is to see and enforce it as coherent in that way'. (*Op. cit.*, p. 167.)

The principle of integrity in adjudication (or, more conveniently, *adjudicative integrity*) 'explains why judges must conceive the body of law they administer as a whole rather than as a set of discrete decisions that they are free to make or amend one by one, with nothing but a strategic interest in the rest', and therefore it may appear that it is only this principle which is relevant to judicial decision-making. However, the principle of integrity in legislation (or, more conveniently, *legislative integrity*) is also relevant, even at the adjudicative stage, since a judge faced with competing interpretations of a legislative provision should seek to adopt the alternative which shows the law as a coherent whole. This will include promoting interpretations which show the provision in question to be the product of legislative integrity.

An important, but easily overlooked, aspect of Dworkin's argument based on rights is his concession that his 'characterization of a right is, of course, formal in the sense that it does not indicate what rights people have or guarantee, indeed, that they have any'. More particularly, in practical terms the content of those rights becomes dependent on the values which are implicit within a given political system. The point is, of course, that these values may change from time to time and from place to place. Even at one time and in one place there may not be unanimity as to what they are. For example, as we shall see in Chapter 11, Dworkin argues for a liberal stance on matters of individual sexual morality, but a judge who takes a different view can justify an anti-liberal decision by appealing to the sort of values which Dworkin argues are the sources of the principles from which his conception of rights flows. Furthermore, rights may conflict with each other.

We come now to the concepts of *justification* and *fit* and their place within Dworkin's theory of interpretation.

7.4 Interpretation: *integrity*, *justification* and *fit*

It is one thing to say that the law not only includes policies and principles, but should also uphold rights, and another to say how, in individual cases, individual judges should make the choices which are open to them. This requires a return to the idea of *political integrity*, and more particularly to that subdivision of that concept which Dworkin labels *integrity in adjudication*, or more conveniently, *adjudicative integrity*.

According to Dworkin, the idea of *adjudicative integrity* requires judges to decide hard cases

> 'by trying to find, in some coherent set of principles, about people's rights and duties, the best constructive interpretation of the political structure and legal doctrine of their community. They try to make that complex structure and record the best these can be... [This] will include convictions about both fit and justification.' (*Op. cit.*, p. 255.)

The ideas of *justification* and *fit* may be explained by way of analogy with the writing of a chain novel (where each chapter is contributed by a different author), or, more realistically in the modern world, by a television soap opera, whose scripts are written by many hands. The broad situations and characterizations are established in the early stages of such a writing project, with the result that successive contributors are constrained to some extent as to how they develop the story lines, but within those constraints there is nevertheless some scope for creativity. Occasionally, there may even be major shifts. For example, the sudden and unexpected death of a leading character may open up previously unimagined possibilities of plot development, just as ground-breaking decisions such as *Donoghue v Stevenson* [1932] AC 562 (which laid the foundations of the modern law of negligence), open up whole new areas of legal development. However, such fundamental changes cannot occur in every chapter, or every week, otherwise the sense of continuity which is necessary to both a chain-written work and a legal system would be destroyed.

It follows that, when exercising judicial discretion, judges should look to the coherence of the legal system as a whole; and that a decision which promotes that coherence is, in a real sense of the word, *better* than one which detracts from it. If there are disputes as to what the promotion of coherence actually requires in terms of a decision in a specific case, judges must, in the final analysis, simply make up their own minds.

> '[A judge] must rely on his own judgment... not because he thinks his opinions are automatically right, but because no one can properly answer any question except by relying at the deepest level on what he himself believes.' (*Op. cit.*, pp. 313–314.)

Three points must immediately be made. First, the judge's personal beliefs will by no means always be objectively reasoned:

> 'Any judge will develop... a fairly individualized working conception of law on which he will rely... in making... judgments... and the judgments will then be, for him, a matter of feel or instinct rather than analysis.' (*Op. cit.*, p. 256.)

Secondly, however, judges' beliefs are unlikely to be highly idiosyncratic because 'most judges will be like other people in their community'. (*Ibid*.)

Thirdly, even judges with unusually eccentric or radical opinions are under a duty to adopt solutions which will 'show the community's record in the best light' rather than pursuing their own idiosyncrasies. (*Ibid*.).

7.5 The nature of legal theory and the 'semantic sting'

By this stage it should be apparent that Dworkin's view of the nature of the whole enterprise of legal theory departs from the common perception which sees the subject in terms of abstract, academic debate.

More particularly, Dworkin argues that, since both legal theorists and practising lawyers are seeking the best constructive interpretation of the law, it follows that the differences between their activities are really matters of degree rather than of kind. In other words, the essential difference between the two groups is the degree of abstraction or particularity at which each functions.

Additionally, Dworkin argues that his view of the seamless connection between legal theory and legal practice, illustrates the fundamental inadequacy of positivist theories in general and Hart's version of positivism in particular (see Chapter 4 for discussion of Hart's theory). More particularly, those theories are based solely on detailed analyses of the purely semantic question of what words such as *law* mean, to the exclusion of any evaluation of the content of the law. They are, therefore, necessarily detached from the daily experience of the courts, where judges must constantly consider moral issues such as justice and fairness when seeking to identify the best versions of disputed propositions of law.

Furthermore, even though positivists base their positions on definitions, Dworkin argues that their disagreements commonly arise from the real differences between their definitions, but that their arguments conceal these differences. Where this happens,

> 'they are not really disagreeing about anything.... They are only talking past one another. Their arguments are pointless in the most trivial and irritating way, like an argument about banks when one person has in mind savings banks and the other riverbanks. Worse still, even when lawyers appear to agree about what the law is, their agreement turns out to be fake as well, as if the two persons I just imagined thought they agreed that there are many banks in North America.' (*Op. cit.*, p. 44.)

Dworkin concludes that those who base themselves solely on semantics are 'stung' by the inadequacy of semantics and semantic arguments to deliver answers to the real questions; or, putting this in a different grammatical form, they suffer what he calls 'the semantic sting'. (*Op. cit.*, p. 45.)

7.6 The problem of identifying rights in practice

7.6.1 Introduction

The importance which Dworkin attaches to rights may be intuitively attractive to those of a liberal disposition, but it is worth remembering (from p. 119) that he specifically concedes that his concept of rights is formal, rather than prescribing content. It is also worth remembering that in some cases the choice before the court is not between a policy and right, but between two conflicting rights, both of which may be supported by equally persuasive policies.

We will consider each point in turn.

7.6.2 Identifying rights

The difficulty which arises where judges have to identify rights in individual cases may be illustrated by the case of *Harrogate Borough Council v Simpson* (1986) 2 FLR 91. The facts were that a Mrs Rodrigo and a Miss Simpson were a lesbian couple who regarded themselves as husband and wife. Mrs Rodrigo was the masculine and Miss Simpson the feminine partner. They lived in a council house. The tenancy, which was in the sole name of Mrs Rodrigo, was a periodic one and was what is technically known as a 'secure tenancy'. The cohabitation lasted approximately two-and-a-half years, until it was terminated by Mrs Rodrigo's death. The council sought to recover possession of the house from Miss Simpson, and obtained judgment in the county court accordingly. Miss Simpson appealed unsuccessfully to the Court of Appeal.

An assessment of this case must begin with the relevant provisions of s. 30 of the Housing Act 1980:

> '(1) Where a secure tenancy is a periodic tenancy and, on the death of the tenant, there is a person qualified to succeed him, the tenancy vests by virtue of this section in that person...

'(2) A person is qualified to succeed a tenant under a secure tenancy if he occupied the dwelling-house as his only or principal home at the time of the tenant's death and either (a) he is the tenant's spouse; or (b) he is another member of the tenant's family and has resided with the tenant throughout the period of twelve months ending with the tenant's death.'

The relevant part of the definition of 'family' was to be found in s. 50(3):

'A person is a member of another's family... if she is his spouse... or if they live together as husband and wife.'

Miss Simpson sought to establish her claim by relying on the equivalent statutory provisions governing rights of succession to protected tenancies in the private sector, and, in particular, the way in which those provisions had been interpreted in the context of unmarried heterosexual couples. However, Watkins LJ felt that the heterosexuality of the couples involved in the earlier cases made those decisions clearly distinguishable:

'If Parliament had wished homosexual relationships to be brought into the realm of the lawfully recognized state of a living together of man and wife for the purpose of the relevant legislation, it would plainly have so stated in that legislation, and it has not done so.... It would be surprising in the extreme to learn that public opinion is such today that it would recognize a homosexual union as being akin to a state of living as husband and wife. The ordinary man and woman... would in my opinion not think even remotely of there being a true resemblance between those two very different states of affairs.'

Why did Watkins LJ not conclude that respect for adjudicative integrity requires homosexual and heterosexual couples to be treated in the same way in relation to security of tenure? The answer lies in his appeal to the views of the 'ordinary [i.e. heterosexual] man and woman', whom he appears to regard as the guardians of society's values in relation to the matter of sexual orientation. In other words, even if ordinary people might feel initially that all couples should be treated equally in terms of security of tenure, they would give even greater weight to the cultural preference for heterosexuality over homosexuality. The consequence is that homosexual individuals are denied what would have been their rights if another reading of society's values had prevailed.

Admittedly, this case was decided at a time when the law was inclining somewhat against homosexuals, as evidenced by s. 28 of the Local Government Act 1988, which introduced a general prohibition on local authorities intentionally promoting homosexuality, and a specific prohibition on the teaching in maintained schools of 'the acceptability of homosexuality as a *pretended* family relationship'. (Emphasis added.) (The provision which became s. 28 was originally introduced into Parliament in early 1987, but when a general election was called it was withdrawn along with a number of other provisions, in order that other, non-contentious, material contained in the same Bill could be enacted before the dissolution of Parliament.) Nevertheless, it remains true that Miss Simpson's choice of a lesbian lifestyle as an essential element of 'the good life' resulted in her being denied a property right which she would have enjoyed if her orientation and lifestyle had been heterosexual. In other words, even if s. 28 of the 1988 Act is treated as evidence of a prevailing climate of discrimination against homosexuals, and therefore as helping to justify the decision in terms of Dworkinian 'fit', it remains strongly arguable that her Dworkinian right should have been held to prevail.

The issue of whether a homosexual partner may succeed to a tenancy on the death of the tenant came before the court again in *Fitzpatrick v Sterling Housing Association Ltd* [1997] 4 All ER 991. The facts involved gay men and the law related to the provisions governing private sector tenancies, but the issue of principle was indistinguishable from that in *Harrogate Borough Council v Simpson*. More particularly, the issue was whether the survivor fell within the scope of the Rent Act 1977; and, if so, whether he was a *member of the tenant's family* (in which case he would have been entitled to an *assured tenancy*) or the tenant's *spouse* (in which case he would have been entitled to a *statutory tenancy*, which would have been more advantageous than an *assured tenancy*).

All three judges in the Court of Appeal were plainly sympathetic. Thus Roch LJ said that

'[allowing the survivor to succeed] would... be consistent not only with social justice but also with the respect accorded by modern society to those of the same sex who undertake a permanent commitment to a shared life.'

Nevertheless, both he and Waite LJ concluded that it was a matter for consideration by Parliament, and that it would be improper for the court to introduce the change which would be necessary if the survivor were to succeed. On the other hand, Ward LJ, in a dissent which Roch LJ described as 'interesting and elegant', had no such constitutional qualms.

'To exclude same-sex couples from the protection of the 1977 Act proclaims the inevitable message that society judges their relationships to be less worthy of respect, concern and consideration than the relationship between members of the opposite sex. The fundamental human dignity of the homosexual couple is severely and palpably affected by the impugned distinction. The distinction is drawn on grounds relating to their personal characteristics, their sexual orientation. If the law is as my Lords state it to be, then it discriminates against a not insignificant proportion of the population who will justly complain that they have been denied their constitutional right to equal treatment under the law.'

Two points may be noticed in passing. First, Ward LJ approved Dworkin's comment (*Law's Empire*, 1986, p. 348) that

'[the judge] interprets not just the statute's text but its life, the process that begins before it becomes law and extends far beyond that moment... [the judge's] interpretation changes as the story develops.'

Secondly, just as the climate of opinion which gave rise to the enactment of s. 28 of the Local Government Act 1988 formed part of the contemporary context of the decision in *Harrogate Borough Council v Simpson*, so s. 145 of the Criminal Justice and Public Order Act 1994, which reduced the age of consent for homosexual acts between consenting males from 21 to 18, may have contributed to the sympathy of the majority, and the support of the minority, in the Court of Appeal, in *Fitzpatrick*.

Against this background, it is worth noticing that when the Appellate Committee of the House of Lords dealt with the case (see [1999] 4 All ER 705), the Commons and the Lords were engaged in a long-running constitutional wrangle. Briefly, a proposal to reduce the age of consent still further (to 16), was passed by the House of Commons as a private member's amendment to the Bill which became the Crime and Disorder Act 1998, but was rejected by the House of Lords. The Commons did not press the issue, and therefore the provision did not appear in the Act itself. However, in late 1998 the proposal returned to the Commons as a government measure in the form of the Sexual Offences (Amendment) Bill. It was again passed by a large majority but, on 13 April 1999, a large majority of the Lords effectively rejected the Bill by voting to postpone its second reading for six months.

Meanwhile, on 13 and 14 April 1999, the Appellate Committee heard argument in *Fitzpatrick*. When the Appellate Committee gave judgment, on 28 October 1999, Lord Nicholls, in the majority of three to two in favour of allowing the appeal, said:

'In one respect of crucial importance there has been a change in social attitudes over the last half-century. I am not referring to the change in attitude toward sexual relationships between a man and a woman outside marriage or toward homosexual relationships. There has been a widespread change in attitude toward such relationships, although differing and deeply felt views are held on these matters. These differing views are to be recognized and respected. The crucial change to which I am referring is related but different. *It is that the morality of a lawful relationship is not now regarded as relevant when the court is deciding whether an individual qualifies for protection under the Rent Acts.*' (Emphasis added.)

On the other hand, Lord Hutton (a member of the minority) was not only against the survivor on the merits but also took the view that the whole matter was one for Parliament and not for the courts. Similarly, Lord Hobhouse (Lord Hutton's companion in the minority) said:

'The developments for which [counsel for the surviving partner] contends involve developments of social policy and fall far outside the proper ambit of statutory construction.'

It is difficult to avoid the conclusion that the Lords' second rejection of the measure, which clearly represented the continuing will of the Commons, must have had at least some impact on the minds of the Appellate Committee, even if the impact varied from one mind to another.

Almost finally, it may be worth recording that, having been reintroduced in the following session of Parliament, in February 2000 the Bill was again passed by the Commons. This time the Lords accepted the Bill but only subject to an amendment which stipulated a differential age of consent to anal sex. Because the House of Lords had not accepted the Bill in the form in which it had been approved by the House of Commons, they had rejected it for the purposes of the Parliament Acts 1911–1949. Accordingly, under the terms of the 1911–1949 Acts, the Bill was able to receive the Royal Assent and become the Sexual Offences (Amendment) Act 2000.

The House of Lords returned to the issue of homosexual partners' rights of succession to tenancies in *Ghaidan v Mendoza* [2004] 3 All ER 411. On this occasion, taking the final step beyond *Fitzpatrick*, the House held (by a majority of 4:1) that for the purposes of the Rent Act 1977, a homosexual partner may be more than merely a *member of the tenant's family*, and may fall within the meaning of the word *spouse*. (The effect of this decision was that the surviving partner would inherit the more advantageous *statutory tenancy*, rather than the less advantageous *assured tenancy*.) More particularly, the House held that there was no reason to exclude the survivors of stable homosexual relationships from the statutory protection which would clearly have applied to the survivors of identical heterosexual relationships; and that, therefore, the denial of that protection constituted unjustifiable discrimination against homosexuals.

The House was not bound by *Fitzpatrick* because that decision pre-dated the interpretative obligation imposed by s. 3 of the Human Rights Act 1998. (Section 3 requires courts to read and apply legislative provisions in such a way as to make them compatible with Convention rights under the Act, where it is possible to do so. The Convention rights which arose for consideration in *Ghaidan* are contained in articles 8 and 14 of the ECHR, relating respectively to respect for the home and the grounds on which discrimination is prohibited.) In passing, and pursuing the contextual nature of the foregoing discussion, *Ghaidan* was decided after the general climate of legislative opinion in relation to gay and related rights had moved on in at least three respects. First, the Local Government Act 2003 had repealed s. 28 of the Local Government Act 1988. Secondly, the Sexual Offences Act 2003, which had largely replaced the Sexual Offences Act 1967, had totally abolished the offences of buggery and gross indecency between consenting male adults. Thirdly, the enactment – on 1 July 2004 – of the Gender Recognition Act 2004, which enables transsexuals to obtain legal recognition of their acquired gender, was imminent. (The decision in *Ghaidan* was handed down on 21 June 2004.)

7.6.3 Where rights conflict

Turning to the situation in which the court must choose between conflicting rights, it is instructive to consider the case of *R v R (Rape: Marital Exemption)* [1991] 4 All ER 481. A husband who had been charged with attempting to rape his wife wished to argue by way of defence that English law did not recognize the possibility of a man raping his wife, and therefore he could not be convicted of attempting to do something which was not an offence. However, in the face of an adverse ruling of law from the judge, he abandoned his defence and pleaded guilty. In due course the House of Lords confirmed the correctness of the trial judge's ruling and therefore upheld the conviction. The basis of the decision was that the modern view of the nature of marriage, and more particularly of equality within marriage, meant that the old rule (according to which a woman, on marriage, gave irrevocable consent to sexual intercourse) had become offensive to the point where it could no longer be sustained. On the judicial assumption about the nature of marriage, the decision provides a clear example of adjudicative integrity. However, it is inescapable that protecting the wife's right necessarily involved violating the husband's right not to be retrospectively penalized.

When the case (along with another, essentially similar, one) reached the European Court of Human Rights, there was held to be no breach of art.7 of the European Convention on Human Rights, which generally prohibits retrospective penalization. The reasoning was partly based on the proposition that, if the husband had taken legal advice, he could reasonably have foreseen the way in which the law had been held to have developed, and partly on the proposition that

'[the] debasing character of rape was so manifest that... [the decision of the English court]... could not be said to be at variance with the object and purpose of art.7, namely to ensure that no-one should be subjected to arbitrary prosecution, conviction or punishment.'

Additionally the English courts'

'[rejection of the former doctrine] was in conformity not only with a civilized concept of marriage, but also, and above all, with the fundamental objectives of the Convention, the very essence of which was respect for human dignity and human freedom.' (*SW v United Kingdom and CR v United Kingdom* (1995) 23 EHRR 363.)

7.7 Legitimacy, law, ethics, morality, justice, interpretation and value: how to be a hedgehog

7.7.1 Introduction

This part of this chapter introduces Dworkin's book *Justice for Hedgehogs* (2011), the enigmatic title of which can be traced back to the ancient Greek poet, Archilochus (c. 680 BCE – c. 645 BCE), according to whom the fox knows many things but the hedgehog knows one big thing. The fox is, of course, proverbially cunning and it would be impracticable to attempt to list everything that the fox knows. The hedgehog, on the other hand, has very little reputation for anything, but he does know that he can protect himself against predators by rolling himself up into a prickly ball when threatened. So, more or less come what may, the simple little hedgehog will gain the most desirable prize of all – survival – merely by knowing one thing. Dworkin regards most recent and contemporary philosophers as being foxes, but he sets out to argue the case for a unifying theory of law, justice, ethics and morality, thereby creating one big thing. Although his theory is not only complex and subtle in content, but also lengthy in exposition, the unity which is its central characteristic is one big thing, which places Dworkin among the apparently humble hedgehogs rather than the fashionable foxes.

Dworkin's conception of unity involves a set of separate values which, when bundled together, combine into a unity of value. We begin by considering the legitimacy of state power before outlining some of the relationships which exist within the fields of ethics, morality, law, justice and interpretation. We then consider what might be meant by the idea of truth in legal theory and conclude with the status of legal theory as a subdivision of political theory.

7.7.2 The legitimacy of state power

According to Dworkin, the legitimacy of any state depends on its acceptance of two 'reigning principles' which 'place boundaries around acceptable theories of distributive justice'. (*Justice for Hedgehogs*, p. 2.) (See p. 41, above, for the meaning of *distributive justice*.) Although Dworkin uses the word *government* here, in many of the contexts in which he uses it when developing his theory the word *state* seems more naturally to represent what appears to be his meaning. Accordingly, in this part of this chapter, the word *state* will generally be used, leaving Dworkinian purists to undertake any mental substitution they may consider to be appropriate.

> 'First, [the state] must show equal concern for the fate of every person over whom it claims dominion. Second, it must respect fully the responsibility and right of each person to decide for himself how to make something valuable of his life.' (*Ibid.*)

Dworkin provides an example of how a state may fail to satisfy these two principles of legitimacy as follows. A *laissez faire* economic system cannot be legitimate because it is in the nature of *laissez faire* economics that some people will grow rich at the expense of others. (As the old saying goes, freedom for the pike is death for the minnows.) Therefore, the state which tolerates such a system does not show equal concern for both those whom the system enriches and those whom it impoverishes. Nor can the state seek to rely on Dworkin's second reigning principle – that people must take responsibility for their own lives – because, under such a *laissez faire* system, there is nothing that many people can realistically do to improve their lot. Taking an example which Dworkin himself does not use, the received wisdom among paediatricians is that persistent and significant malnutrition during the first three years or so of life will irretrievably harm the development of a child's cognitive functioning. Therefore, it can be credibly argued that a society which values and rewards educational achievement and which values intellectual work more highly than manual work has not shown equal concern for the well-being of children who experience such malnutrition as it has shown for the well-being of children brought up in more affluent circumstances.

This is not to say that state toleration of child poverty necessarily indicates a total lack of equal concern which would result in a total lack of legitimacy even in the field of child welfare, let alone across the board of all state activity. For example, the state may still be able to advance an entirely credible claim that, for example, all children have received equal concern under the laws which protect them against sexual abuse.

Broadening the scope of the discussion, the principle of equal concern does not make state legitimacy depend on an equal distribution (and still less a continuing redistribution) of wealth. A state based on this principle would breach Dworkin's second reigning principle by failing 'to respect people's responsibility to make something of their own lives'. (*Op. cit.*, p. 3.) There is, for example, no duty on a state to protect people against the ordinary hazards of human life, such as bad luck, or against the consequences of making bad decisions in terms of personal relationships, financial investments and many other matters. But it is to say that the legitimacy of a state which tolerates a system that necessarily leads to child poverty is flawed.

7.7.3 The relationship between ethics and morals

Many people use the words *ethics* and *morals* more or less interchangeably; and even people who are careful to maintain a distinction between the two often disagree as to precisely what that distinction is. It is not surprising, therefore, that Dworkin is careful to identify the meaning he attributes to each word and, therefore, the sense in which he uses them throughout his book:

> 'Ethics... is the study of how to live well, and morality... is the study of how we must treat other people.' (*Op. cit.*, p. 13.)

Obviously, this raises the question of what it means to live well.

Essentially, Dworkin's answer is that 'we each have a sovereign ethical responsibility to make something of value of our own lives' and 'living in the foothills of death as we do... we must find the value of living... in living well, just as we find value in loving or painting or writing or singing or diving well'. Furthermore, 'dignity and self-respect – whatever these turn out to mean – are indispensable conditions of living well'. This means, he continues, 'our various responsibilities and obligations to others flow from that personal responsibility for our own lives', (*ibid.*) thus unifying ethics and morality as he conceives them to be.

One difficulty with this kind of answer is that, in itself, it tells us very little, because it is expressed in terms which themselves require interpretation; and it is highly likely that at least some of the words in at least some of the interpretations will themselves require further interpretation; and so on.

Of course, lawyers are no strangers to the need for interpretation in many contexts, including judgments of the courts, statutes, delegated legislation and contracts, not to mention treaties, conventions and other international agreements. And, as we have seen (at pp. 120–121), Dworkin has very definite views on the role of integrity in interpretation. On the face of it, therefore, you may be forgiven for thinking it is also obvious that the same interpretative process is appropriate when seeking to identify the meanings of all words, including those which represent ethical and moral concepts such as *dignity* and *self-respect* (and many others, such as *justice*). If you do think this, you may be gratified to discover that Dworkin agrees with you. However, Dworkin goes further, saying that some kinds of concepts are themselves *interpretative* concepts (although he naturally uses the American English term *interpretive* rather than the British English term *interpretative* which, equally naturally, is used in this book). The immediate question, therefore, is: *what does it mean to say a concept is interpretative?*

The answer is that concepts can be classified in various ways, but those falling within the interpretative category cannot be discussed without also being interpreted. This may sound too obvious to be worth saying, but it may nevertheless be useful, by way of contrast, to consider briefly another category of concepts, namely those which depend on *criteria*. Taking an example which Dworkin does not take, the essential criterion for distinguishing a *bicycle* and a *tricycle* is that the former runs on two wheels (as indicated by the *bi* element in its name) while the latter runs on three wheels (as indicated by the *tri* element in its name). Therefore, leaving aside only the possibility of any express, context-specific definition to the contrary, anyone who asserts that a three-wheeler is a *bi*cycle is simply wrong. Admittedly, not all criterial concepts are as precise as those of *bicycle* and *tricycle*. As Dworkin says (*op. cit.*, p. 159), you and I may have a mutual friend who suffers from hair loss. We may also share an understanding of the concept of baldness as being *significant hair loss*, without necessarily agreeing whether our friend's hair loss is significant enough to bring it within the scope of that concept. The nature of our disagreement, therefore, arises from the intrinsic vagueness of the concept of baldness rather than from any differences between our respective understandings of the concept itself.

Finally, for an example of a criterial concept of law, you may recall Austin's view that a law is a *command*, issued by a *sovereign* to a subject, backed by a *sanction* (see p. 66), in which the three criteria are clearly identified.

Interpretative concepts are different. For example, *moral* concepts, such as *justice*, arise in the field of social practices; and, for Dworkin, even law itself is a moral concept. For the moment, however, we will take the example of the concept of justice, which arises within the field of social interaction, either between the state and the individual or between individuals. There are many situations in which the concept causes no difficulty. (Even the most ardent supporter of capital punishment could scarcely argue that it would be just to impose the death penalty on motorists who exceed the speed limit.) However, once we move beyond standard (or *paradigm*) cases, serious and extensive disagreements about moral concepts can – and often do – arise.

Obviously, such disagreements will arise where philosophers are arguing about the concepts themselves. Crucially, however, they may also arise where the disputants are ostensibly arguing *about something else* – such as whether a party to a particular contract is required to act in good faith. Equally crucially, a number of factors (not the least of which is the way that lawyers' reasoning tends to be dominated by particular fact-situations) may contribute to the parties losing sight of the fact that they are really arguing about the concept itself (which, in our example, means they are concerned with the nature and meaning of *good faith*). In other words, unlike the case of the difference between a bicycle and a tricycle, they cannot resolve their disagreements by reference to agreed criteria. (However, even though they will be arguing about the concept, they must nevertheless have *some* shared understanding of the concept, because if they have no shared understanding, they will be simply talking past each other (to adopt one of Dworkin's favourite phrases) and their disagreement will be illusory rather than real.)

Putting all this another way, disputants who share a sufficient understanding of a concept can move straight to the application of the concept to their specific dispute, but they can do this only because they have previously undertaken the task of interpreting the concept in order to arrive at the understanding they are able to share. Where the disputants do not share a sufficient understanding to enable them to move straight to the application of the relevant concept, they must identify the meaning of the concept itself as one of the heads of argument in their dispute. And the process of identifying that meaning will inescapably be *interpretative*, which is an essentially different process from identifying both bicycles and tricycles and the limits of a vague criterion (such as baldness) in order to apply it in individual cases.

The next question which arises is *how are we to talk about interpretative concepts*? Dworkin's answer is essentially little more than a reformulation of his notions of *integrity, justification* and *fit*, which we encountered at pp. 120–121 in the context of adjudication. It is this. When we think about our values we tend to think about a number of specifics, such as equality, the freedom of the individual, the protection of the community, the observance of the requirements of due process of law, the predictability of law (which enables people to plan what they will and will not do), the flexibility of law (which enables outcomes to be varied in order to meet the particular circumstances of individual cases), and many more. Dworkin argues that, when properly understood, our specific values, taken together, constitute a coherent unity composed of mutually supporting elements (or, perhaps more accurately, they should constitute such a unity).

Developing the process of *interpretation* for the present purposes, Dworkin's point is that when dealing with interpretative concepts we must base ourselves on our values. So, for example, a Dworkinian way of defending the idea of individual freedom in a particular context could be to point out that individuals without freedom are not able to make something valuable of their lives (in the words of Dworkin's second reigning principle, which we encountered at p. 128). Thus freedom is an essential precondition to the enjoyment of a basic value. But other cases will be more complex.

For example, most people regard individual liberty and democracy as important values. However, it is perfectly obvious that democratic processes will result in restrictions on individual liberty. For example, the incidence and level of taxation are determined by democratic processes, but no modern, complex state could continue to function if the idea of individual freedom were interpreted as making such payments entirely voluntary. In practice, the legal regime which underpins the system of taxation will include enforcement procedures; but this appears to contravene Dworkin's principle of the unity of values – which is hardly surprising since the relevant values appear to be in straightforward conflict with each other. However, the conflict which requires prioritization of one value over the other can be avoided by interpreting one or both of the key terms appropriately. In the case of the present example, Dworkin is unpersuaded by 'a majoritarian or statistical conception' of democracy, preferring a 'partnership conception', according to which

> 'each citizen participates as an equal partner, which means more than just that he has an equal vote. It means that he has an equal voice and an equal stake in the result. On that conception... [which Dworkin defends]... democracy itself requires the protection of justice and liberty that democracy is sometimes said to threaten' . (*Op. cit.*, p. 5.)

This quotation neatly illustrates Dworkin's claim that what appear to be competing values should, in reality, be interpreted in such ways that each is mutually supportive of the other and both combine (along with other values) to create a single unity of value.

In practical terms, for example, the values which underpin both individual liberty and democracy can be supported by (and, in turn, support) the value of fairness (or proportionality), which (in the present context) requires state action (say, taxation) to be proportionate to the outcome (say, the social desirability of the expenditure which the taxation will support). Additionally, the state's budgetary allocations to various government departments must themselves be proportionate, not only on the basis outlined immediately above and in relation to each other, but also in relation to the taxpayers' ability to pay, having regard to matters such as trends in the cost of living and the overall state of the economy. If it is argued that this whole structure is essentially circular, with everything ultimately being supported by everything else, it may also be defended on the basis that it offers an alternative to the more conventional view that where there are conflicts between values (or rights, or interests, or whatever other word may be used), some have to prevail and others have to yield, according to more or less arbitrary preferences resulting from the party-political composition of the government at the time or the felt political exigencies of the moment.

Finally, before leaving the technique of interpretation in the context of values, it is worth recalling Dworkin's view (see p. 121) that, in the context of their participation in interpretation, the difference between legal theorists and their practitioner counterparts is a matter of degree rather than of kind, being based only on the differing levels of abstraction at which they each work, thus reinforcing the argument that a grasp of legal theory is (or should be) an integral of the education of legal practitioners.

7.7.4 Truth and value

It is important to understand that Dworkin emphatically rejects the widely held view that statements of ethics, morality and other values are no more than matters of opinion and, as such, can be neither true nor false. He also rejects the widely held view that Hume's argument (to the effect that no amount of empirical evidence as to what *is* the case can produce any true conclusion as to what *ought to be* the case) can be said to establish the impossibility of establishing the truth or falsity of moral propositions. Instead, Dworkin argues that what Hume really establishes is 'the independence of morality as a separate department of knowledge with its own standards of inquiry and justification' (*op. cit.*, p. 17). Advancing his own theory, Dworkin says:

> 'Value judgments are true, when they are true ... in view of the substantive case that can be made for them. *The moral realm is the realm of argument, not brute, raw fact.*' (*Op. cit.*, p. 11; emphasis added.)

And, he argues, the case that can be made for the capacity of statements of value to be true depends on establishing their place in the realm of values, all of which are capable of being true in the Dworkinian way. If you wish to argue that this proposition makes value-based truth into something totally different from fact-based truth, Dworkin would simply reply: 'Precisely so!' and go on his way, happy that you have understood what he is saying.

7.7.5 Law as a topic within political theory

If state power is legitimate only when it comes within the scope of Dworkin's two reigning principles (see p. 128), the essentially moral nature of those principles means that morality is an intrinsic part of law. This leads Dworkin to conclude that the two-system model of morality and law fails to fit the facts in such a fundamental way that it is untenable. The question then becomes: what consequences flow from this conclusion?

In terms of legal practice, the answer, in most cases, may be 'very little'. After all, practitioners and judges already commonly appeal to the requirements of justice, the moral nature of which would be difficult to deny. However, viewing law and justice as one integrated topic, rather than as two complementary ones, would equip the courts to make intellectually respectable decisions in exceptional cases such as *Airedale National Health Service Trust v Bland* [1993] 1 All ER 821. In that case, Lord Browne-Wilkinson confessed that he had difficulty in finding a moral reason why it was lawful to allow a patient in a persistent vegetative state to starve to death (albeit under sedation and, therefore, painlessly), but unlawful to end his life with a lethal injection. Nevertheless, as he said, this was 'undoubtedly the law'. (The decision in *Bland* is discussed in more detail at p. 229.)

In terms of legal education, the answer is that adopting the Dworkinian position would be much more significant. Once it is accepted that legal theory is part of political theory, there is an unanswerable case for including political theory as an element in all undergraduate law courses. Indeed, for those degree programmes which enjoy *qualifying law degree* status, the case for making it a compulsory element is similarly unanswerable, even in the face of predictable protestations from the legal educational establishment about the undergraduate syllabus being already overloaded with compulsory elements as a result of the legal profession's dictatorial tendencies.

Summary

▶ Dworkin sees law as essentially an *interpretative* (or, to use the American form of the word which he favours, *interpretive*) process.

▶ Dworkin began by denying that judges make law but more recently he has played down this aspect of his theory.

▶ Dworkin rejects the idea that the meaning of the word *law* can usefully be approached as a semantic exercise.

▶ Dworkin's use of the word *law* includes *policies* and *principles*, as well as the authoritative texts.

▶ Dworkin takes rights seriously.

▶ Dworkin emphasizes the unity of value.

▶ Dworkin's later work emphasises his claim to have developed a theory of law and not simply a theory of adjudication, as well as arguing for the importance of value and suggesting that legal theory is really part of political theory.

Further reading

Austin, John, *Jurisprudence*, 5th edn, 1885
Dworkin, Ronald, *A Matter of Principle*, 1986
Dworkin, Ronald, *Is Law a System of Rules?* in *The Philosophy of Law*, 1977
Dworkin, Ronald, *Justice for Hedgehogs*, 2011

Further reading cont'd

Dworkin, Ronald, *Justice in Robes*, 2006

Dworkin, Ronald, *Law's Empire*, 1986

Dworkin, Ronald, *Pragmatism, Right Answers and True Banality* in Brint, M. and Weaver, W., (eds), *Pragmatism in Law and Society*, 1991

Dworkin, Ronald, *Taking Rights Seriously*, 1977

Edmund-Davies, *Lord, Judicial Activism* [1975] *Current Legal Problems*

Harris, J.W., *Legal Philosophies*, 2nd edn, 1997

Hart, H.L.A., *The Concept of Law*, 2nd edn, 1994

Kelly, J.M., *A Short History of Western Legal Theory*, 1992

Chapter 8

American realism

Introduction

The movement known as American realism dominated American legal theory for roughly the first half of the 20th century, reaching its peak in the 1920s and 1930s. It constitutes a fairly broad church, but the common creed is scepticism about the role of rules in judicial decision-making, and an insistence that the way to discover what the courts do is to examine the law in action, rather than indulging in abstract theorizing. In *A Realistic Jurisprudence: the Next Step* (1930) 30 Colum L Rev 431 (reprinted in *Jurisprudence: Realism in Theory and Practice*, 1962), Karl Llewellyn (1893–1962), one of the movement's leading members, summarizes one of its main tenets by distinguishing what he calls the *real rules* (which, he says, are in fact 'the practices of the courts' and not rules at all) from what he calls the *paper rules*. The real rules are 'on the level of isness and not of oughtness; they seek earnestly to go no whit, in their suggestions, beyond the remedy actually available'.

The effective thrust of American realism is clearly, therefore, in the direction of a theory of interpretation within the context of adjudication. This may seem rather narrow. After all, a great deal of the work of lawyers involves clients whose affairs will never trouble any court, and even where proceedings are commenced, it is not uncommon in civil cases for the parties to settle out of court, and in criminal cases for guilty pleas to be entered, thus depriving the court of its decision-making role, save for the exercise of discretion as to sentencing in criminal cases. However, the importance of the activities of the courts within any legal system can hardly be doubted.

The reasons for the emergence of American realism are complex, but at least three elements may be identified.

First, it is a commonplace comment that American legal theorists tend to concentrate to a much greater extent than their English counterparts on the functioning of the judicial process. The equally commonplace explanation for this emphasizes the fact that the American legal system has a genuinely supreme court, with the power to quash legislation on constitutional grounds, and concludes that this power of an unelected judiciary over the products of an elected legislature is itself sufficient to justify giving the closest possible scrutiny to the judicial process. (In the context of the English legal system, of course, no court – not even the new Supreme Court which replaced the Appellate Committee of the House of Lords in October 2009 – is supreme in the sense of having the power to quash statutes, quite apart from the oddity that the Supreme Court Act 1981 defined the 'supreme court' as consisting of the Court of Appeal, the High Court and the Crown Court, with the notable omission of the Appellate Committee of the House of Lords.)

Secondly, the idea of a sovereign (which, as we saw in Chapter 4 is one of the key elements in Austin's command theory of law, which dominated English-language legal theory at the time of the emergence of American realism) does not fit easily into the American legal system, which is based on a political structure consisting of a federal legislature and a multiplicity of state legislatures.

Thirdly, the dominant influence on American legal education at the end of the 19th century was Christopher Columbus Langdell, Dean of the Harvard Law School. In the preface to his *Selection of Cases on the Law of Contracts* (1871), Langdell asserts that 'It is indispensable to establish at least two things, first that law is a science; secondly that all the available materials of that science are contained in the printed books'. As Gary Minda puts it, 'Langdellians believed that the object-forms of law were immune from the ever-changing nature of society. Society might change, but they thought that the universal principles of law would endure forever.' (*Postmodern Legal Movements*, 1995, pp. 15–16.) While this position is plainly untenable when viewed from the modern perspective, it equally plainly commanded widespread support at the time. However, there were sceptics even then, principal among whom was Oliver Wendell Holmes (1844–1935), who is generally considered to be the founding father of American realism and who became a distinguished member of the Supreme Court.

8.2   The basis of American realism

Although, as we shall see, there are differences of opinion and emphasis between various members of the American realist movement, in *Some Realism About Realism* (1931) 44 Harv LR 1222, Llewellyn identifies nine 'points of departure' to which all would be willing to subscribe. Briefly, these nine points come down to saying that the problems of the law should be approached in the light of certain propositions which may be condensed into the following summary.

- ▶ Law is a means to a social end, rather than being an end in itself, and therefore it should be evaluated in terms of its effects.
- ▶ Both law and society are in a constant state of flux, although legal change typically lags behind social change, so there is a need to keep the law under constant review.
- ▶ Value judgments are essential when identifying the objectives which the law should seek to achieve, but while the law is being critically examined, *is* must be divorced from *ought* otherwise our perception of how things *are* is likely to be tainted by our belief as to what they *ought* to be.
- ▶ Legal rules and concepts should be distrusted where they purport to

describe what actually happens within the legal system, and legal theory should be distrusted where it suggests that legal rules govern the decisions of the courts.

▶ Cases and legal situations should generally be grouped together into narrower rather than broader categories, and this is particularly so where the rules and concepts are expressed in simple language, because this tends to conceal the complex range of situations to which they apply.

8.3 Law as prophecy

In one of American realism's most famous texts, Oliver Wendell Holmes says:

'Take the fundamental question, what constitutes the law? You will find some text writers telling you that it is something different from what is decided by the courts of Massachusetts or England, that it is a system of reason, that it is a deduction from principles of ethics or admitted axioms or what not, which may or may not coincide with the decisions. But if we take the view of our friend the bad man we shall find that he does not care two straws for the axioms or deductions, but that he does want to know what the Massachusetts or English courts are likely to do in fact. I am much of his mind. *The prophecies of what the courts will do in fact, and nothing more pretentious, are what I mean by the law.*

'Take again a notion which as popularly understood is the widest conception which law contains; – the notion of legal duty.... We fill the word with all the content which we draw from morals. But what does it mean to a bad man? Mainly, and in the first place, a prophecy that if he does certain things he will be subject to disagreeable consequences by way of imprisonment or compulsory payment of money.' (Emphasis added. *The Path of the Law* (1897) 10 Harv LR pp. 460–461.)

The importance of making prophecy (or, to use a less emotive term, prediction) as accurate as possible may be self-evident, but this does not prevent Holmes from spelling it out:

'In societies like ours the command of the public force is entrusted to the judges in certain cases, and the whole power of the state will be put forth, if necessary, to carry out their judgments and decrees. People want to know under what circumstances and how far they will run the risk of coming against what is so much stronger than themselves.... The object of our study, then, is prediction, the prediction of the incidence of the public force through the instrumentality of the courts.' (*Op. cit.*, p. 457.)

Holmes' realism may sound entirely practical and, in that sense, too anti-intellectual, or even too untheoretical, to qualify as a serious contribution to legal theory. Indeed, William Twining argues that, when full regard is had to its context, *The Path of the Law* 'should be interpreted more as a contribution to legal education than to legal philosophy'. (*Other People's Power: the Bad Man and English Positivism*, at p. 110, in *Globalisation and Legal Theory*, 2000, being a shortened version of a paper first published in (1997) 63 Brooklyn LR 189.) On this reading of the evidence, Holmes' argument is best seen as a device to encourage law students to 'substitute for the point of view of the appellate judge the lowly one of an ordinary citizen or his/her legal adviser (counsellor) and make that citizen amoral... [so that the students]... could see law from a perspective that is both hard-nosed and closer to the realities of everyday legal practice.' (*Op. cit.*, p. 111.)

In support of this view, Twining points out that Holmes' emphasis on the bad man and the prediction of judicial outcomes, concentrates exclusively on the judicial function. However, an emphasis on judicial outcomes is common among American legal theorists (forming, for example, a significant part of Dworkin's theory of law, which is discussed in Chapter 7); and at least some teachers of law like to think that legal theory suffuses much of their work. Those teachers would, therefore, see no basis for Twining's apparent suggestion that a contribution to legal education cannot also be a contribution to legal theory.

Irrespective of the label under which his comments are presented, however, Holmes may be said to be seeking to advance an enlightened view of the way in which the law functions. His view is characterized by a recognition of the place of the law in the real world, which it both informs and is informed by. The true significance of this view, when it is placed in its historical context, is the extent to which it represents a significant departure from the spuriously scientific conceptualization of Langdell, which at that time represented the established orthodoxy in American law schools and consequently in the American legal profession.

Finally, the emphasis on the importance of the courts and their role leads one American realist to resurrect an old argument to the effect that even statutes do not have the status of law, being at most a source on which the courts draw in order to make law.

'It has been sometimes said that the Law is composed of two parts – legislative law and judge-made law, but in truth all the Law is judge-made law. The shape in which a statute is imposed on the community as a guide for conduct is that statute as interpreted by the courts. The courts put life into the dead words of the statute. To quote... from Bishop Hoadley [an 18th century English clergyman]... "Nay, whosoever hath an absolute authority to interpret any written or spoken laws, it is He who is truly the law Giver to all intents and purposes, and not the Person who first wrote or spoke them".' (John Chipman Gray, *The Nature and Sources of the Law*, 1909, pp. 119–120.)

While this view may overstate the case, it undoubtedly provides food for thought.

8.4 Rule-scepticism

The scepticism of rule-sceptics relates not to the existence of legal rules but to their role in the judicial decision-making process. There is no better starting point than the opening passage of the first page of Holmes' textbook *The Common Law*, published in 1881:

'The object of this book is to present a general view of the Common Law. To accomplish the task, other tools are needed besides logic. It is something to show that the consistency of a system requires a particular result, but it is not all. *The life of the law has not been logic*, it has been experience. The felt necessities of the time, the prevalent moral and political theories, intuitions of public policy, avowed or unconscious, even the prejudices which judges share with their fellow men, have had a good deal more to do than the syllogism in determining the rules by which men should be governed.' (Emphasis added.)

Elsewhere, he develops the relationship between logic and the judicial process thus:

'The training of lawyers is a training in logic.... The language of judicial decision is mainly the language of logic. And the logical method and form flatter that longing for certainty and for repose which is in every human mind. But certainty generally is an illusion, and repose is not the destiny of man. *Behind the logical form lies a judgment as to the relative worth and importance of competing legislative grounds, often an inarticulate and unconscious judgment it is true, and yet the very root and nerve of the whole proceeding.* You can give any conclusion a logical form.' (Emphasis added. *Op. cit.*, p. 461.)

In other words, and bearing in mind (as Holmes expressly acknowledges in the passage taken from *The Common Law*) the central position of syllogistic reasoning within judicial method (where the major premise is a proposition of law and the minor premise is a finding of fact), there may well be what is often termed an 'inarticulate major premise', which precedes, and effectively governs the outcome of, the express and formal part of the judge's reasoning. Of course, the fact that an inarticulate major premise is, in its very nature not articulated, may mean that its content (or even its existence) is very difficult (or even impossible) to identify in individual cases. However, while giving judgment a judge will sometimes articulate what could have been left inarticulate, thus making it much easier to understand the fundamental importance of the kind of intellectual or emotional starting point which Holmes has in mind. Two examples will suffice.

In *Bourne v Norwich Crematorium Ltd* [1967] 1 All ER 576, the issue was whether expenditure on a furnace chamber and chimney tower built by a crematorium company qualified for a tax allowance. This depended upon whether it was 'an industrial building or structure' for the purposes of the Income Tax Act 1952, and this in turn depended upon whether it was used

'for a trade which consists in the manufacture of goods or materials or the subjection of goods or materials to any process.'

In the course of his judgment, Stamp J said:

'I would say at once that my mind recoils as much from the description of the bodies of the dead as "goods or materials" as it does from the idea that what is done in a crematorium can be described as "the subjection of" the human corpse to a "process". Nevertheless, the taxpayer so contends and I must examine that contention.'

Given this as the judge's starting point, it is not surprising that the statutory 'rule' was interpreted in such a way that the taxpayer lost.

In *R v West Dorset District Council ex parte Poupard* (1987) 19 HLR 254, Mr and Mrs Poupard had capital assets but they were meeting their weekly living expenses by drawing on an overdrawn bank account. They applied to the council for housing benefit. This benefit was subject to a means test, and therefore the question arose as to whether the drawings were 'income'. If they were, the amounts involved were sufficient to disqualify the applicants from receiving assistance under the relevant Regulations.

The council's Housing Review Board concluded that the drawings were income. The High Court held that in each case it was a question of fact whether specific sums of money were 'income', and that this question was to be decided on the basis of all that the council and their Review Board knew of the sources from which an applicant for benefit was maintaining himself and paying his bills. The conclusion was that on the present facts the local authority and their Review Board had made no error of law, and had acted reasonably in reaching their decision.

On his way to reaching his decision, Macpherson J, adopting an argument advanced by counsel for the local authority, said:

'The scheme [of Housing Benefit] is intended to help those who do not have the weekly resources to meet their bills, or their rent, and it is not intended to help comparatively better-off people (in capital terms) to venture into unsuccessful business and not to bring into account moneys which are regularly available for day-to-day spending, albeit that the use of moneys depletes their capital.'

Although the Court of Appeal (reported at (1988) 20 HLR 295) upheld this decision, it will nevertheless be apparent that, with equal or even greater logic, a court with different sympathies could have upheld the argument that the weekly drawings were outgo, rather than income, because each drawing increased the drawer's indebtedness to the bank. After all, it can be argued that if Parliament had intended to exclude people such as the applicants from eligibility for housing benefit it would have been a simple enough matter to enact an appropriate definition of what was meant by 'income' for the purposes of the means test.

It must be emphasised that cases such as *Bourne* and *Poupard* are wholly exceptional. More particularly, judges very seldom explicitly acknowledge that the psychological realities of life in general apply also to the realm of judicial decision-making, and that the judges' individual values and preferences may impact on their decisions. However, Baroness Hale (who was a Law Lord before becoming a Justice of the Supreme Court) did address the matter specifically in a lecture given at City University on 30 April 2008, under the title of *Leadership in the Law: What is a Supreme Court For?* Having commented that the House of Lords usually functioned through panels of five members, Baroness Hale said:

'Many, perhaps most, other Supreme Courts sit *en banc*. That is, all the judges sit on all the cases. This eliminates the risk that the selection of the particular panel to hear the case may affect the result. *We can all think of cases in which the result would probably have been different if the panel had been different*, although that raises interesting questions about how predictable the decision of any particular judge either is or should be. The listing is done in the judicial office and the allocation of judges to the panels is agreed with the two senior law lords in what is known as the "horses for courses" meeting. The aim is to have those with the most relevant expertise together with some generalists. I cannot think that either the judicial office or the two seniors give any thought to the likely outcome of the case if X sits instead of Y. But even without sinister intent, the selection may affect the outcome.

'This is solved by having us all sit. But it would halve the number of cases we could take. It is hard enough narrowing them down now and would be much worse then. It would also shift the focus to the appointments process. In other parts of the world, it clearly increases the desire of the politicians who make the appointments to fill the court with people of their own political persuasion. That does not happen here. Colleagues in the US are amazed that I do not know my colleagues' politics. We have not had political appointments to the Law Lords for many decades and the risk is even less now that we are to have an independent Judicial Appointments Commission. But I doubt whether we shall change our practice of sitting in panels rather than *en banc*.' (Emphasis added.)

By way of an aside, it is worth saying that, since Baroness Hale delivered her lecture, the conversion of the former Middlesex Guildhall into the building which houses the new Supreme Court has been completed, and the assumption that sittings will not be *en banc* has been reflected in the fact that the principal court room has been designed to accommodate a maximum of nine justices. (The Appellate Committee of the House of Lords usually sat with five members, although panels of seven – and occasionally even nine – were not unknown, and petitions for leave to appeal were heard by panels of three).

Finally, before leaving rule-scepticism, it is worth emphasizing that its adherents do not deny the relevance of legal rules altogether: they merely stress the importance of other factors within the process of judicial reasoning. As Llewellyn puts it (*op. cit.*, p. 37):

'Rules, concepts, ideology... ideological stereotypes... [and]... patterns... are, by themselves, confusing, misleading, inadequate to describe and explain. But a jurisprudence which was practically workable could not be built in terms of them, if they had not contained a goodly core of truth and sense.'

8.5 Fact-scepticism

Jerome Frank (1889–1957), whose personal preference would have been for American realism to be called *constructive scepticism* (see *Law and the Modern Mind*, preface to the sixth printing, 1949, p. vii), identifies a variety of realism which he labels *fact-scepticism*. This may be best described as a form of ultra-realism, which builds on, rather than being an alternative to, rule-scepticism.

Frank puts his own commitment to rule-scepticism beyond question, at the same time as explaining the basis of fact-scepticism:

> 'Rules (whether made by legislatures or judge-made) are embodiments of social policies, values, ideals, and... for that reason... should be recurrently and informedly re-examined...
> 'But the rules, statutory or judge-made, are not self-operative. They are frustrated, inoperative, whenever, due to faulty fact-finding in trial courts, they are applied to non-existent facts.' (*Op. cit.*, p. xxiv.)

Frank plainly regards fact-scepticism as being even more realistic than rule-scepticism.

> 'Generally, most of the rule-sceptics, restricting themselves to the upper-court level, live in an artificial two-dimensional legal world, while the legal world of the fact-sceptics is three-dimensional. Obviously, many events occurring in the fact-sceptics' three-dimensional cosmos are out of sight, and therefore out of mind, in the rule-sceptics' cosmos.' (*Op. cit.*, p. ix.)

Putting his argument in rather more detail, Frank points out that when trial courts receive conflicting oral evidence, they have to decide which witnesses they believe, or, as he puts it, 'a fact-finder... is himself a witness – a witness of witnesses'. (*Op. cit.*, pp. xx–xxi.) In English terms, the decision-makers on matters of fact will be either judges, jurors or magistrates, depending on the level of the court and the type of proceedings, but whoever they are, the fact that they are human means that they may well have prejudices which will colour the way they view the parties, the witnesses or even the lawyers. Those prejudices may be relatively easily identifiable where they are based on racial, religious, political or economic factors, but those which involve attitudes to women or to 'men with deep voices or high-pitched voices, or fidgety men, or men who wear thick eyeglasses, or those who have pronounced gestures or nervous tics' will be much more likely to go undetected. (The placing of sexual prejudice in a different category from its racial and religious counterparts provides an interesting insight into the attitudes of the times.) For Frank, therefore,

> 'the chief obstacle to prophesying a trial-court decision is... the inability, thanks to these inscrutable factors, to foresee what a particular trial judge or jury will believe to be the facts.' (*Op. cit.*, p. xi.)

Having considered both the mainstream varieties of American realism, we can now turn to a later stage in Llewellyn's career when the emphasis shifts from straightforward scepticism to the development of the concept of *law-jobs*.

8.6 Law-jobs

Llewellyn's emphasis on the importance of the effects of law (see p. 137) leads him in his later work to develop the idea of law as an institution which exists to ensure that certain jobs (which he calls 'law-jobs') are done. These law-jobs are common to all societies because they are essential if society is to be prevented from disintegrating. The essence of these law-jobs is those activities which would now be called problem avoidance and dispute resolution, as well as the allocation and exercise of public authority. Since these jobs have to be done, it is not surprising that people develop the skills (which he calls 'law-crafts') to do them. These law-crafts include not only the major activities of advocacy, advising clients, judging, legislating and administering, but also things such as policing, teaching and scholarship.

As far as advising clients is concerned, there remains, of course, the problem of whether the judicial decision-making process is predictable (or, to use Llewellyn's own term 'reckonable'):

> 'The average lawyer has only to shift his focus for a few hours from "what was held" in a series of opinions to what was bothering and what was helping the court as it decided... [and] there can be no question as to the gain in predictive power. Spend a single thoughtful weekend with a couple of recent volumes of reports from your own supreme court, read this way, and you can never again, with fervour or despair make that remark about never knowing where an appellate court will hang its hat. Spend five such weekends, and you will be getting a workable idea of the local geography of hat-racks.' (*The Common Law Tradition: Deciding Appeals*, 1960, p. 179.)

The law-jobs aspect of Llewellyn's theory, therefore, clearly reinforces the basic tenet of American realism that judges who are trying to apply legal rules to the fact-situations which come before them must recognize that the function of those rules is limited to guiding, rather than controlling, the decision-making process. More particularly, he says that the judges will be guided in each case by what he calls their *situation-sense*. His own account of this phrase is less than lucid, but in essence it involves categorizing both the interests which are in conflict, and any relevant policy considerations, as well as the facts which give rise to the case in the first place.

To take an English example of Llewellyn's situation-sense in action, the case of *Beatty v Gillbanks* (1882) 9 QBD 308 arose because parades by the Salvation Army through Weston-super-Mare had provoked violent opposition from an organization calling itself the Skeleton Army. The High Court allowed an appeal against an order of the magistrates' court binding over certain members of the Salvation Army. On the issue of principle, Field J said:

> 'What has happened here is that an unlawful organization has assumed to itself the right to prevent the appellants and others from lawfully assembling together, and the finding of the justices amounts to this, that a man may be convicted for doing a lawful act if he knows that his doing of it may cause another to do an unlawful act. There is no authority for such a proposition.'

On the other hand, in *Duncan v Jones* [1936] 1 KB 218, Duncan, a left-wing activist, wished to address a public meeting outside a training centre for the unemployed in an exceptionally depressed part of London. On a previous occasion when she had done so, there had been a disturbance at the training centre, and accordingly a police officer tried to move the meeting some 175 yards away to a different street. When Duncan refused to move, she was arrested for wilfully obstructing the police in the execution of their duty. The question which arose, therefore, was whether the police officer had been acting in the execution of his duty. Upholding her conviction by the magistrates' court, Lord Hewart CJ said:

'If I thought that the present case raised [the] question... [of]... whether an assembly can properly be held to be unlawful merely because the holding of it is expected to give rise to a breach of the peace on the part of persons opposed to those who are holding the meeting... I should wish to hear much more argument before I expressed an opinion. This case, however, does not even touch that important question.

'...in my view *Beatty v Gillbanks* is apart from the present case. No such question as that which arose there is even mooted here.'

When viewed in Llewellyn's terms, it can be said that the judges in these cases had different situation-senses. In *Beatty v Gillbanks* the judge saw the Salvation Army as merely exercising a lawful right, whereas in *Duncan v Jones* the judge did not see the case as raising an issue as to the right (if any) of public assembly. Whether the difference in situation-sense can be justified is, of course, another matter. It could be argued that, in terms of the preservation of public order (which must be at least one of the functions of law), there is a valid distinction between the activities of a socially accepted and charitably oriented Christian organization in a sedate Victorian seaside resort, and those of a left-wing agitator in a depressed area of London at a time of high unemployment. On the other hand, approaching the question from a standpoint which emphasizes the importance of individual rights, you could argue that it was the duty of the police in *Duncan v Jones* to ensure that Duncan could address her meeting without a disturbance occurring; or at least to arrest anyone who caused a disturbance.

Apart from its application to the facts as well as the law, it will be apparent that Llewellyn's situation-sense is a kind of precursor of Dworkin's concepts of *justification* and *fit*, which are discussed at pp. 120–121.

Developing the idea of judging as a law-craft, Llewellyn speaks of the *period style* of judgments, in which connection he distinguishes the *formal style* from the *grand style*. Clarifying the basic terminology, he says:

'*Style* refers in this connection not to literary quality or tone but to the manner of doing the job, to the way of craftsmanship in office, to a functioning harmonization of vision with tradition, of continuity with growth, of machinery with purpose, of measure with need.' (*Op. cit.*, p. 37.)

Proceeding to the distinction between the two styles, he says the *formal style* of judgment involves the application of established legal rules, and is essentially backward-looking. Judges who adopt this style believe that

'the rules of law are to decide cases; policy is for the legislature, not for the courts, and so is change even in pure common law. Opinions run in deductive form with an air or expression of single-line inevitability. "Principle" is a generalization producing order which can and should be used to prune away those "anomalous" cases or rules which do not fit, such cases or rules having no function except, in places where the supposed "principle" does not work well, to accomplish sense – but sense is no official concern of a formal-style court.' (*Op. cit.*, p. 38.)

On the other hand, the *grand style* of judgment (which is 'a way of ongoing renovation of doctrine') welcomes precedents, and may find them very persuasive, but will nevertheless 'almost always' test them 'against three types of reason'. Llewellyn explains the 'three types of reason' thus:

'The reputation of the opinion-writing judge counts heavily (and it is right reason to listen carefully to the wise). Secondly, "principle" is consulted to check up on precedent, and... in this way of work "principle" means no mere verbal tool for bringing large-scale order into the rules, it means a broad generalization which must yield patent sense as well as order, if it is to be "principle". Finally, "policy", in terms of prospective consequences of the rule under consideration, comes in for explicit examination by reason in a further test of both the rule in question and its application.... The better and best law is to be built on and out of what the past can offer; the quest consists in a constant re-examination and reworking of a heritage...' (*Op. cit.*, p. 36.)

Furthermore,

'[the grand style of judgment] is the best device ever invented by man for drying up that free-flowing spring of uncertainty, conflict between the seeming commands of the authorities and the felt demands of justice.' (*Op. cit.*, pp. 37–38.)

Llewellyn himself provides what is perhaps the best summary of his version of American realism:

'Realism is *not* a philosophy, but a technology ... What realism was, and is, is a method, nothing more.' (Original emphasis. *Op. cit.*, p. 510.)

8.7 American realism and after

In terms of American politics, the economic and social turmoil which flowed from the Wall Street crash of 1929 and the ensuing Great Depression, gave rise to Roosevelt's New Deal, with its emphasis on welfare liberalism in general and the legitimacy of the regulatory role of the state in particular. Furthermore, this political philosophy was necessarily unsympathetic to the primacy of individual rights and freedoms which had characterized much of the 19th century common law and which had largely provided the basis for Langdell's conception of the scientific principles of law. Quite apart from any immediate impact it may have had on practitioners, therefore, American realism had an important role to play in seeking to change the aims and objectives of American legal education. Neil Duxbury puts it thus:

> 'Whereas a basic tenet of realism was that the abstract concepts of legal formalism must be brought down from the clouds and shown for what they are – that is, limited, pliable, often flawed tools for dealing with disputes and social problems – an equally basic requirement of the New Deal agencies... was a legal staff trained to treat law as a tool for shaping social policy.' (*Patterns of American Jurisprudence*, corrected edn, 1997, p. 155.)

In order to assess the longer term impact of American realism, Minda emphasizes the subdivision of the movement as a whole into *radical* realism and *progressive* realism. (*Op. cit.*, pp. 28–33.) Radical realism was the more politically motivated version, while progressive realism 'rejected the conceptualism of legal formalists and turned to social science approaches in developing new objective policy analyses of the law'. (*Op. cit.*, p. 30.) However, the progressive realists' redefinition of the conceptual framework was not as liberating as they imagined it would be, because their thought became limited by the social scientific concepts which they had adopted, just as Langdell's perspective had become limited by the concepts which he had formulated.

In the medium term, a more widespread acceptance of the legitimacy of the state's role in relation to welfare and regulation led to radical realism losing its specific identity. Similarly, progressive realism developed into the *law in context* approach which has come to be a major part of the mainstream of legal scholarship.

In the longer term, however, the politically questioning impetus which gave rise to radical realism reasserted itself in the origins of critical legal studies, to which we will return in Chapter 9.

Summary

▶ American realism places the emphasis on *law in action* rather than *law in books*. Accordingly, while realists accept that legal rules exist and are important, they are sceptical of claims that the rules determine the outcome of legal disputes, and point to a variety of other factors which also contribute to the decision-making process. (Realists who emphasize this aspect of realism are *rule-sceptics*.) Additionally, some realists (*fact-sceptics*) emphasize that in practice the courts' core task is often fact-finding, and therefore the way in which this process operates is central to the judicial process.

▶ Llewellyn's version of realism sees law as a craft, within which there are certain *law-jobs* which have to be done.

▶ American realism is, to some extent, the forerunner of critical legal studies.

Further reading

Duxbury, Neil, *Patterns of American Jurisprudence*, corrected edn, 1997

Frank, Jerome, *Law and the Modern Mind*, 6th printing, 1949

Gray, John Chipman, *The Nature and Sources of the Law*, 1909

Holmes, Oliver Wendell, *The Common Law*, 1881

Holmes, Oliver Wendell, *The Path of the Law* (1897) 10 Harv LR 461

Langdell, Christopher Columbus, *Selection of Cases on the Law of Contracts*, 1871

Llewellyn, Karl, *A Realistic Jurisprudence: the Next Step* (1930) Colum L Rev 431

Llewellyn, Karl, *The Common Law Tradition: Deciding Appeals*, 1960

Llewellyn, Karl, *Some Realism About Realism* (1931) 44 Harv LR 1222

Minda, Gary, *Postmodern Legal Movements*, 1995

Twining, William, *Other People's Power: the Bad Man and English Positivism* in *Globalisation and Legal Theory*, 2000

Chapter 9
Critical perspectives on law

9.1 Introduction

Although there is a sense in which the whole of legal theory must be critical if it is to be valuable, this chapter takes a very specific sense of the term *critical*, in order to group together, albeit loosely, four perspectives on law and legal theory which proceed from bases other than those which underpin the traditional analysis into the *positivist* and *natural law* traditions. They may be labelled *sociological jurisprudence, Marxism, critical legal studies* and *feminism*. We shall consider each in turn, but before doing so it is important to realize that they are by no means watertight compartments.

In particular, Marxism may be said to be one example of socio-legal studies (which, in turn, are often said to be closely related to, if not a version of, sociological jurisprudence) as well as being a major influence on critical legal studies, while feminism may be seen variously as a subdivision within critical legal studies and as a separate movement. (Procrustean beds – see p. 6 – are, of course, as dangerous here as elsewhere.)

Furthermore, critical legal studies and some forms of feminism may both be seen as aspects of a wider intellectual movement known as *postmodernism*, which originates far beyond the limits of traditional legal theory in the world of art and architecture, from which it permeates a range of other humane and social scientific disciplines, including social theory, history and politics.

In passing, it may be helpful to say that the *modernism* which preceded *postmodernism* was (and for many people still is) based on the conviction that truth is discoverable, and progress is attainable, by human reason, applied, where necessary, to the interpretation of observable facts. For reasons which are beyond the scope of the present discussion, this mindset came to be challenged during the 20th century, and it is the relationship of this new sceptical mindset to the pre-existing one which gives rise to the term *postmodernism*.

The essence of postmodernism is difficult for many lawyers to grasp, because it is directed to challenging the most fundamental assumptions that many lawyers make without, in many cases, even being aware that they are making them. Thus postmodernism argues that the actors within the legal system and the observers who comment on it are all products of the social environment which produced the law. The consequence of this is that all objectivity is impossible. The structures and systems which are the stock-in-trade of lawyers become subject to interpretation which deconstructs them, and shows them as being nothing other than instruments of political power.

Some legal theorists find postmodernism so alien that they reject it altogether; and sometimes do so in no uncertain terms. For example, Kramer, in the context of a book review, contrasts the rigorous scholarship of the book under review, with 'the lazy, self-indulgent prattle of postmodernism' and refers to 'the proponents of postmodernist mumbo-jumbo'. (See [1998] *CLJ*, pp. 612 and 614.)

9.2 Pound's sociological jurisprudence

9.2.1 Introduction

In common with many other general headings in legal theory, the phrase *sociological jurisprudence* covers a variety of different approaches. However, the discussion here will be restricted to the ideas advanced by Roscoe Pound (1870–1964), who was Dean of the Harvard Law School from 1916 to 1936, before returning to being an 'ordinary' professor for the following ten years (and continuing to work until he was turned 90). Incidentally, it should perhaps be said that the use of the word *jurisprudence*, rather than the phrase *legal theory*, in relation to Pound's work reflects his own usage (as well as reflecting American usage across the field as a whole) and must not be taken as having any significance.

Pound was principally concerned with the way the law develops. More particularly, an account of his approach is included within a chapter dealing with *Critical Perspectives on Law* because he was concerned not with the analysis and interpretation of legal texts contained in statutes and cases, but with the relationship between law and society, and how this relationship leads (or fails to lead) to law reform. As he himself puts it, 'in the past century we studied law from within. The jurists of today are studying it from without'. (*The Spirit of the Common Law*, 1921, p. 212.)

Two concepts are at the core of Pound's sociological jurisprudence, namely *legal interests* and *jural postulates*.

9.2.2 Legal interests

According to Pound, legal interests fall into three categories, namely *individual*, *public* and *social*, which he differentiates from each other as follows.

Individual interests are 'claims or demands or desires involved immediately in the individual life and asserted in title of that life'. (*A Survey of Social Interests* (1943) 57 Harv LR, pp. 1–2.) Because many of these interests immediately involve only individuals, they may seem to fall largely within the scope of *private* law. However, as we have just seen, Pound's classificatory scheme is more a matter of perspective than of substance.

Public interests 'are claims or demands or desires involved in life in a politically organized society and are asserted in title of that organization.

They are commonly treated as the claims of a *politically* organized society thought of as a *legal* entity.' (Emphasis added. *Op. cit.*, p. 2.) Many of them are conventionally classified as being the concern of criminal law, from which perspective their overlap with individual interests becomes obvious.

Pound originally conceived *social* interests as being a distinct category from *public* interests, with the former being conceived, as their labels indicate, in essentially social terms and the latter in essentially legal ones. 'Social interests are claims or demands or desires involved in social life in civilized society and asserted in title of that life. It is not uncommon to treat them as claims of the *social group as such.*' (Emphasis added. *Ibid.*) However, since some kind of legal system is a basic requirement of social life, the distinction between public and social interests seems less than clear-cut, and even Pound himself came to concede that, reduced to their basics, they come down to the same thing, namely social interests in the 'security of social institutions'. (*Jurisprudence*, vol. 3, 1959, p. 236.)

Despite his terminology, Pound did not really see the three different types of interests as being distinct entities, but rather as being three different perspectives on a single – and essentially individual – set of interests. For example, the elimination of corruption in public life may appear to be a public, or social, interest. However, Pound saw the true interest as being that of the individual (from whose perspective corruption distorts the lawfully authorized and just allocation of public resources), with the public, or social, interests being merely different ways of looking at the same thing.

Three points arise. First, whether or not a particular matter involving private interests may also be viewed from a public or social perspective may vary from time to time. For example, historically, the law of residential landlord and tenant was regarded as being a matter of contract, in relation to which the doctrine of freedom of contract meant that the parties could make any agreement they wished. Subsequently, protection of the individual's home came to be seen as a matter of social significance, as a result of which security of tenure legislation was enacted. Equally, however, re-classification may take the form of movement in the opposite direction, as illustrated by the progressive decriminalization of homosexual conduct between consenting adult males (and, including now, non-adults, provided they are at least 16 years old). (See p. 126.)

Secondly, interests come into existence before the laws which protect them. Thus, although it can be said that tenants have security of tenure because the relevant legislation confers that security upon them, when viewed in terms of causation it is more accurate to say that the relevant legislation confers the security of tenure because tenants were claiming it, and the law recognized the legitimacy of their interest in asserting that claim. In other words, the claim caused the legislation. The contrast between the legalistic and sociological approaches to the emergence of security of tenure is clear. Similarly, the Civil Partnership Act 2004, which enables same-sex couples to register what amount to quasi-marital relationships, provides another, and more recent, example. Pound illuminates this process by saying that 'pictures of an ideal social order, which come to enter into the law as part of the authoritative guides to determination of controversies, are not photographs or even idealized photographs of the social order of the time and place. They are instead much more idealized pictures of the social order of the past, *undergoing a gradual process of re-touching* with reference to details of the social order of the present'. (Emphasis added. *Social Control Through Law*, 1942, p. 142.) Of course, not all developments in the law come about as a way of meeting new claims. At this point it is worth remembering that Pound's concept of interests (which are, of course, the source of claims) includes *social* interests. This explains how statutes imposing new taxes may fall within his scheme of things, even though they will seldom, if ever, result from claims arising from *individual* interests.

Thirdly, when it becomes necessary to prioritize one kind of interest over another (which is, after all, an inevitable part of the functioning of any legal system), it is interests within a single category – or, as Pound puts it, *on the same plane* – which must be compared.

It is now necessary to turn to the second of Pound's core concepts, namely *jural postulates*.

9.2.3 Jural postulates

According to Pound, the process of evaluating different interests, and therefore of resolving conflicts between them, is to be undertaken within the framework of relevant *jural postulates* (by which he means, in more everyday language, basic assumptions relating to rights and obligations). Clearly, these assumptions will vary both from one legal system to another and from time to time within a single legal system. However, by way of example, towards the middle of the 20th century Pound formulated the American legal system's approach to the law relating to possession, property and legal transactions, and this formulation provides the flavour of the concept. While Pound may, perhaps, be laying himself open to a charge of ethnocentricity, there can be no doubt that the American version will certainly sound familiar to English lawyers, even in the subsequent century. It may be summarized as follows.

- People must be able to assume that others will not be intentionally aggressive.
- People must be able to assume that they can control things that they have discovered, created or legitimately acquired.
- People must be able to assume that other people will honour reasonable expectations which they create and undertakings which they give, as well as making restitution in respect of unjust enrichment which they could not reasonably have expected to receive.
- People must be able to assume that other people will act with due care not to create an unreasonable risk of injury to others.
- People must be able to assume that other people will control things which they maintain on their land and which are likely to escape and cause damage.

A final insight may be derived from the following statement, which contains a restatement of the basis of Pound's views, and with which he concludes one of his later articles.

'I have come to feel that instead of putting the task of the law... in terms of satisfying as much as we can of the total human demands, we do better to speak of providing as much as we may of the total of men's reasonable expectations in life in civilized society with the minimum of friction and waste.' (*The Role of the Will in Law* (1954) 68 Harv LR 19.)

Quite apart from the fact that the comment as a whole indicates a refreshing willingness to refine his ideas even into old age, its closing words (emphasizing as they do the minimization of friction and waste) go some way to illustrating why Pound's approach to law is sometimes described as a form of 'social engineering'. However, this description misses one essential point. Pound's position is that law is reactive in the sense that it responds to claims which are made. Engineering, on the other hand, is proactive, in the sense that engineers begin with plans which they then execute.

By way of conclusion, it is worth noticing that Karl Llewellyn, whom we encountered in the previous chapter, sums up the significance of Pound's contribution to legal theory by saying that he 'provided half of the commonplace equipment on and with which our work since has been builded (*sic*)'. (Book review in (1960) 28 U Chi L Rev 175.)

9.3 Marxism

Marxism, in common with all other major political philosophies, embraces a wide range of views, but it rests on two basic ideas, namely a progressive view of history, and an insistence that economic relations are inevitably the driving force behind that progression. More particularly, Marxists argue that history is – and always has been – moving inexorably towards the emergence of a communist society, with the historical phenomena of *primitive communalism*, *slavery*, *feudalism* and *capitalism* being no more than provisional stages along the way.

Moving to an explicitly legal perspective, the essence of the Marxist argument is that law is an instrument of class domination which serves to preserve economic inequalities. Accordingly, once a communist society comes into existence, there will be no further need for law, because at that stage there will no longer be any economic inequalities to be preserved. Ultimately, this is the condition in which not only the law but even the state itself will wither away.

Viewed a little more closely, the Marxist argument divides the whole social enterprise into two components, namely the *base* and the *superstructure*. The base of any human society lies in the conditions of production and the economic relationships of those engaged in production. This base gives rise to, and determines the nature of, a whole range of social institutions which together constitute the superstructure.

Somewhat surprisingly to those who, having been brought up on non-Marxist thought, tend to regard law as basic to human society, the Marxist analysis places law within the *superstructure* rather than the *base*. In other words, law is seen as being simply 'one aspect of a variety of political and social arrangements concerned with the manipulation of power and the consolidation of modes of production of wealth'. (Hugh Collins, *Marxism and Law*, 1982, p. 13.) One aspect of this is, naturally, that where the base is capitalist, the law will serve the interests of capitalists.

It is, of course, easy to accept that certain aspects of the law and the legal system reflect the nature of the society within which they operate, but it is much less obvious that they are *merely* part of the superstructure, rather than being part of the fabric of the society itself. For example, even a primitive communalist society of the hunter–gatherer type is likely to have a rule which requires able-bodied adult males to join in the process of hunting and gathering. As Collins points out, this rule is likely to be 'supported by such sanctions as ostracism, removal of privileges, or even expulsion from the community'. (*Op. cit.*, p. 33.) Admittedly, when viewed from the Marxist perspective, such a rule may not be properly regarded as *law* at all (since it does not spring from conditions of economic inequality), being perhaps more accurately categorized merely as a rule of morality or social convention; but whatever its character may be, it clearly remains a rule. What is less clear is whether it belongs within the base (because it is part of the arrangements for the provision of food) or within the superstructure (because it is, at least, a law-like requirement, even if it is not technically a law).

Moreover, practical examples such as this show that it may even be difficult to maintain the distinction between the base and the superstructure at all. Collins (*op. cit.*, p. 79) develops this point by reference to *Duke of Buccleuch v Alexander Cowan & Sons* (1866) LR 2 AC 344, a Scottish case on the law of nuisance. The facts were that the plaintiff, an agricultural landowner, was seeking an injunction to restrain the defendant, an industrial landowner, from polluting a stream which served both the agricultural and the industrial land holdings. Viewed in Marxist terms, therefore, the case clearly involved a dispute over the stream as a productive resource, since the plaintiff wished to use it to water his cattle, while the defendant wished to use it for the drainage of industrial effluent, even if this was harmful to the plaintiff's cattle. The question is whether a legal dispute of this kind can genuinely be seen as being *superstructural*? Suggesting a negative answer, Collins says:

'The legal rule provides the stability and reliability which any set of relations of production requires in order to flourish. It defines the reciprocal expectations and the basis upon which the landowner conducts his farming. In this sense, relations of production have to be constituted by normative frameworks...' (*Op. cit.*, p. 81.)

On this analysis, therefore, where the law *constitutes* the relations of production rather than *being constituted* by them, it is difficult to maintain the Marxist view of the distinction between the base and the superstructure. Moreover, even if the distinction can be maintained, it is by no means necessary to accept the Marxist version of where that distinction lies:

> 'Into [social] interactions go such matters as culture, ethical or other beliefs and inherited concepts of solidarity as well as purely economic factors. To concentrate solely upon economics as the base factor is severely to limit the analysis and to interpret all other factors in its light actually involves a distortion.' (McCoubrey, *The Development of Naturalist Legal Theory*, 1987, p. 109.)

Whatever view is taken of the persuasiveness of Marxism in general, its modern significance to legal theory lies principally in its influence on the *critical legal studies movement*, to which we now turn.

9.4 The critical legal studies movement

As we saw in Chapter 8, the impetus behind American realism was a desire to replace the traditional focus of *law in books* with an examination of *law in action*. A superficially similar, yet crucially different, sceptical stance provides the starting point for the critical legal studies movement (which is commonly known simply as *CLS*, with its proponents being known as *crits*). This movement originated in America in the late 1970s and spread to England in the mid-1980s, where it has remained a distinctly minority interest.

The sceptical essence of CLS is neatly conveyed thus:

> 'Legal doctrine not only does not, but also cannot, generate determinant results in concrete cases. Law is not so much a rational enterprise as a vast exercise in rationalization. Legal doctrine can be manipulated to justify an almost infinite spectrum of possible outcomes. Moreover, a plausible argument can be made that any such outcome has been derived from the dominant legal conceptions. Legal doctrine is nothing more than a sophisticated vocabulary and repertoire of manipulative techniques for categorising, describing, organizing and comparing: it is *not* a methodology for reaching substantive outcomes.' (Original emphasis. Hutchinson and Monahan, *Law, Politics and Critical Legal Scholars: The Unfolding Drama of American Legal Thought* (1984) 36 Stan Law Rev 199.)

The difference between this scepticism and that of American realism lies in the latter's focus on seeking a deeper understanding of the way in which law works, in order to make it work better, rather than simply seeking to explore the way in which the law perpetuates injustice in general and inequality in particular. Moreover, American realism's scepticism emphasizes the significance of extra-legal factors such as political and economic reality, but does not extend to questioning those factors themselves. The scepticism of the crits, on the other hand, goes significantly further by denying that legal reasoning has any distinct existence: 'Law is politics. It does not have an existence outside of ideological battles within society'. (Freeman (ed.), *Lloyd's Introduction to Jurisprudence*, 8th edn, 2008, p. 1041.) According to the crits, therefore, law and legal reasoning are merely techniques used by those who hold power within society in order to preserve their own position:

'Critical legal theory... sees the whole enterprise of jurisprudence... as operating to confer a spurious legitimacy on law.... Furthermore, by treating law as a discrete and distinct object, jurisprudence reinforces... the idea of law... separated from politics, morality and everyday conversation. In denying this separation... critical legal theory attempts to reconnect law with everyday political and moral argument, struggles and experiences, with all their attendant incoherences, uncertainties and indeterminacies. Most importantly... critical legal theorists reveal... law as the expression and medium of power.' (Alan Thomson, in Ian Grigg-Spall and Paddy Ireland (eds), *The Critical Lawyers' Handbook*, 1992, pp. 2–3.)

Against such sentiments, Stephen Guest argues that 'much of [the crits'] work can be criticized in ways which are sad rather than serious; it is trendy; it appeals to the less bright student who wants a quick answer...' (*Why the 'Critical Theorists' Miss the Point* or *The Human Face of Law* [1993] *Current Legal Problems*, p. 234.) In particular, he argues that crits are short on constructive criticism. If they are criticizing law as such, rather than merely bad law, they should be willing to deal with the established literature covering theories of justice and the idea of law itself.

Furthermore, according to one leading English commentator, 'one gets a sense, even from across the Atlantic, that critical legal studies peaked in the American law schools in the mid-1980s and has been losing momentum ever since'. (Duxbury, *Patterns of American Jurisprudence*, corrected edn, 1997, p. 426). On the other hand, whatever the fate of CLS itself may be, there is no doubt that its depiction of the study and practice of law as being unavoidably politically conditioned and directed, is also seen in feminist legal theory, to which we now turn.

9.5 Feminism in legal theory

9.5.1 Introduction

The feminist movement is often perceived to be a 20th century phenomenon and – except for the women's suffrage movement – largely confined to the period from the 1960s onwards. In fact, the roots of feminism can certainly be traced substantially further back, to at least the 18th century. More particularly, Mary Wollstonecraft's *A Vindication of the Rights of Woman* (first published in 1792) provides what is probably the first systematic account of the social reasons for the subjection of women, together with a passionate plea for their independence.

'There is a homely proverb, which speaks a shrewd truth, that whoever the devil finds idle he will employ...

'It is vain to expect virtue from women till they are, in some degree, independent of men.... Whilst they are absolutely dependent on their husbands they will be cunning, mean and selfish...' (Dover Thrift edition, 1996, pp. 145–146.)

Similarly:

> 'From the tyranny of man, I firmly believe, the greater number of female follies proceed; and the cunning, which I allow makes at present a part of their character... is produced by oppression...
>
> 'Asserting the rights which women in common with men ought to contend for, I have not attempted to extenuate their faults; but to prove them to be the natural consequence of their education and station in society. If so, it is reasonable to suppose that they will change their character, and correct their vices and follies, when they are allowed to be free in a physical, moral and civil sense.
>
> 'Let woman share the rights and she will emulate the virtues of man; for she must grow more perfect when emancipated.' (*Op. cit.*, pp. 200–201.)

Moving forward to the second half of the following century, in Part II of his essay on *The Subjection of Women* (written in 1861 but remaining unpublished until 1869), John Stuart Mill comments on the status of wives thus:

> 'I am far from pretending that wives are in general no better treated than slaves; but no slave is a slave to the same lengths, and in so full a sense of the word, as a wife is.... Above all, a female slave has (in Christian countries) an admitted right, and is considered under a moral obligation, to refuse to her master the last familiarity. Not so the wife: however brutal a tyrant she may unfortunately be chained to... he can claim from her and enforce the lowest degradation of a human being, that of being made the instrument of an animal function contrary to her inclinations.' (*On Liberty and Other Essays*, Oxford World's Classics edition, 1998, ed. John Gray, p. 504.)

On the assumed superiority of males and maleness, Mill observes:

> 'Think what it is to be a boy, to grow up to manhood in the belief that without any merit or exertion of his own, though he may be the most frivolous and empty or the most ignorant and stolid of mankind, by the mere fact of being born male he is by right the superior of all and every one of an entire half of the human race.... What must be the effect on his character of this lesson?' (*Op. cit.*, pp. 558–559.)

9.5.2   The modern context

Turning to the modern context, feminist legal theory, as currently conceived, comes in a variety of forms. However, it always has two unifying, and closely linked, characteristics.

First, there is 'a belief that society, and necessarily legal order, is patriarchal'. (*Lloyd's Introduction to Jurisprudence*, 8th edn, 2008, p. 1124.)

Secondly, 'it seeks to analyse the contribution of law in constructing, maintaining, reinforcing and perpetuating patriarchy and it looks at ways in which this patriarchy can be undermined and ultimately eliminated.' (*Ibid.*)

A third common, but by no means universal, characteristic (which is fuelled by the genuine and often justified anger of the feminists), is a tendency to overstate the case, or at least to state it more forcefully than the immediate argument warrants. (See, for example, the passage quoted from Robin West at p. 160.) One unfortunate consequence of such overstatement may be that that part of the audience which is unsympathetic to the feminist case becomes unreceptive even to those of its elements which cannot reasonably be refuted.

Feminism generally, and feminist legal theory in particular, may usefully be considered under four broad headings, namely *liberal, cultural, radical* and *postmodern*. Before considering each in turn, however, it is worth noticing Patricia A. Cain's comment on the achievements of feminism in legal theory generally:

> 'Feminist theorists have made valuable contributions to law by adding a female perspective to legal discussions. But feminist theorists should not privilege one perspective over another. Our contributions are especially valuable, not because we speak from a female perspective, but because we speak from a previously-silenced perspective.' (*Feminism and the Limits of Equality* (1990) 24 Georgia Law Rev 803 at p. 845.)

Despite the force of feminism, there are few English examples of judges adopting an explicitly feminist standpoint. However, the case of *Radmacher v Granatino* [2010] UKSC 42, [2011] 1 All ER 373, is an instructive exception, albeit only in a dissenting judgment delivered by a minority of one. The case arose from an ante-nuptial agreement or, in other words, an agreement (sometimes known as a *pre-nuptial* agreement or a *pre-nup*), made before marriage, dealing with financial provision and the division of assets if the marriage breaks down. The all-male majority of the Supreme Court decided there was a presumption that the courts should give effect to such agreements provided they had been freely entered into and were, in all the circumstances, fair. The basis of this decision was said (at para. [78]) to be 'respect for individual autonomy.... It would be paternalistic and patronising to override... [the]... agreement simply on the basis that the court knows best'. So, a spouse wishing to challenge an ante-nuptial agreement must prove either that it was not freely entered into or that it is unfair.

Against the presumption favoured by the majority, Lady Hale dissented on the basis that a marriage contract creates status. She elaborated on this (at para. [132]) as follows.

> 'This means two things. First, the parties are not entirely free to determine all its legal consequences for themselves. They contract into the package which the law of the land lays down. Secondly, their marriage also has legal consequences for other people and for the state.'

Lady Hale, from her standpoint as the only female Supreme Court Justice and the court's only family law specialist, also made the point that in a typical case involving an ante-nuptial agreement (although this was not so in the present case) the wife would be more dependent on a favourable financial outcome than her husband would be. She put the feminist point bluntly (at para. [173]):

'In short, there is a gender dimension to the issue which some may think ill-suited to decision by a court consisting of eight men and one woman.'

Lady Hale, therefore, rejected the idea of a presumption in favour of upholding ante-nuptial agreements, taking the view that each agreement (provided, of course that it had been freely entered into and was fair) should simply be put into the balance, together with all the other relevant factors in each case, thus enabling the court to make a fair decision on each case as a whole.

9.5.3 Liberal feminism

The liberal variety of feminism was the original, and so far the most successful, subdivision of the feminist movement as a whole. It sought, and largely secured, acceptance of the idea that women should have the same legal rights and privileges as men in terms of matters such as the suffrage, and the right to graduate from the universities and to enter the professions.

However, some feminists object that a high price was paid for gaining these equalities:

'Liberal feminism's central ideal amounted to a strategy of assimilation of women to a standard set by and for men. The rights assigned to men as legal subjects had to be made available to women wherever a comparison between the treatment of the two revealed a disparity: the equalization was almost invariably in one direction – towards a male norm.' (Nicola Lacey, *Feminist Legal Theory: Beyond Neutrality* [1995] *Current Legal Problems*, p. 6.)

Furthermore, by concentrating on the elimination of the visible manifestations of sexual inequality, liberal feminism distracts attention from the attempt to understand its origins. In other words, eliminating symptoms is a poor substitute for identifying and eradicating causes.

The other versions of feminism seek to avoid what their proponents see as the liberal feminist trap of seeking to make women into 'honorary men'.

9.5.4 Cultural feminism or *difference theory*

The second variety of feminist legal theory, often associated with the work of Carol Gilligan, an American educational psychologist, is known alternatively as cultural feminism, or difference theory. The essence of this school of thought is that there are genuine differences between the sexes, but that the distinctively female contribution is at worst unrecognized, and at best under-valued, by a male-dominated world, rather than being accepted and valued.

'Gilligan identifies the female voice with caring and relationships. Woman's moral vision encompasses this different voice. Woman's difference is good. Feminists in the Gilligan camp are interested in changing institutions to give equal weight to woman's moral voice. They argue that the category "woman" has not been so much misdefined by men, as it has been ignored and undervalued. Yes, women are nurturing. Yes, women value personal relationships. These attributes are to be valued. Using equality rhetoric, cultural feminists argue for material changes in present conditions that would support woman-valued relationships.' (Patricia A. Cain, *Feminism and the Limits of Equality* (1990) 24 Georgia Law Rev, p. 836.)

Without seeking to detract from difference theory in general, it is sometimes difficult to avoid the conclusion that some of its arguments may be overstated. Take, for example, the following passage, in which Robin West, having argued that men see the world as being made up of fundamentally separate and autonomous individuals, contrasts

'[women, who] are not essentially, necessarily, inevitably, always, and forever separate from other human beings... [but] are in some sense 'connected' to life and to other human beings during at least four recurrent and critical material experiences: the experience of pregnancy itself; the invasive and 'connecting' experience of heterosexual penetration, which may lead to pregnancy; the monthly experience of menstruation, which represents the potential for pregnancy; and the post-pregnancy experience of breast-feeding.' (*Jurisprudence and Gender* (1988) 55 U of Chi L Rev, pp. 2–3.)

The implicit exclusion not only of chaste heterosexual women and lesbians (both of whom lack 'the "invasive and connecting" experience of heterosexual penetration'), but also of post-menopausal women (who lack 'the monthly experience of menstruation') and of those women who have never given birth (and who therefore lack 'the post-pregnancy experience of breast-feeding'), may all be thought to be unduly dismissive of a significant number of women.

9.5.5 Radical feminism

Radical feminists see women as a class which is subject to male domination. As one leading radical feminist puts it:

'The state is male jurisprudentially: meaning that it adopts the standpoint of male power on the relation between law and society.... Those who have freedoms like equality, liberty, privacy, and speech socially keep them legally, free of government intrusion. No one who does not have them socially is granted them legally.' (Catherine A. MacKinnon, *Toward a Feminist Theory of the State*, 1989, p. 163.)

In the context of legal theory, therefore, one of the principal tasks for radical feminists is to secure changes in the law which will end the fundamental inequality of the sexes. More particularly, radical feminists differ from liberal feminists, whose aim they see as being assimilation into a male world, arguing instead that women must be seen in their own terms, rather than having the concept of 'woman' defined by men. They also reject the cultural feminist position:

'Difference is the velvet glove on the iron fist of domination. The problem then is not that differences are not valued; the problem is that they are defined by power. This is as true when difference is affirmed as when it is denied, when its substance is applauded or disparaged, when women are punished or protected in its name.' (MacKinnon, *op. cit.*, p. 219.)

A useful illustration of the radical feminist position may be found in MacKinnon's statement of one way in which the law fails to recognize, and still less to reflect, the interests of women:

'Pornography is neither harmless fantasy nor a corrupt and confused mis-representation of an otherwise natural and healthy sexual situation. It institutionalizes the sexuality of male supremacy, fusing the eroticization of dominance and submission with the social construction of male and female.... Men treat women as who they see women as being. Pornography constructs who that is.' (*Pornography, Civil Rights and Speech*, in *Pornography: Women Violence and Civil Liberties: a Radical New View*, ed. Catherine Itzin, 1993, p. 462.)

9.5.6　Postmodernist feminism

Cain (*op. cit.*, p. 838) explains the application of postmodernism (see p. 149) to feminism thus:

'Postmodern feminists eschew the idea of unitary truth, of objective reality. They readily admit that categories, especially gender categories, are mere social constructs. Equality, too, is a social construct. It is true that these constructs, as products of patriarchy, are in need of a feminist reconstruction. But postmodern feminism tells us to beware of searching for a new truth to replace the old. There simply is no such thing as the essential 'woman'. There is no such thing as the woman's point of view. There is no single theory of equality that will work for the benefit of all women. Indeed there is probably no single change or goal that is in the best interest of all women.'

Bearing in mind the use of the word *crits* explained at p. 155, it is not surprising that feminists of this persuasion are sometimes called *fem-crits*.

9.5.7　Why has feminism had so little impact?

One puzzle arising from feminist legal theory is why the movement has had such little impact on the wider field of law and legal theory. Ngaire Naffine suggests that the answer lies partly in the ambiguity of the law's concept of *personality*, and partly the adaptability of the law when faced with new challenges.

She develops the first point by noting that although personality is one of law's central concepts, it has also been a source of significant confusion. More particularly, the word 'person' is sometimes used to mean 'human being', but is also sometimes used 'in a more restrictive manner to refer to that which possesses the formal ability or capacity to bear a legal right or duty'. (See *In Praise of Legal Feminism* (2002) 22 LS 71, at p. 95.)

'One upshot for feminists of this persisting uncertainty about law's central term is that there is simply no well-developed and coherent body of theory about the person (unlike the flourishing jurisprudence of property) with which to engage. It is difficult to demonstrate incongruities and anomalies in a sustained and systematic manner, indeed to obtain an intellectual purchase, when the concept of the legal person itself is so poorly theorized and so inconsistently deployed. In short, we lack a clear target.' (*Op. cit.*, p. 96.)

Naffine's second point recognizes that the law has accorded women full rights of property ownership, full rights to hold public office, and so on. In other words, 'law has managed, at least partially, to accommodate women in its concept of a person. It has, therefore, bent to the demands of feminism, not broken'. (*Op. cit.*, p. 98.) However,

'[while feminists may] concede the creative and supple nature of personality as a legal device... [they should insist] that it is not at present neutral as between men and women. Rather... law... still harbours an idea of a certain sort of autonomous individuated male as the ideal rights-holder.' (*Op. cit.*, p. 100.)

Naffine concludes that 'fair minded men (and women)... must suspend old ways of thinking and embrace open scholarly debate'. (*Op. cit.*, p. 101.) Although it is tempting to see this as an adverse comment on those representatives of patriarchal legal theory who may have failed to give feminist legal theory the serious consideration it deserves, it is clear that feminists may not be entirely outwith the scope of the criticism. More particularly, four pages containing a reading from the work of Catherine MacKinnon were physically cut out of the first printing of *Jurisprudence and Legal Theory: Commentary and Materials* (Penner, Schiff, Nobles *et al.*, 2002) because 'the anticipated permission... was refused by Professor MacKinnon in view of the authors' [Emily Jackson and Nicola Lacey] commentary on her work'. (See an insert to the book as sold, appearing between pp. 806 and 811.) While academics, in common with everyone else, enjoy intellectual property rights in the fruits of their labours and are, therefore, perfectly entitled to withhold permission for reproduction, such permission is, in practice, given as a matter of course, in the interests of, among other things, 'open scholarly debate'.

Summary

- Roscoe Pound's sociological jurisprudence uses the ideas of legal interests and jural postulates as the basis for explaining how the law develops.

- The Marxist theory of law regards the base of any society as consisting of the conditions of production and the economic relationships of those engaged in

Summary cont'd

production. A superstructure of social institutions, including law and the legal system, is constructed on this base.

▶ The critical legal studies movement sees law and the legal process as being part of politics. It rejects the conventional analyses of legal theory which tend to see law and legal reasoning as discrete entities, preferring to see law in terms of power.

▶ Feminist legal theories all agree that law is the product of a society which is fundamentally patriarchal. Beyond this, there are significant differences between *liberal* feminists, *cultural* feminists, *radical* feminists and *postmodern* feminists.

Further reading

Cain, Patricia A., *Feminism and the Limits of Equality* (1990) 24 Georgia Law 803

Collins, Hugh, *Marxism and Law*, 1982

Duxbury, Neil, *Patterns of American Jurisprudence*, corrected edn, 1997

Freeman, M.D.A. (ed.), *Lloyd's Introduction to Jurisprudence*, 8th edn, 2008

Guest, Stephen, *Why the 'Critical Theorists' Miss the Point or The Human Face of Law* [1993] *Current Legal Problems*

Hutchinson, Alan C., and Monahan, Patrick J., Law, *Politics and Critical Legal Scholars: The Unfolding Drama of American Legal Thought* (1984) 36 Stan LR 199

Lacey, Nicola, *Feminist Legal Theory: Beyond Neutrality* [1995] *Current Legal Problems*

Llewellyn, Karl, *Review of Pound's Jurisprudence* (1960) 28 U Chi L Rev 175.

MacKinnon, Catherine A., *Pornography, Civil Rights and Speech*, in Itzin, Catherine (ed.), *Pornography: Women, Violence and Civil Liberties: a Radical New View*, 1993

MacKinnon, Catherine A., *Toward a Feminist Theory of the State*, 1989

McCoubrey, Hilaire, *The Development of Naturalist Legal Theory*, 1987

Mill, John Stuart, *On the Subjection of Women*, 1869, is widely reproduced. See, for example *John Stuart Mill On Liberty and Other Essays*, Oxford World's Classics, John Gray (ed), 1991

Naffine, Ngaire, *In Praise of Legal Feminism* (2002) 22 LS 71

Penner, Schiff, Nobles and others, *Jurisprudence and Legal Theory: Commentary and Materials*, 2002

Pound, Roscoe, *The Spirit of the Common Law*, 1921

Pound, Roscoe, *Social Control Through Law*, 1942

Pound, Roscoe, *A Survey of Social Interests* (1943) 57 Harv LR 1

Pound, Roscoe, *The Role of the Will in Law* (1954) 68 Harv LR 1

Pound, Roscoe, *Jurisprudence*, vol. 3, 1959

Thomson, Alan, in Grigg-Spall, Ian and Ireland, Paddy, (eds) *The Critical Lawyers' Handbook*, 1992

West, Robin, *Jurisprudence and Gender* (1988) 55 U of Chi L Rev 1

Chapter 10

Theories of justice

10.1 Introduction

As we have seen, the ideas of justice and injustice have a long history within legal theory. More particularly, having dealt with Aristotle's theory of justice and having seen the importance of the idea of unjust laws to the Thomist theory of natural law (in Chapter 3), and having seen (also in Chapter 3) how the revival of interest in natural law theory during the latter part of the 20th century emphasizes its evaluative, rather than constitutive, function, we now return to the same theme. More particularly, this chapter will consider utilitarianism, the economic analysis of law, Rawls' *Theory of Justice* and *Political Liberalism*, and Nozick's *Anarchy, State and Utopia*.

By way of a preliminary observation, it may seem obvious that lawyers regard the pursuit of justice as an integral part of the legal enterprise, even if those in professional practice seldom have the time or the inclination to step back from the fray to ask themselves what exactly they think 'justice' means. Nevertheless, it is worth noticing the possibility of extreme scepticism. In the words of Alf Ross, a Danish legal theorist

> 'To invoke justice is the same thing as banging on the table: an emotional expression which turns one's demand into an absolute postulate. That is no proper way to mutual understanding. It is impossible to have a rational discussion with a man who mobilizes "justice" because he says nothing that can be argued for or against. His words are persuasion, not argument. The ideology of justice leads to implacability and conflict, since on the one hand it incites to the belief that one's demand is not merely the expression of a certain interest in conflict with opposing interests, but that it possesses a higher, absolute validity; and on the other hand it precludes all rational argument and discussion of a settlement.' (*On Law and Justice*, 1958, p. 274.)

However, most commentators are more constructive, and it is to some of those that we now turn.

10.2 Utilitarianism

As we have already seen (p. 66), Austin's command theory of law is based on the work of his predecessor and mentor, Jeremy Bentham (1748–1832). At this juncture it is appropriate to return to Bentham, and to consider the doctrine which he calls 'the principle of utility'. Two preliminary points may be made.

The first, which is purely terminological, is that the more common usage of *utilitarianism* seems to have been coined not by Bentham himself but by John Stuart Mill (1806–73), in order 'to denote the position of those attached to the doctrine of utility as the measure of laws and institutions'. (Kelly, *A Short History of Western Legal Theory*, 1992, pp. 317–318.) The second is that Bentham totally rejects the then prevailing natural law tradition, as evidenced by his oft-quoted dismissal of the idea of natural rights as 'nonsense on stilts'.

Turning to the substance of the topic, Davies and Holdcroft summarize the nature of utilitarianism thus:

> 'Utilitarianism is a goal-based theory which evaluates actions in terms of their propensity to maximize goodness, however this is defined. Hence, it takes the view that our conception of what is right depends on our conception of what is good, since a right action is defined as one which produces more good than any alternative. So that only if a person has a conception of what is good can he or she have one of what is right.' (*Jurisprudence: Texts and Commentary*, 1991, p. 205.)

In the first chapter of *An Introduction to the Principles of Morals and Legislation*, Bentham argues that humankind is subject to 'two sovereign masters, pain and pleasure' and that the principle of utility allows us to rank actions according to their tendency 'to augment or diminish the happiness of the party whose interest is in question'. In this context, *utility* is the capacity to 'produce benefit, advantage, pleasure, good, or happiness (all this in the present case comes to the same thing), or (what comes again to the same thing) to prevent the happening of mischief, pain, evil, or unhappiness to the party whose interest is considered'. When the party being considered is the community as a whole, it will be the happiness of the community which counts, but the community is essentially a fiction, so the interest of the community is the sum of the interests of its members.

Bentham says that if an action conforms to the principle of utility, 'one may always say either that it is one that ought to be done, or at least that it is not one that ought not to be done'. Another way of putting this is that 'it is right it should be done; or at least it is not wrong it should be done: that it is a right action; at least that it is not a wrong action'. This leads him to the conclusion that, when they are 'thus interpreted, the words *ought*, and *right* and *wrong*, and others of that stamp, have a meaning: when otherwise, they have none'.

Bentham accepts that the principle of utility cannot be directly proved, since

> 'that which is used to prove every thing else, cannot itself be proved: a chain of proofs must have their commencement somewhere. To give such proof is as impossible as it is needless.'

Pausing only to comment that Bentham's proposition that 'chains of proofs must have their commencement somewhere' is clearly a close relative of Kelsen's assertion that the *grundnorm* is a logical necessity (see p. 84), we must proceed to examine what Bentham calls the *felicific calculus*, which is simply a rather obscure label for the process by which he believes it is possible to quantify (or calculate) the amount of pleasure or pain which will ensue from any specific action.

The basis of the felicific calculus is that there are various qualities (namely, *intensity, duration, certainty, propinquity, fecundity, purity* and *extent*) each of which has to be assessed in order to assess the utility of an act. The meaning of most of these elements is self-evident, but it may be worth commenting that by *fecundity* Bentham meant the chance of the same kind of pleasure or pain being repeated; by *purity* he meant the chance of the act in question *not* being followed by the opposite sensation; and by *extent* he meant the number of people who would experience either the pleasure or the pain (as the case may be).

The discussion so far has dealt with the utility of acts, and is therefore known as *act utilitarianism*, but it is possible to formulate another version, namely *rule utilitarianism*, according to which 'the rightness or wrongness of an action is to be judged by the goodness or badness of the consequences of a rule that everyone should perform the action in like circumstances'. (J.J.C. Smart, in Smart and Williams (eds), *Utilitarianism: For and Against*, 1973, p. 9.) This version of utilitarianism is particularly relevant when legal theorists are talking about justice, because typically they will be talking about the justice (or injustice) of a rule.

Having outlined the basis of utilitarianism, it is appropriate to consider some of the arguments which are commonly raised against it.

One of the most obvious objections is that, in reality, the felicific calculus will usually be unworkable. First, there is the difficulty of quantifying both pleasure and pain. For example, how can anyone calculate *how much* pleasure I get out of, say, clay-pigeon shooting on my land, and *how much* pain my neighbour suffers through having to endure the noise of my shooting?

Secondly, even if such calculations could be undertaken with precision, there remains the problem of predicting consequences, in an inevitably uncertain future. In other words, even leaving aside the problem of quantification, utilitarianism is intrinsically better suited to evaluating events which have occurred than to prescribing future conduct.

Other objections may, however, be met with answers which may be found convincing. For example, it is not difficult to imagine a situation in which utilitarianism may be employed to justify using an individual as no more than a means to an end. A classic example of this objection involves supposing both that a murder is committed in a community which has a race problem, and that the ethnic majority suspect a member of the ethnic minority is guilty. If there is a delay in bringing a suspect to trial, racial tensions will increase, and may result in many people suffering a great deal of harm in consequence of rioting, looting and general public disorder. In this situation, therefore, the greatest happiness of the greatest number may be served by arresting, trying, convicting and sentencing a member of the ethnic minority group with as little delay as possible, whether or not the suspect is guilty, and even if it is necessary to fabricate evidence against him. However, an answer to this objection may be found in *rule utilitarianism*, since a general practice (or rule) of scapegoating the innocent is likely to undermine confidence in the administration of justice, with even more harmful consequences for society as a whole than those flowing from an outburst of public disorder.

Similarly, it is commonly objected that utilitarianism's crude majoritarianism is intrinsically likely to be anti-liberal, and therefore to produce consequences which many people will find unacceptable.

Once again, however, if the focus is placed on the utility of rules rather than individual acts, the problem may be seen differently, since the happiness of the majority may be enhanced by living in a tolerant society. (The extent to which the law should be tolerant of the exercise of individual freedom of choice is discussed in Chapter 11.)

Another problem which may be more apparent than real is that utilitarianism's emphasis on pleasure makes it seem more than somewhat selfish, and therefore – at least to those conditioned by those moral traditions which emphasize the importance of self-denial and service to others – correspondingly unattractive. Moreover, utilitarianism's intrinsic subjectivity appears to result in an inability to discriminate between the pleasures of conspicuous consumption on the one hand and self-control on the other, and therefore to validate hedonism. Similarly, if value is subjective, there can be no distinction between the pleasure to be derived from reading literary classics on the one hand and pot-boilers on the other.

The following responses may be offered. First, it is a common experience that altruism may be a source of pleasure. Secondly, it is possible to argue that some activities and experiences may have value independently of the pleasure which they generate. Thus, acquiring knowledge may be argued to be good, whether or not it is pleasant. (Cf. knowledge as a basic good in the context of Finnis's theory of natural law, discussed at p. 105.) Alternatively, Mill argues that there is a hierarchy of pleasures, so that, for example, the pleasure to be derived from reading a literary classic is better than the pleasure to be derived from reading a pot-boiler. This version of utilitarianism, therefore, 'seems to imply that pleasure is a necessary condition for goodness but that goodness depends on other qualities of experience than pleasantness and unpleasantness'. (J.J.C. Smart, *Utilitarianism: For and Against*, Smart and Williams (eds), 1973, p. 13.)

10.3 The economic analysis of law and justice

The economic analysis of law, which lies in a direct line of descent from utilitarianism, substitutes the more easily measurable criterion of *economic efficiency* for the felicific calculus's criteria of pleasure and pain. The economic approach originated, and has been most highly developed, in America, although it has some presence in English academic law, and, as we shall see, it is not unknown for English judges to take their perception of economic factors into account when deciding cases.

Beginning with a classic American case where a cost–benefit analysis was used as the basic test for establishing liability for negligence, in *United States v Carroll Towing Co* 159 F2d 169 (2nd Cir 1947) the issue was whether the owner of a barge which had been left unattended for several hours in a busy harbour was liable when the barge broke away from its moorings and damaged another vessel. In all the circumstances of the case the court did hold the owner liable, but the enduring interest of the case lies in the way in which Judge Learned Hand formulated the relevant principle.

'Since there are occasions when every vessel will break from her moorings, and since, if she does, she becomes a menace to those about her, the owner's duty, as in other similar situations, to provide against resulting injuries is a function of three variables: (1) The probability that she will break away; (2) the gravity of the resulting injury, if she does; (3) the burden of adequate precautions. Possibly it serves to bring this notion into relief to state it in algebraic terms: if the probability be called P; the injury [sc. loss] L; and the burden B; liability depends on whether B is less than L multiplied by P; i.e., whether $B < PL$...'

Although English judges are much less likely to express themselves in such formally algebraic terms, the same approach may readily be discerned. As Denning LJ said, in *Watt v Hertfordshire County Council* [1954] 2 All ER 368:

'It is well-settled that in measuring due care one must balance the risk against the measures necessary to eliminate the risk.'

Thus, for example, in *Bolton v Stone* [1951] 1 All ER 1078, a cricket ball was hit out of the ground, injuring a passer-by on the highway. In the previous 30 years, the ball had been hit out of the ground on only six occasions and in the entire 90 year history of the ground no similar injury had occurred. Furthermore, the boundary fence was effectively 29 feet high, being a 12 feet high fence on top of a 17 feet high bank. Finding against the plaintiff, Lord Reid said the test to be applied was

'whether the risk of damage to a person on the road was so small that a reasonable man..., considering the matter from the point of view of safety, would have thought it right to refrain from taking steps to prevent the danger.'

It follows that the court will impose liability more readily if there is a risk of greater injury, as in *Paris v Stepney Borough Council* [1951] 1 All ER 42, where a one-eyed mechanic was struck and blinded by a piece of metal. Although there was overwhelming evidence that goggles would not be supplied to two-eyed workers, the House of Lords found negligence. In Lord Morton's words:

'In considering generally the precautions that the employer ought to take... it must... be right to take into account both elements, the likelihood of an accident happening and the gravity of its consequences.'

However, considerations of the public good may also enter the picture, in the sense that the social utility of the activity which causes the harm may be an important factor when assessing the cost of avoiding the risk. In *Watt* the accident happened when an unsuitable fire-brigade vehicle was answering an emergency call, leading Denning LJ to comment:

> 'If this accident had occurred in a commercial enterprise without any emergency, there could be no doubt that the [plaintiff] would have succeeded. But the commercial end to make profit is very different from the human end to save life and limb... [which]... justifies taking considerable risk.'

Similarly, in *Daborn v Bath Tramways* [1946] 2 All ER 333, the court had to decide whether there was contributory negligence on the part of the driver of a left-hand drive ambulance (in England) which was involved in an accident while overtaking. Finding in favour of the driver, Asquith LJ said:

> 'In determining whether a party is negligent... a relevant circumstance... may be the importance of the end to be served in behaving in this way or that. As has often been pointed out, if all the trains in this country were restricted to a speed of five miles an hour there would be fewer accidents but our national life would be intolerably slowed down.... During the war... it was necessary for many highly important operations to be carried out by means of motor vehicles with left-hand drives, no others being available.... It would be demanding too high and an unreasonable standard of care from the drivers of such cars to say to them: "Either you must give signals which the structure of your vehicle renders impossible or you must not drive at all".'

Another economic aspect arose in *Stovin v Wise (Norfolk County Council, Third Party)* [1996] 3 All ER 801, where the House of Lords said that where a public body fails to exercise a statutory power, individuals who are claiming damages in respect of harm which they allege to be due to that failure will be more likely to succeed where the statutory power is intended to protect people against risks which they cannot guard against in other ways, such as insurance. In other words, since the nature of insurance is a sharing of risk, have the individuals chosen to accept the risk, rather than sharing it with others?

The cases outlined above may seem unexceptional, but more startling results flow from what has become known as the *Coase theorem*, which states that where people are willing and able to negotiate without cost, property rights will go to those who value them most highly. The theorem originated in *The Problem of Social Costs* (1960) 3 J L & Econ 1, by Ronald H. Coase, an English economist working in America. (As an economist, of course, Coase assumes that people generally behave in a rational and self-interested way. While recognizing that this assumption will not be true of every individual, economists nevertheless proceed on the basis that, taking the population as a whole, it will be true by and large, and may therefore be adopted as a reasonable basis for decision-making.)

Coase illustrates the theorem by examining the case of *Sturges v Bridgman* (1879) 4 CPD 172, where a confectioner and a doctor were neighbours. For several years they coexisted peacefully, even though the confectioner's kitchen, which was located at the end of his garden, housed certain machinery which caused noise and vibration. When the doctor built a consulting room on part of his land which adjoined the confectioner's kitchen, the noise and vibration became a problem. The court granted the doctor an injunction restraining the confectioner from causing the nuisance.

From the legal perspective, the decision of the court in a case such as this will determine the future use of each piece of land. However, to an economist making the assumption that the parties are willing and able to negotiate, the decision of the court is only one factor in the overall process which determines the use to which each piece of land is ultimately put. In outline, the economic argument turns on how highly each party values his use of his own land. If the confectioner values his use more highly than the doctor values his, the former will buy out the latter by paying him not to enforce the injunction. Similarly, if the court withholds the injunction, but the doctor values his use more highly than the confectioner values his, the doctor will pay the confectioner to cease the harmful use. Of course, if the injunction is granted and the doctor values his use of his own land more than the confectioner values his, the injunction will be effective. Equally, if there is no injunction and the confectioner values his use more than the doctor values his, the harmful use will continue. In other words, whatever the decision of the court may be, the market will establish the most efficient use of the land. It can be argued, therefore, that the law ought to reflect the facts of economic life by imposing or withholding liability in accordance with the demands of economic efficiency.

Whether you wish to substitute this kind of economic calculation for more traditional ideas of justice is a matter of individual judgment, although some people may be wary of bringing themselves too readily within the scope of Oscar Wilde's definition of a cynic as 'A man who knows the price of everything and the value of nothing'. (*Lady Windermere's Fan*, Act 3.)

In practice, however, economic theorists of law need not be wholly devoted to the criterion of economic efficiency. For example, Guido Calabresi, the author of a leading study entitled *The Costs of Accidents: A Legal and Economic Analysis*, first published in 1970, argues that the law should be such that it reduces both the costs which result from accidents happening and the costs incurred in avoiding accidents. Nevertheless, he insists that economic analysis is only one way of arriving at a judgment, and that there are some things (such as murder and prostitution) which the law may properly prohibit on the basis that they are immoral, irrespective of any economic benefit which they may produce.

More generally, Calabresi argues that the state must, through the agency of law, decide not only what entitlements are to be allocated to each person, but also how those entitlements are to be protected. Additionally, it must decide whether people who hold particular entitlements should be allowed either to transfer them to others or to forego them altogether. (See *Property Rules, Liability Rules, and Inalienability: One View of the Cathedral* (1972) 85 Harv LR 1089.)

Putting Calabresi's point into context, the bulk of substantive law is, of course, concerned with allocating rights, duties, powers and immunities in all sorts of situations. An example of limited protection in English law may be found in the principle in *Barraclough v Brown* [1895–99] All ER Rep 239, which states that where a statute simultaneously creates a specific right and a corresponding remedy, that remedy will be the only means of enforcing that right. The facts of the case were that the undertakers who were responsible for a waterway had a statutory right to remove and sell any boat which sank within their jurisdiction. Furthermore, if the proceeds of sale were less than the cost of removal, the statute gave the undertakers a specific right to recover the balance in the magistrates' court. In the instant case, the undertakers wanted to recover £3,000, which was a substantially larger sum than those which normally came within the jurisdiction of the magistrates. Accordingly, they brought their claim in the High Court. However, that court held that the proceedings could be brought only in the magistrates' court, because both the right of recovery and the means of enforcing that right had been created by the same statute. In a case falling within the *Barraclough v Brown* principle, therefore, the fact that the lower court may be an unsuitable forum for bringing a claim (whether through lack of experience, inadequacy of enforcement power, or for any other reason) is legally irrelevant. In economic terms, however, the unsuitability of an initial forum may be seen as a source of inefficiency, since it increases the probability of an appeal.

For an example of entitlements which cannot be foregone, the Unfair Contract Terms Act 1977 provides that, in certain types of contract, exemption clauses may be simply ineffective, or their effectiveness may be subject to a test of reasonableness. In other words, as a matter of legislative policy, a party who would gain an entitlement under a contract if there were no exemption clause may still gain that entitlement despite the presence of such a clause.

10.4 Rawls' *justice as fairness*

10.4.1 Introduction

John Rawls, a Harvard Professor of Politics, adopts the title *justice as fairness* for his sophisticated reworking of the old idea of the social contract (some earlier versions of which are discussed at pp. 50–53). At its most basic, the distinction between Rawls and his predecessors lies in a fundamental difference as to their aims. Rawls is concerned with principles of justice in relation to the distribution of social goods (which include traditional aspects of liberty such as freedom of speech, and assembly, as well as 'the social bases of self-respect' (by which he means those things which are 'normally essential if citizens are to have a lively sense of their worth as persons'). (*Justice As Fairness: A Restatement*, 2001, §17.2.)

His predecessors, on the other hand, generally aim to defend (or to challenge) the legitimacy of specific legal systems or regimes. However, Rawls tends to blur the distinction between *legitimacy* and *justice* by placing his theory firmly within the liberal tradition, before explaining the *principle of liberal legitimacy* as meaning that

> 'political power is legitimate only when it is exercised in accordance with a constitution ... the essentials of which all citizens, as reasonable and rational, can endorse in the light of their common reason.' (*Op. cit.*, §12.3.)

Furthermore, Rawls says that, in the light of this principle, it is highly desirable that contentious laws 'should... be settled, so far as possible, by guidelines and values that can be similarly endorsed'. (*Ibid.*) Rawls' blurring of the distinction between *legitimacy* and *justice* flows from the fact that *justice as fairness* also very largely depends on the acceptability of conclusions which are derived from a basis of common reasonableness that, as we shall shortly see, Rawls calls an 'overlapping consensus'.

Having first presented *justice as fairness* in *Theory of Justice* (1971), Rawls develops and refines his argument further through a number of essays as well as *Political Liberalism* (1993) and *Justice As Fairness: A Restatement* (2001, ed. Kelly). (The three books are cited in the remainder of this discussion as *Theory*, *Liberalism* and *Restatement*.)

The best way to approach Rawls is through *Restatement*, which is not only the shortest and most lucid statement of his position, but also contains many cross-references back to the earlier works for those who wish to study the evolution of his thinking in depth. The focus of the following discussion is, therefore, primarily on *Restatement*, although occasional reference is also be made to the earlier works.

Rawls is careful to restrict his argument to the field of political theory, which, he emphasizes, is only part of the wider moral picture, thus avoiding an earlier suggestion that it could, potentially at least, be developed into a more general moral theory. He is also careful to make clear that 'justice as fairness is a political conception of justice for the special case of the basic structure of a *modern democratic society*'. (Emphasis added. *Restatement*, §5.2.) Rawls clarifies the nature of a democratic society as being one which 'not only professes but wants to take seriously the idea that citizens are free and equal, and tries to realize that idea in its main institutions'. (*Op. cit.*, §12.1.)

One key factor influencing the final formulation of *justice as fairness* is Rawls' recognition of the fact that it is unrealistic to assume that each society is unified not only by a shared base of religious and moral belief, but also by general agreement as to what constitutes a good life. More particularly, he had originally based his argument on the old-fashioned assumption of underlying unity, before coming to appreciate the need to adapt his thinking in order to take account of 'the fact of reasonable pluralism... [as]... a permanent condition of a democratic society'. (*Op. cit.*, §11.3.) Thus, the final version of the theory presents a conception of justice which recognizes that society embraces a wide variety of doctrines, each of which is reasonable in itself while also differing significantly from each of the others. The crux of Rawls' argument on this point is that, despite their manifest and manifold differences, these doctrines will generally share enough common ground to enable an 'overlapping consensus' to be identified. (Of course, Rawls accepts that it is in the nature of any pluralistic society that there will always be some doctrines which remain wholly outside the overlapping consensus, but this does not trouble him unduly because he never suggests that universal acceptance is an essential precondition to the existence and identification of an overlapping consensus.)

Consistently with his basic liberal values, Rawls rejects any attempt to be prescriptive as to the relationship between political doctrines and their comprehensive moral counterparts, leaving this as a matter that individuals must decide for themselves.

Against this background, we can now consider how Rawls identifies the principles of justice.

10.4.2 How are the principles of justice identified?

Introduction to the key concepts

The process of identifying the principles of justice involves two key concepts: *the original position* and *the veil of ignorance*. By *the original position*, Rawls means the position before the principles of justice are formulated; and by *the veil of ignorance* he means the circumstances which disqualify the individuals who are formulating those principles from knowing how their content will affect individual cases. However, before considering the original position and the veil of ignorance in more detail, it must be said that Rawls is not suggesting that these two concepts represent any factual reality. Indeed, having accepted that the process which is central to his theory is 'hypothetical and nonhistorical' (*Liberalism*, Lecture VII, §6), he gives further emphasis to the point by describing the people who formulate the principles of justice as 'artificial persons' who are created solely because they 'have a part to play in our thought-experiment'. (*Restatement*, §23.4.)

The original position

The *original position* is the phrase which Rawls uses to indicate the point of departure for the people who are entering into the agreement, in which capacity they are required 'as representatives of free and equal citizens [to] act as trustees or guardians'. (*Restatement*, §24.2.) Although Rawls would like the people in the original position to argue deductively (that is, from propositions to conclusions), rather than inductively (that is, from empirical observations to conclusions), he concedes that deriving the principles of justice in this way 'would be a complicated business and a distraction from our practical aim'. (*Op. cit.*, §23.4.) Therefore, he says, we simply require the parties to choose from a list, which he likens to a menu, containing important ideas within the Western tradition of political philosophy. Rawls takes the view that the fundamentals should be limited to those which are 'truly essential', such as the right to private property, because 'whenever we enlarge the list of basic liberties we risk weakening the protection of the most essential ones.' (*Liberalism*, Lecture VIII, §2.)

Rawls corrects the view he expressed in *Theory* (at §3.15 and §9.47) that the rational processes of those in the original position can establish what the principles of justice ought to be. His final view is that 'this is simply a mistake' and that the true position is that rational choice 'is itself part of a political conception of justice, one that tries to give an account of reasonable principles of justice'. (*Restatement*, §23.3, n.2.) In other words, while both rationality and reasonableness are important, reasonableness prevails over rationality. (Although the meaning of the distinction between the two is adequately clear as a matter of intuitive interpretation, Rawls offers little assistance when he declines to define either term, preferring to say simply that 'we gather their meaning by how they are used and by attending to the contrast between them'. (*Op. cit.*, §23.3.))

The veil of ignorance

While keeping in mind the idea that those who are in the original position are representatives of the individuals who constitute the community at large, we must now move to the *veil of ignorance*. The question is simple: how do those representatives know what is in the best interests of the individuals whom they represent? The answer is correspondingly simple: they do not know – or, more accurately, they do not know what is in the best interests of any particular individuals. Although this may sound paradoxical, it is merely Rawls' way of imposing, so far as it is reasonably possible to do so, objective constraints on the thought processes of those who are in the original position. More particularly, they will lack the following information about those whom they represent, namely: their social position; their comprehensive doctrines (such as their religious beliefs, if any); their race, ethnicity and sex; and their natural abilities. (*Op. cit.*, §6.2.)

If by this stage you are beginning to think that the nature of the Rawlsian thought-experiment is so unrealistic as to be unhelpful (perhaps even to the point of being incomprehensible), it may be useful to consider a very concrete, if somewhat simplified, example. Imagine yourself as someone in the original position, and having to decide on the justice (or injustice) of abortion. Although you will almost certainly have your own views on the matter, you will recall that Rawls requires you to exercise your decision-making powers as a trustee, and therefore you must act in the best interests of the person you represent rather than in accordance with your own views. The problem, of course, is that the veil of ignorance means that you do not know whether the person you represent is (a) male or female; and (if female) (b) whether she is sterile or fertile; and (c) if fertile, whether she is pregnant; and, if so, (d) whether the pregnancy has occurred (i) within the context of a stable and loving relationship, or (ii) as the result of a casual but consensual sexual encounter, or (iii) as the result of rape; or (e) assuming still that she is pregnant but irrespective of the circumstances surrounding the conception (i), whether the child she is carrying is or may be suffering from some serious disability; or (ii) whether the continuation of the pregnancy may be seriously inconvenient in terms of the mother's career progression or her social circumstances. Now imagine that, once you have fully debated the matter with your fellow decision-makers and formulated a collective view of the requirements of justice, the veil of ignorance is lifted. Since you will no doubt have considered all the alternatives outlined above (and possibly many others as well) while you were beneath the veil of ignorance, neither you nor the person you are representing can legitimately complain about the way the ensuing law operates in any particular case.

Having established the role of the original position and the state of knowledge of those who are in it, we can now consider Rawls' account of the content of the principles of justice.

10.4.3 The content of the principles of justice

The principles of justice emerge in their final form as:

> '(a) Each person has the same indefeasible claim to a fully adequate scheme of equal basic liberties, which scheme is compatible with the same scheme of liberties for all; and
> '(b) Social and economic inequalities are to satisfy two conditions: first, they are to be attached to offices and positions open to all under conditions of fair equality of opportunity; and second, they are to be to the greatest benefit of the least advantaged members of society (the difference principle).' (*Op. cit.*, §13.1.)

At its most basic, the distinction between the two principles is that the first deals with constitutional fundamentals, while the second, which itself has two limbs, deals with the operation of those fundamentals.

More particularly, Rawls says that the first principle covers the traditional freedoms of thought, conscience and association as well as freedom of the person and the interests protected by the rule of law. He clearly intends the second principle to cover 'institutions of social and economic justice in the form most appropriate to citizens seen as free and equal' (*op. cit.*, §13.6), although it must be conceded that this is not immediately apparent from his choice of words.

The next matter to be considered is the relationship between the two principles. The short point is that Rawls presents them in descending order, so the first principle takes priority over the second and the first limb of the second principle takes priority over the second limb. However, two elements need to be unpacked here, namely why is the order of priority the way that it is; and what does it mean to say that one principle, or limb, takes priority over another?

The reason for the priority of the first principle over the second is twofold. First, constitutional fundamentals are the product of the highest form of political power, namely 'the power of the people to constitute the form of government', which may be contrasted with 'the ordinary power exercised routinely by officers of a regime'. (*Op. cit.*, §13.5.). Secondly, the 'basic liberties' to which it relates exist in order to 'protect fundamental interests that have a special significance'. (*Op. cit.*, §30.2.)

As far as the two limbs of the second principle are concerned, the first limb takes priority over the second limb on the simple and logical basis that institutions must exist before they can function.

Turning to what it means to say that one principle takes priority over another, two points arise. First, as we have just seen, the form of power which is exercised in order to produce the first principle is higher than the form of power which is exercised to produce the second principle. Secondly, and less obviously, Rawls says that the consequence of the priorities is that, when applying the second principle, we must assume that the first principle has been satisfied. Similarly, when applying the second limb of the second principle, we must assume that both the first principle and the first limb of the second principle have been satisfied.

Finally, Rawls identifies a common misunderstanding that the second limb of the second principle (the 'difference principle') is an application of the *maximin* principle. (This principle requires decision-makers to imagine the worst of all possible outcomes flowing from all possible solutions to a given problem, and then to choose the solution which provides the least bad outcome – or, in other words, they are required to *maxi*mize the *min*imum outcome.) Having identified this misunderstanding, Rawls nevertheless does accept that the maximin principle does have some, albeit limited, relevance, to the extent that it may illuminate the theory, but not to the extent that it becomes part of it. One key element underlying the limited relevance which Rawls accords to the maximin principle is that the principle does not take into account the relative probabilities of the various alternatives actually happening. For example, it is not rational to reject an alternative on the basis that it produces a very poor possible minimum (in the sense of a very unfavourable outcome for the least advantaged) if the chances of that outcome actually materializing are remote in the extreme.

10.4.4　From the original position to a fully functioning legal system

The principles of justice and their application to the legal system cannot be fully identified from the original position, but will emerge through a four-stage process. This process begins with people adopting the principles of justice, while in the original position and subject to the veil of ignorance. (The veil of ignorance is not, however total, being subject, at this stage, to the exception that the principles of social theory are known: *Theory*, §31.) The parties' knowledge then increases progressively through the subsequent stages. Thus, at the second stage, the first principle will be applied by a convention held for the purpose of drawing up a constitution and the veil of ignorance is lifted to the extent that the kind of society is known. At the third stage, the principles of justice are applied to the enactment of legislation in accordance with both the constitution and, of course, the principles of justice. At the fourth stage, when the veil of ignorance is lifted in its entirety, the laws which have been enacted are administered, interpreted and enforced on a day-to-day basis, in the context of a fully functioning legal system.

10.4.5 The *just savings* principle

We have, so far, been dealing only with the problem of justice within a given society and it has been implicit that we have also been limiting our discussion to a given point of time within that society. However, in all three books, Rawls extends his idea of justice so that it applies between generations, rather than simply between contemporaries, and it is to this aspect of his thinking that we finally turn.

Rawls responds to the need for *inter-generational equity*, which requires each generation to see itself as being merely one stage in the general progression through all the generations of history, by formulating what he calls the *just savings principle*. In its final version the 'correct principle' becomes

> 'that which the members of any generation (and so all generations) would adopt as the one their generation is to follow and as the principle they would want preceding generations to have followed (and later generations to follow), no matter how far back (or forward) in time.' (*Liberalism*, Lecture VII, §6.)

In other words, the idea underlying *just savings* is essentially the same as the idea underlying the *difference principle*, with only the time frame being different. In practical terms, of course, the opportunities for its application are enormously varied, covering matters as diverse as the disposal of nuclear waste and other aspects of energy policy, and social welfare policy in relation to the changing age structure of the population.

10.5 Nozick and the minimal state

In his book *Anarchy, State and Utopia* (1974), Robert Nozick, a Harvard Professor of Philosophy, argues for the idea of a *minimal state*, which is based on *just entitlements*, and in which the notion of *social* or *distributive* justice has no place. While Nozick shares with Rawls both a common starting point in the tradition of social contractarianism and an emphasis on the interests of the individual, there are also detailed, but fundamental, differences between them. More particularly, Rawls begins by presuming equality, any departure from which will require justification. Nozick, on the other hand, begins by presuming that the current distribution of resources is just, unless and until the contrary is proved; and he goes on to argue that there is only a very limited basis on which the contrary may be proved.

The shared emphasis of both Nozick and Rawls on the importance of individual liberty means that both may legitimately claim to be liberals, but this claim must not be allowed to obscure the extent to which they differ on the crucial question of the extent to which the state may legitimately interfere with the interests (or, to put it more bluntly, infringe the liberty) of the individual. Indeed, Nozick's restrictive view of the legitimacy of state intervention is such that some people may be tempted to place him some significant way towards the right wing end of the political spectrum and well outside the liberal camp altogether.

Turning to the elements of Nozick's theory, the crucial question centres on the legitimacy of the power which is vested in the state. Nozick argues that, in the earliest stages of the evolution of a state, people must form protective associations in order to safeguard their rights. For some time there will be several such associations, but one will inevitably become dominant and when that dominance can be said to amount to a monopoly of power, that association has become a state. However, the fact that the state has emerged as the culmination of a process of self-protection means that power which is vested in the state should be kept to the minimum required for that purpose. The extent of that minimum power is simply that which is necessary in order to provide both machinery for identifying rights and protective force for protecting them once they have been identified. (This explains why Nozick's theory leads to what is often called a *night-watchman state*.)

More particularly, and with only one possible exception (see below), it is no part of the state's legitimate activities to become involved in *distributive* justice. Nozick comes to this conclusion by arguing that the ideas of *liberty* and *equality* (which are, of course often linked in popular political slogans) are, in fact, mutually inconsistent to the extent that the provision and maintenance of equality necessarily involves infringements of liberty. More particularly, his argument for the rejection of distributive justice has two elements. First, the whole concept rests on a misapprehension:

> 'We are not in the position of children who have been given portions of a pie by someone who now makes last minute adjustments to rectify careless cutting. There is no central distribution, no person or group *entitled* to control all the resources, jointly deciding how they are to be doled out. What each person gets, he gets from others who give to him in exchange for something, or as a gift. In a free society, diverse persons control different resources, and new holdings arise out of voluntary exchanges and actions.... There is no more a distributing... of shares than there is a distributing of mates in a society in which persons choose whom they shall marry. (Emphasis added. *Op. cit.*, pp. 149–150.)

Secondly, what is commonly described as distributive justice is, when properly analyzed, '*re*distributive' (original emphasis) which, in Nozick's view, 'involves the violation of people's rights'. (*Op. cit.*, p. 168.) Thus, for example, Nozick regards the redistribution of wealth by means of income tax as being tantamount to forced labour exacted by the state from the taxpayer. This argument is based on the proposition that if an individual chooses to work less in order to enjoy more leisure, nobody would seek to argue that any of that leisure time should be expropriated by the state, in order that it may be deployed for the public good. By parity of reasoning, therefore, those who choose to work more, and in consequence enjoy less leisure, should not have their earnings expropriated by way of income tax which will then be used for the purposes of distributive justice. As Nozick puts it:

'Why should the man who prefers seeing a movie (and who has to earn money for a ticket) be open to the required call to aid the needy, while the person who prefers looking at a sunset (and hence need earn no extra money) is not?' (*Op. cit.*, p. 170.)

By way of another example, take successful entertainers who make large sums of money out of very large numbers of individuals paying relatively small sums of money to see them perform. Why should the entirely voluntary transfer of money from audiences to entertainers give the state any entitlement whatsoever to take a percentage by way of taxation (beyond, of course, that percentage which it would take from anyone who earns money in order to help finance the minimal activities which the state may legitimately perform)?

The exceptional case in which Nozick does recognize the legitimacy of redistributing wealth arises where property has been acquired unjustly at some time in the past, even if there is no injustice in the way its present owner has come by it. At this stage, therefore, we need to consider Nozick's argument dealing with *just entitlements*, which breaks down into *justice in acquisition*, *justice in transfer* and *justice in rectification*.

Fairly obviously, *justice in acquisition* and *justice in transfer* include, for example, purchase, receipt of gifts and inheritance, but not theft. On the other hand, *justice in rectification* is more problematic. Clearly there may be a need for rectification where, for example, a purchaser acting in good faith has bought property from a thief. In a simple case such as this, the injustice of the thief's acquisition may be rectified by restoring the property to its former (historically rightful) owner. But Nozick acknowledges that other cases may be more difficult. For example, 'how far back must one go in wiping clean the historical slate of injustices? What may victims of injustice permissibly do in order to rectify the injustices being done to them, including the many injustices done by persons acting through their government?'. (*Op. cit.*, p. 152.)

Many people would accept that survivors of the Nazi concentration camps may legitimately claim compensation, at least for themselves and perhaps also on behalf of their relatives who did not survive. But should the descendants of those survivors (and of those who did not survive) also receive compensation? (After all, if the compensation had been paid during the lifetime of the victims, the descendants might well have inherited it; and the possibility that they might not have done so could be reflected by reducing the amount of compensation, in the same way as damages are commonly reduced to take account of contingencies.)

The greater remoteness in time of the injustice perpetrated during the age of American slavery makes the claims to compensation advanced by some contemporary African-Americans rather more problematic. And would anybody seriously suggest that the modern Scandinavian states should compensate the present inhabitants of the United Kingdom for the raping and pillaging inflicted by the Vikings more than a thousand years ago? While the drawing of lines is frequently unavoidable when dealing with practical problems, it is a peculiarly difficult enterprise in the present context.

It is hardly surprising that Nozick's work is controversial. Perhaps the most obvious point is that by no means everyone would accept that the current distribution of resources is just, thus rejecting Nozick's basic premise. Additionally, Hart makes the following three points. First, any amount of taxation still leaves the individual free to choose whether or not to work, and to choose what work (if any) to do. Can taxation, therefore, really be equated with forced labour? Secondly, 'can one man's... relief from great suffering not outweigh a small loss of income imposed on another to provide it?'. Thirdly, and more positively, 'it is, of course, an ancient insight that for a meaningful life not only the protection of freedom from deliberate restriction but opportunities and resources for its exercise are needed'. (*Between Utility and Rights*, in *Essays in Jurisprudence and Philosophy*, 1983, pp. 206–207.)

Summary

- ▶ Utilitarianism sees the greatest happiness of the greatest number as the proper objective of law. However, this gives rise to difficulties of quantifying pleasure and pain.

- ▶ The economic analysis of law sees the promotion of economic efficiency as being an important part of the proper objective of law.

- ▶ Rawls presents a version of the social contract theory according to which justice is identified in terms of what people would have agreed to accept if they did not know how it would affect themselves.

- ▶ Nozick's theory of justice argues that the state should do as little as possible beyond providing for the security of those who live within it.

Further reading

Bentham, Jeremy, *An Introduction to the Principles of Morals and Legislation* (1780)
Calabresi, Guido, *Property Rules, Liability Rules, and Inalienability: One View of the Cathedral* (1972) 85 Harv LR 1089

Further reading cont'd

Calabresi, Guido, *The Costs of Accidents: A Legal and Economic Analysis*, 1970

Coase, Ronald H., *The Problem of Social Costs* (1960) 3 J L & Econ 1

Davies, Howard and Holdcroft, David, *Jurisprudence: Texts and Commentary*, 1991

Hart, H.L.A., *Between Utility and Rights*, in *Essays in Jurisprudence and Philosophy*, 1983

Kelly, J.M., *A Short History of Western Legal Theory*, 1992

Nozick, Robert, *Anarchy, State and Utopia*, 1974

Rawls, John, *Justice as Fairness: A Restatement*, 2001, Kelly, E, (ed.)

Rawls, John, *Political Liberalism*, 1993

Rawls, John, *Theory of Justice*, 1971

Ross, Alf, *On Law and Justice*, 1958

Smart, J.J.C. and Williams, B. (eds), *Utilitarianism: For and Against*, 1973

Chapter 11

Law and morality

11.1 Introduction

Having considered the relevance of morality to the distinction between natural law and positivist theories, it is now appropriate to come down to the more immediate and specific question of the extent (if any) to which the law may properly seek to enforce individual morality. Admittedly, the central question discussed in this chapter is sometimes expressed rather differently, in terms of the legal enforcement of *private* morality, but this formulation is best avoided, at least as a starting point, because it assumes that there is such a thing as private morality; and, as this chapter will demonstrate, in some situations at least, the validity of this assumption may well be at the heart of the debate.

Many of the issues discussed in this chapter are essentially concerned with the acceptability (or otherwise) of liberalism and its insistence on the intrinsic and fundamental worth of individual freedom. There are, of course, many variations within the general area of liberalism, and nothing more than a broad-brush approach can be attempted here. However, it is worth recalling that we have already considered two variations, in the form of the theories of Dworkin and Rawls (see, respectively, pp. 113 and 171). We have also noted that Nozick's position may be characterized as being essentially liberal despite its apparently right-wing nature (see p. 177).

Of course, all governments must govern, which is simply another way of saying that the essential function of government is to seek to control the conduct of those who are being governed; and it is obvious that this control must inevitably restrict individual freedom. From the liberal standpoint, therefore, while the fact of interference with individual freedom must be accepted as necessary, each specific instance of interference will nevertheless require specific justification. It follows that the arguments for and against liberalism will turn on assessing the extent (if any) to which such interference can be justified.

The rest of this chapter discusses a variety of arguments in a variety of contexts. Before turning to this material, however, it may be worth dealing with one general objection which some opponents of liberalism sometimes raise, namely that the whole liberal enterprise is based on a fundamentally self-contradictory proposition and is therefore irremediably flawed.

The substance of this objection is that liberalism, while proclaiming the importance of freedom of choice, nevertheless asserts that it, and it alone, is right. According to this objection, therefore, liberalism is based on the self-contradictory proposition that freedom is compulsory.

Those whose instincts are authoritarian may find this objection compelling. On the other hand, those whose instincts are located towards the liberal end of the spectrum may prefer the argument that liberalism does not seek to prevent individuals from voluntarily submitting to the authority of others, because such submission is the exercise of, rather than being inconsistent with, the freedom which liberalism values so highly. But, in the absence of any convincing argument to the contrary, liberalism does reject the imposition of authority on those who do not voluntarily accept it. The arguments to the contrary which are most commonly accepted as being convincing are the protection of the legitimate interests of other people and, perhaps, paternalism. However, the balancing of individuals' rights against those of other individuals and of the community at large, is an intrinsic element of government in a liberal democracy; and it can be argued that paternalism may be seen as being only a limitation on, rather than the rejection of, liberalism. On this basis it is, therefore, possible to reject the contention that liberalism is intrinsically self-contradictory.

No attempt to resolve this disagreement will be made here. Indeed, those who are sympathetic to the views of Barney Reynolds and Oliver Wendell Holmes (see pp. 225–226), may conclude that any such attempt would be futile, on the basis that the disagreement is of the type which is beyond argument anyway.

Returning more specifically to the context of legal theory, the enforcement of individual morality is usually discussed in relation to criminal law. The question may, however, arise equally in a civil context. For example, in the well-known case of *Pearce v Brookes* (1866) LR 1 Exch 213, a prostitute had entered into a contract of hire purchase in respect of an ornamental carriage for use while plying her trade. Declining to enforce the contract against her, Pollock CB said that the plaintiff had no cause of action because the carriage had been 'furnished to the defendant for the purposes of enabling her to make a display favourable to her immoral purposes'.

Although the fundamental issue is ageless, two particularly famous contributions to the debate were made in the second half of the 19th century, by John Stuart Mill and Sir James Fitzjames Stephen. The debate became particularly topical again a century or so later with the publication, in 1957, of the *Wolfenden Report* on homosexuality and prostitution. The views of Mill and Stephen will form the starting point of this chapter, which will then proceed through *Wolfenden* to some further contributions to the debate, before considering the ways in which English law reflects the various theoretical standpoints when dealing with conduct which is, at least arguably, immoral. It will conclude with perhaps the most basic of all moral problems, namely those arising from abortion and euthanasia.

11.2 The debate in the 19th century

11.2.1 John Stuart Mill (1806–73)

In his *Essay on Liberty*, published in 1859, John Stuart Mill states the classic liberal view of the relationship between law and morality. This statement is in terms of what is generally known as the *harm principle* or the *harm condition*, which he formulates thus:

> 'The only purpose for which power can be rightfully exercised over any member of a civilized community, against his will, is to prevent harm to others. His own good, either physical or moral, is not a sufficient warrant. He cannot rightfully be compelled to do or forebear because it will be better for him to do so, because it will make him happier, because in the opinion of others, to do so would be wise, or even right.'

Pausing only to emphasize that Mill's view is extensive enough to preclude the law from intervening even on a paternalistic basis ('his own good, either physical or moral, is not a sufficient warrant'), we now turn to a classic statement of the opposing position.

11.2.2 Sir James Fitzjames Stephen (1829–94)

In his essay *Liberty, Equality, Fraternity*, published in 1873, James Fitzjames Stephen (who subsequently became Sir James Fitzjames Stephen on his appointment as a High Court judge and who appears to have had a more authoritarian view of morality than his novelist niece Virginia Woolf), challenges Mill. More particularly, he argues that moral and religious obligations operate as real constraints on individual conduct, and that they cannot be convincingly distinguished from legal constraints.

> 'Criminal legislation proper may be regarded as an engine of prohibition unimportant in comparison with morals and the forms of morality sanctioned by theology. For one act from which one person is restrained by the fear of the law of the land, many persons are restrained from innumerable acts by the fear of the disapprobation of their neighbours, which is the moral sanction; or by fear of punishment in a future state of existence, which is the religious sanction; or by the fear of their own disapprobation, which may be called the conscientious sanction, and may be regarded as a compound of the other two. Now in the innumerable majority of cases, disapprobation, or the moral sanction, has nothing whatever to do with self-protection. The religious sanction is by its nature independent of it. Whatever special forms it may assume, the fundamental condition of it is a being intolerant of evil in the highest degree and inexorably determined to punish it wherever it exists, except upon certain terms. I do not say that this doctrine is true, but I do say that no-one is entitled to assume it without proof to be essentially immoral and mischievous. Mr Mill does not draw this inference, but I think his theory involves it, for I know not what can be a greater infringement of his theory of liberty, a more complete and formal contradiction to it, than the doctrine that

there are a court and a judge in which, and before whom, every man must give an account of every work done in the body, whether self-regarding or not. According to Mr Mill's theory, it ought to be a good plea in the day of judgment to say "I pleased myself and hurt nobody else". Whether or not there will ever be a day of judgment is not the question, but upon his principles a day of judgment is fundamentally immoral. A God who punished anyone at all, except for the purpose of protecting others, would, upon his principles, be a tyrant trampling on liberty...'

'Why draw so strongly marked a line between social and legal penalties? Mr Mill asserts the existence of the distinction.... Yet from one end of his essay to the other I find no proof and no attempt to give the proper and appropriate proof of it. His doctrine could have been proved if it had been true. It was not proved because it was not true.'

11.3 The *Wolfenden Report*

In 1957 the Committee on Homosexual Offences and Prostitution, under the chairmanship of Sir John Wolfenden, published its report (Cmd 247), bringing the issue of the legal regulation of morality once more to the forefront of public attention. By way of an anecdotal aside, while the Report was awaiting implementation, Sir John's homosexual son, Jeremy, was working in Moscow as both a foreign correspondent and part of the British Intelligence Service. On one occasion, the KGB arranged for Jeremy to be placed in an undeniably compromising homosexual situation, so that some of its agents could burst upon the scene and take photographs with a view to blackmail. In fact, when the blackmail reached the stage of confronting Jeremy with the photographs, he was so pleased with them that he asked if he could have a set of enlargements. When Jeremy reported the incident to the staff of the British Embassy, they were equally unperturbed, merely advising him to co-operate with the KGB, but to keep MI5 informed when he was next on leave in London. (See Sebastian Faulks, *The Fatal Englishman*, 1997, pp. 283–284.)

According to para. 13 of the *Wolfenden Report*,

'[the function of the criminal law] is to preserve public order and decency, to protect the citizen from what is offensive or injurious and to provide sufficient safeguards against exploitation or corruption of others, particularly those who are specially vulnerable because they are young, weak in body or mind, or inexperienced.'

Paragraph 61 of the *Report* sums up the committee's fundamental philosophy in the following terms:

'Unless... the sphere of crime [can be equated] with that of sin, there must remain a realm of private morality and immorality which is, in brief and crude terms, not the law's business.'

The *Report* contained two main conclusions. First, and unanimously, prostitution itself should be legal (as indeed it already was) because it harms nobody other than, possibly, the parties to the transaction. However, soliciting in the street for the purposes of prostitution should be an offence, because people who are going about their daily business find it offensive. Additionally, there should remain a whole raft of offences related to prostitution, such as brothel-keeping, living on immoral earnings, procuring, and so on. Secondly, but this time by a majority of 12 to 1, homosexual conduct between consenting male adults in private should not be an offence. (The restriction to males arises from the fact that lesbian conduct had never been an offence anyway.)

The *Wolfenden Report* generated widespread public discussion, as well as a specific exchange of views which is often known as the *Hart–Devlin* debate.

11.4 The *Hart–Devlin* debate

11.4.1 Introduction

In the immediate aftermath of the publication of the *Wolfenden Report*, Sir Patrick Devlin, who was then a High Court judge (and who subsequently became a Law Lord with the very unusual distinction of not being appointed to the Court of Appeal first) gave the British Academy's second Maccabean Lecture in Jurisprudence. (The lecture, which was given in 1959, was first published as *The Enforcement of Morals* in the *Proceedings of the British Academy*, vol. xlv. However, it is more generally accessible under the title of *Morals and the Criminal Law*, as the first essay in a collection to which that essay's original title of *The Enforcement of Morals* was given. The collection was published in 1965.) By way of reply, H.L.A. Hart, whose *Concept of Law* we considered in Chapter 4, delivered a set of lectures at Stanford University in 1962. They were published the following year as *Law, Liberty and Morality*.

We shall consider the contribution of each of the protagonists in turn. However, by way of a preliminary comment, those who believe with Wordsworth that 'the child is father of the man' may find it interesting to note that Devlin was educated by the Jesuits of Stonyhurst. (It is, of course, the Jesuits' proud boast that if they have a child for seven years, they have him for life.) One insight into the deeply conservative nature of Devlin's thought may be derived from a comment that the traditional 'twelve men' of the jury are now 'diluted with women'. (*The Relation Between Commercial Law and Commercial Practice* (1951) 14 MLR 249.)

Hart, on the other hand, although born into a Jewish family who sent him to a boarding school with a separate house for Jewish boys (until declining family fortunes necessitated his withdrawal) 'disliked being... labelled... [and]... was not attracted by the Jewish or other religions, and was very hostile to the enforcement of rules based on religious beliefs'. (Tony Honoré, *Herbert Lionel Adolphus Hart, 1907–92: In Memoriam* (1993) 84 Proceedings of the British Academy 295.)

Perhaps even more significantly, at least in the context of Hart's reaction to the *Wolfenden Report*, is the fact that his emotional make-up contained a substantial element of bisexuality. (See his correspondence to this effect – principally addressed to his future wife – cited by Nicola Lacey in *A Life of H.L.A. Hart*, 2004, Chapter 4.) Although Lacey accepts that 'it is doubtful whether [he] ever acted, physically, on [his homosexual] feelings', she does record that, while in New York in 1957, Hart visited a Greenwich Village restaurant, which he described, in the vernacular usage of that period, as 'pansy'. She then ventures the comment that this was 'an experience which opened up a vista of how his own life might have been had he grown up in a similarly tolerant, diverse environment'. (*Op. cit.*, p. 194.) (The year of this event was, of course, the year the *Wolfenden Report* itself was published.)

11.4.2 Devlin's *Enforcement of Morals*

Devlin asks three questions. First, is society entitled to pass judgment on all moral matters, or can some matters be properly reserved into the private sphere? Secondly, if society is entitled to pass judgment, is it also entitled to use the law as a means of enforcement? Thirdly, if the second question receives an affirmative answer, is society entitled to use the law in all cases, or only in some; and if only in some, how is the dividing line to be drawn? He answers these questions as follows.

First

'The structure of every society is made up of politics and morals ... [and, more particularly] ... society is not something that is kept together physically; it is held by the invisible bonds of common thought.... The bondage is part of the price of society; and mankind, which needs society, must pay its price.' (*Op. cit.*, pp. 9–10.)

Secondly, he likens immoral conduct to treason, on the basis that both threaten the continued existence of society:

'The suppression of vice is as much the law's business as the suppression of subversive activities; it is no more possible to define a sphere of private morality than it is to define a sphere of private subversive activity.' (*Op. cit.*, pp. 13–14.)

With regard to the third question, the problem is to balance public and private interests. No absolute rule can be formulated as to how this should be done, but the general principle is that

'there must be toleration of the maximum individual freedom that is consistent with the integrity of society.' (*Op. cit.*, p. 16.)

Devlin accepts that the limits of tolerance will shift from time to time, but insists that 'tolerance' is not the same thing as 'approval' (*op. cit.*, p. 18), the point apparently being that it is only appropriate to speak of tolerating things which are considered to be wrong.

'[Tolerance should cease where there is] a deliberate judgment that the practice is injurious to society.' (*Op. cit.*, p. 17.)

Crucially, individuals who do not accept the rightness of the common morality must nevertheless accept the need for that morality. Returning to his analogy between subversion and immorality, Devlin says:

'A rebel may be rational in thinking that he is right but he is irrational if he thinks that society can leave him free to rebel.' (*Op. cit.*, p. 25.)

Ultimately, the legitimacy of the law's intervention in matters of individual morality depends on the 'intolerance, indignation and disgust' of ordinary people (*op. cit.*, p. 17), and Devlin is totally confident that ordinary people are capable of differentiating between disapproving of something and being disgusted by it.

Finally, it is interesting to note that, when writing his lectures, Devlin was wholly unaware of Stephen's contribution to the debate in the previous century. (*Op. cit.*, p. *vii*.) While some people may see this as a rather alarming mark of his limited awareness of intellectual history, perhaps it is not surprising that Devlin himself sees it differently.

'The fact that we reached our conclusions independently gives additional force to Professor Hart's comment (which, however it may have been intended, I regard as complimentary) that they reveal "the outlook characteristic of the English judiciary".' (*Ibid.* Footnote omitted.)

Flattered though he may have been, however, the conclusion to the Preface to *The Enforcement of Morals* shows Devlin's awareness of his own limitations.

'The best justification for printing this collection of lectures is the possibility that it may stimulate the professionals to undertake not merely the demolition of amateur work but the construction of something better.' (*Op. cit.*, p. x.)

We must now turn to Hart's explicitly liberal reply to this challenge.

11.4.3 Hart's reply – *Law, Liberty and Morality*

As a preliminary, it is worth commenting that, at an early stage in his argument against Devlin, Hart identifies the issue as one *of*, and not merely *about*, morality. In other words, empirical evidence of what our society, or any other society for that matter, actually does about the legal regulation of individual morality can provide no answer to the question of what ought to be done.

Turning to the substance of Hart's argument, there are four key points. First, he distinguishes between harm being suffered by one person in the form of being offended by witnessing other people's conduct, and harm suffered by one person in the form of being offended by merely knowing what other people do. The first of these, being a matter of public decency, is within the law's proper scope, and therefore the law may legitimately prohibit the conduct which offends others. The latter, being purely private, is outwith the law's proper scope:

> 'Recognition of individual liberty as a value involves, as a minimum, acceptance of the principle that the individual may do what he wants, even if others are distressed when they discover what it is that he does – unless, of course, there are other good grounds for forbidding it.' (*Op. cit.*, p. 47.)

Secondly, Hart says that Devlin's argument that maintaining moral bonds is essential to preserving society itself, rests on

> 'an undiscussed assumption... that all morality – sexual morality together with the morality that forbids acts injurious to others such as killing, stealing, and dishonesty – forms a single seamless web, so that those who deviate from any part are likely or perhaps bound to deviate from the whole.... But there is no evidence to support, and much to refute, the theory that those who deviate from conventional sexual morality are in other ways hostile to society.' (*Op. cit.*, pp. 50–51.)

In passing, it is worth noticing that even those who do deviate more widely within a repressive regime may be doing so because of the nature of that regime. As Leo Abse said in the House of Commons, when opening the debate on the second reading of the Bill which became the Sexual Offences Act 1967, it is not surprising that those whom the law places 'outside the community... should react... in an antisocial manner'. (Quoted in Louis Blom-Cooper and Gavin Drewry (eds), *Law and Morality*, 1976, p. 109.)

Turning to Hart's third point, he argues that any society's morality will change from time to time, and that it is 'absurd' (*op. cit.*, p. 51) to say, as Devlin does, that this means that one society has ceased to exist and another one has taken its place.

> '[Changing morality may more accurately be compared not with] the violent overthrow of government but to a peaceful constitutional change in its form, consistent not only with the preservation of a society but with its advance.' (*Op. cit.*, p. 52.)

Finally, however, Hart, unlike Mill, does accept that paternalism has a role in the legal regulation of morality, provided it is restricted to activities which cause physical (and not merely moral) harm to individuals. He justifies this on the basis that

> '[We have] an increased awareness of a great range of factors which diminish the significance to be attached to an apparently free choice or to consent. Choices may be made without adequate reflection or appreciation of the consequences; or in pursuit of merely transitory desires; or in various predicaments when the judgment is likely to be clouded; or under inner psychological compulsion; or under pressure by others of a kind too subtle to be susceptible of proof in a law court.' (*Op. cit.*, pp. 32–33.)

The point at which paternalistic intervention may be justified is clearly a matter on which opinions are likely to differ widely, but Hart insists that his limited concession to paternalism does not extend to accepting that the law may legitimately enforce individual morality for its own sake.

11.5 The *Williams Report*

In 1979, the Committee on Obscenity and Film Censorship, under the chairmanship of Professor Bernard Williams, a distinguished philosopher, published its report (Cmd 7772). Endorsing Mill's 'harm condition', the committee took the view that the onus of proof was on those who wished to interfere with personal liberty and on this basis concluded that, in general, the case for control had not been established beyond reasonable doubt. However, by way of an exception to its general conclusion, the committee accepted that those who actually take part in the making of obscene photographic and videographic material may be harmed, and therefore it recommended that

'[the law should prohibit material the production of which appears] to have involved the exploitation for sexual purposes of any person where either
(a) that person appears from the evidence as a whole to have been at the relevant time under the age of 16, or
(b) the material gives reason to believe that actual physical harm was inflicted on that person.'

It follows that purely written or auditory material should not be prohibited, since no one is either exploited or harmed by its production.

Additionally, and again by way of exception to its general conclusion, the committee recommended that there should be legal restrictions on the display of material which would offend a reasonable person. For these purposes, the committee thought that the content of the whole material should be relevant, and not merely that part of it (for example, a magazine's cover) which would be visible to the public. (Legislation partially implementing this recommendation is discussed at pp. 206–207.)

11.6 Dworkin's Argument on *Political Integration*

In an essay entitled *Liberal Community*, Dworkin (whose theory we considered generally in Chapter 7) seeks to show the fallacy of both the distinction between private and public morality generally, and, more particularly, the idea that the law is entitled to be authoritarian in respect of individuals' conduct in matters such as their sexual practices. The essay was originally published in (1989) 77 Calif Law Rev 479, but may be more accessible, albeit in a somewhat shortened form, as Chapter 12 of *Communitarianism and Individualism* (Avineri and de-Shalit (eds), 1992, to which the following page references relate.)

Dworkin accepts as

'right and important [the integrationist proposition that] political communities have a communal life, and the success or failure of a community's communal life is part of what determines whether its members' lives are good or bad.' (*Op. cit.*, p. 207.)

However, he continues:

'The argument succumbs to anthropomorphism; it supposes that a communal life is the life of an outsize person, and that it has the same shape, encounters the same moral and ethical watersheds and dilemmas, and is subject to the same standards of success and failure, as the several lives of the citizens who make it up.' (*Op. cit.*, p. 208.)

In order to avoid falling into this error, it is necessary to consider more closely 'what the phenomenon of integration is supposed to be'. (*Ibid.*) He answers his own question thus:

'The collective life of a political community includes its official political acts: legislation, adjudication, enforcement, and the other executive functions of government. An integrated citizen will count his community's success or failure in these formal political acts as resonating in his own life, as improving or diminishing it. On the liberal view, nothing more should be added. These formal political acts of the community as a whole should be taken to exhaust the communal life of a political body, so that citizens are understood to act together, as a collective, only in that structured way.' (*Op. cit.*, p. 217.)

By way of analogy, Dworkin takes an orchestra, whose function is – obviously enough – to make music. This being so, the private sexual conduct of one or more of its members is no concern of the other members, because it does not impinge on the purpose for which the orchestra exists as a community. Although Dworkin does not say so explicitly, it is implicit in his argument that if other members of the orchestra are disturbed by the sexual conduct of one of their colleagues to the point where they are unable to co-operate in the making of music, the remedy lies in those who are disturbed changing their attitudes on the basis of a proper understanding of the nature of an orchestra, rather than in imposing constraints on the person whose conduct disturbs them.

Returning to Dworkin's point that for liberals the quality of life depends on the nature of the community into which they are integrated, he says:

'[The] fusion of political morality and critical self-interest seems to me to be the true nerve of civic republicanism, the important way in which individual citizens should merge their interests and personalities into political community...

'A community of people who accept integration in this sense will always have one important advantage over communities whose citizens deny integration. An integrated citizen accepts that the value of his own life depends on the success of his community as treating everyone with equal concern.' (*Op. cit.*, p. 219.)

11.7 Some practical applications

11.7.1 Introduction

Having considered some theoretical perspectives, it is now appropriate to see how far, and in what ways, English law reflects the various positions. The analysis in this section of this chapter will begin by considering certain areas where legal intervention is said to be justified on the grounds of either preserving the fabric of society, preserving public decency or paternalism; but it is important to appreciate at the outset that this classification is largely a matter of convenience, and that in reality the categories commonly overlap. The next section will consider what are in some ways the most basic questions of all, namely matters of life and death, including abortion, assisted suicide and euthanasia.

11.7.2 Preserving the fabric of society

Introduction

Devlin's argument that the law may legitimately intervene in individual morality in order to preserve the fabric of society may be illustrated by reference to the offence of conspiracy to corrupt public morals and the law relating to sado-masochism and the problem of consent. Since we shall see, in the context of the latter, that the courts may hold cruelty to be intrinsically evil, the basis of the legal protection of animals may also be said to illustrate this ground of the law's intervention. We will consider these topics in turn.

Conspiracy to corrupt public morals

Two cases fall to be considered in relation to the offence of conspiracy to corrupt public morals, namely *Shaw v DPP* [1961] 2 All ER 446 and *Knuller v DPP* [1972] 2 All ER 898.

In *Shaw v DPP*, the defendant had published a booklet which he called *The Ladies' Directory*. This consisted of advertisements which prostitutes inserted and paid for, giving their names, addresses and telephone numbers, and in some cases the services which were available. On these facts, the House of Lords upheld Shaw's convictions for publishing an obscene article, living off the immoral earnings of prostitution and conspiracy to corrupt public morals. It is the third charge, and more particularly the House of Lords' treatment of it, which is of interest for the present purpose.

Stating the view of the majority of four Law Lords, Lord Simonds said:

'When Lord Mansfield, speaking long after the Star Chamber had been abolished, said that the Court of King's Bench was the *custos morum* [i.e. moral guardian] of the people and had the superintendency of offences *contra bonos mores* [i.e. against good morals], he was asserting, as I now assert that there is in that court a residual power, where no statute has yet intervened to supersede the common law, to superintend those offences which are prejudicial to the public welfare. Such occasions will be rare, for Parliament has not been slow to legislate when attention has been sufficiently aroused. But gaps remain and will always remain, since no one can foresee every way in which the wickedness of man may disrupt the order of society. Let me take a single instance.... Let it be supposed that at some future date, perhaps early, homosexual practices between adult consenting males are no longer a crime. Would it not be an offence if even without obscenity such practices were publicly advocated and encouraged by pamphlet and advertisement? Or must we wait till Parliament finds time to deal with such conduct? I say, my Lords, that if the common law is powerless in such an event then we should no longer do her reverence. But I say that her hand is still powerful and that it is for Her Majesty's judges to play the part which Lord Mansfield pointed out to them.'

Lord Reid, in a minority of one, thought that the offence of conspiracy to corrupt public morals did not exist, but that if it did, it ought to be used only in those cases where there was general agreement as to the conduct which ought to be criminal. He concluded that

'[the majority view had the unacceptable consequence that] "you cannot tell what is criminal except by guessing what view a jury will take, and juries" views may vary and change with the passing of time.'

In passing it may be noted that while Lord Reid's analysis is undoubtedly accurate, both the retroactivity of judicial decisions and the unpredictability of their content in specific cases are deeply ingrained in the English legal tradition generally. (For the retroactivity of judicial decision-making generally, see, for example, *R v R (Rape: Marital Exemption)* [1991] 4 All ER 481, and *Kleinwort Benson Ltd v Lincoln City Council* [1998] 4 All ER 513, while for the unpredictability of judicial outcomes generally, see, for example, *Fitzpatrick v Sterling Housing Association* [1997] 4 All ER 991 and [1999] 4 All ER 701 (HL), noting the divisions of opinion both within and between the Court of Appeal and the House of Lords.)

Knuller v DPP [1972] 2 All ER 898 presented the House of Lords with an opportunity to reconsider *Shaw*, in the light not only of the controversy which that decision had aroused, but also of the *Practice Statement: Judicial Precedent* [1966] 3 All ER 77, which gave the House power 'to depart from a previous decision [of its own] when it appears right to do so'. The facts of the case involved a journal entitled *International Times* which carried advertisements by means of which homosexual men sought to meet new partners. The parallel between this situation and that envisaged by Lord Simonds in *Shaw* is, of course, remarkably close, save that in *Knuller* there was merely facilitation (rather than advocacy and encouragement) of homosexual practices. A seven-member House decided to follow *Shaw*.

Finally, it must be said that even if the decision in *Knuller* is still an accurate statement of the common law, there seems to be a general acceptance that this aspect of the law should not be enforced. As any perusal of a number of quality newspapers (such as *The Independent* and *The Observer*) will show, advertisements intended to bring about homosexual encounters are commonplace; and they clearly no longer provoke the wrath of the prosecuting authorities.

Sado-masochism and the problem of consent

The issue in *R v Brown* [1993] 2 All ER 75 was whether homosexual sado-masochists who inflicted harm on others, with their consent, could properly be convicted of assault occasioning actual (or grievous) bodily harm contrary to s. 47 (or s. 20) of the Offences Against the Person Act 1861.

Answering this question in the affirmative, the majority of the House of Lords (Lords Templeman, Jauncey and Lowry) held that the common law does not recognize the general defence of consent to the infliction of bodily harm, and that it is only in special circumstances, such as lawful sports, and surgery, that consent is effective. Lord Templeman summarized the majority view thus:

'In principle there is a difference between violence which is incidental and violence which is inflicted for the indulgence of cruelty. The violence of sado-masochistic encounters involves the indulgence of cruelty by sadists and the degradation of victims. Such violence is injurious to the participants and unpredictably dangerous. I am not prepared to invent a defence of consent for sado-masochistic encounters which breed and glorify cruelty and result in offences under ss. 47 and 20 of the Act of 1861.'

And even more briefly:

'Society is entitled and bound to protect itself against a cult of violence. Pleasure derived from the infliction of pain is an evil thing. Cruelty is uncivilized.'

On the other hand, Lord Slynn, as part of the dissenting minority, endorsed the written submission of the Director of Public Prosecutions:

'In the end it is a matter of policy. Is/are the state/courts right to adopt a paternalistic attitude as to what is bad or good for subjects, in particular as to deliberate injury?'

Lord Slynn then dealt with the problem of who should make such decisions thus:

'It is a matter of policy in an area where social and moral factors are extremely important and where attitudes can change. In my opinion, it is a matter of policy for the legislature to decide. If society takes the view that this kind of behaviour, even though sought after and done in private, is either so new or so extensive or so undesirable that it should be brought now for the first time within the criminal law, then it is for the legislature to decide. It is not for the courts in the interests of "paternalism"... or in order to protect people from themselves, to introduce into existing statutory crimes relating to offences against the person, concepts which do not properly fit there. If Parliament considers that the behaviour revealed here should be made specifically criminal, then the Offences Against the Person Act 1861 or, perhaps more appropriate, the Sexual Offences Act 1967 [which, as we have seen, de-criminalized homosexual acts between consenting male adults in private] can be amended specifically to define it.'

Whether the homosexual background to *Brown* influenced the House (and if so, to what extent) is unclear. However, the case of *R v Wilson* [1996] 2 Cr App R 241 provides a heterosexual contrast. The facts were that a husband burnt his initials into his wife's buttocks with a hot knife. The branding was not only with her consent but at her instigation. (She had originally wanted a tattoo, but her husband lacked the necessary expertise.) The trial judge, reluctantly held himself to be bound by *R v Brown*, so that 'anyone who injures his partner, spouse, or whatever, in the course of some consensual activity is at risk of having his or her private life dragged before the public to no good purpose'.

In due course, however, even though the issues of harm and consent may seem to make this case indistinguishable from *Brown*, the Court of Appeal held that there had been no offence. The decision rests in part on the proposition that tattooing, which the court was unable to distinguish logically from the branding which actually occurred, would have been lawful; and in part on the proposition that 'consensual activity between husband and wife, in the privacy of the matrimonial home, is not, in our judgment, a proper matter for criminal investigation, let alone criminal prosecution'. At the more general level, the court observed:

'In this field, in our judgment, the law should develop on a case by case basis rather than upon general propositions to which, in the changing times in which we live, exceptions may arise from time to time not expressly covered by authority.'

In passing, it may be observed that the idea that the law should be slow to intervene in marital relationships is also apparent in other areas of the law. For example, in *Wennhak v Morgan* (1888) 20 QBD 635, a statement made by one spouse to another was said not to have been published for the purposes of the law of defamation.

However, whatever the context may be, any manifestation of judicial policy based on marital status is less than even-handed between heterosexuals and homosexuals, since Lord Penzance's definition of marriage, in *Hyde v Hyde* (1866) LR 1 P&D 130, as 'the voluntary union for life of one man and one woman to the exclusion of all others' plainly excludes members of homosexual unions. Neither the Gender Recognition Act 2004 – see p. 126 – nor the Civil Partnership Act 2004, seriously detracts from this comment, since the former relates only to transsexuals and the latter falls short of permitting homosexual marriages as such.

Animals: moral status, interests and rights

Introduction

The idea that cruelty is harmful to the fabric of society is also apparent in certain aspects of the law relating to animals. Furthermore, the final quarter of the last century saw a significant increase in both scholarly and popular interest in questions involving the moral status of animals. Putting these two propositions together suggests that the emerging moral arguments may provide an illuminating framework within which to consider the law; and the discussion which follows will, indeed, adopt this approach.

The seminal work relating to the moral status of animals is Peter Singer's *Animal Liberation: a New Ethics for our Treatment of Animals* (first published in 1975; 2nd edn, 1990, reissued, simply as *Animal Liberation*, with a new Preface in 1995). Pausing only to comment that Singer is a leading consequentialist philosopher (see p. 10 for the nature of consequentialism), the starting point is that, having identified the Black Liberation and Gay Liberation movements as leading modern examples of their type, Singer explains his title by way of the following comment on the nature of liberation movements generally:

> 'A liberation movement is a demand for an end to prejudice and discrimination based on an arbitrary characteristic like race or sex ... A liberation movement demands an expansion of our moral horizons. Practices that were previously regarded as natural and inevitable come to be seen as the result of an unjustifiable prejudice.' (*Op. cit.*, Preface to the first edition, reproduced in the 1995 reissue of the second edition, p. xii.)

Singer is also at pains to distinguish the *animal liberation movement* from groups which are commonly and collectively called the *animal liberation front*. The distinguishing feature between the two is clearly the latter's willingness to use unlawful violence in the pursuit of their cause – a practice which Singer rejects thus:

> 'the strength of the case for Animal Liberation is its ethical commitment; we occupy the high moral ground and to abandon it is to play into the hands of those who oppose us.' (*Op. cit.*, Preface to the 1995 reissue of the second edition, p. xxiv.)

We can now proceed to classify, and then to consider, some ways of thinking about the issue of animal liberation.

Classifying the arguments

Tom Regan, an American academic philosopher and one of the leading proponents of animal rights, suggests a useful classification of the arguments which are commonly encountered when discussing humankind's moral response to animals, namely the *indirect duty* view and the *direct duty* view. (See Chapters 14 and 15 of Carl Cohen and Tom Regan, *The Animal Rights Debate*, 2001.) However, before considering both views, it may be useful to comment on the distinction between *interests* and *rights*. Take, for example, my authorship of this book. Fairly obviously, I have an *interest* in as many copies as possible of this book being sold. In fact, this interest has a number of elements, two of which are that I receive a royalty on every copy that is sold, and, the academic world being what it is, authorship of a widely used textbook would enhance my reputation. However, it is equally obvious that my interest in the sales of this book cannot credibly be said to give me any *right* that people should buy it. In this context, a *right* could arise only where my interest is deemed to be of such significance that it prevails over other people's interests (for example, their power to choose how to spend their own money) and this is clearly not the case in the example under discussion.

Returning to the distinction between the *indirect duty* and *direct duty* views, and taking the *indirect duty* view first, the starting point is that if the animal kingdom is seen as a self-contained entity, it is neither moral nor immoral but simply amoral. In other words, an animal cannot make a decision by reference to a moral framework, and therefore cannot be said to be a *moral agent*. Thus, for example, when an animal predator kills and devours its prey, it is absurd to say either that the predator is exercising its own rights or that it is infringing the rights of its prey. Cohen argues the matter thus:

> 'Animals cannot be the bearers of rights because the concept of right is *essentially human*; it is rooted in the human moral world and has force and applicability only within that world ... To say of a pig or a rabbit that it has rights is to confuse categories, to apply to its world a moral category that can have content only in the human moral world. (Original emphasis. *Op. cit.*, p. 30.)

On the other hand, Cohen does accept that 'denying the reality of animal rights does not entail the denial of our obligations to animals'. (*Op. cit.*, p. 27.) Thus animals may be *moral patients*, in the sense that they may be subject to either moral or immoral conduct on the part of humankind. However, according to the *indirect duty* view, it does not follow from the proposition that humankind may have moral duties which *involve* animals, that those duties are owed *to* animals. More particularly, according to this view, humankind's concern with animal welfare arises only *indirectly*, in the sense of being a consequence of some other, morally relevant, interest which is itself of *direct* concern.

For example, if your cruelty to animals causes me to suffer unnecessary and avoidable distress, your conduct may be said to be morally wrong on the basis of its interference with my interests, without the need to impute any interests to your animal victims. In other words, the ground on which your cruelty is open to moral condemnation is, from the point of view of the animals, *indirect* in the sense that it arises only as a consequence of the effect which your conduct has on my interests.

Secondly, there is the *direct duty* view, which itself divides into two limbs. One limb relies on the argument that animals have *interests* which have *direct* moral relevance for humankind, while the other limb goes one stage further by arguing that animals actually have *rights*.

We will consider each of these views in turn.

The 'indirect duty' view

The traditional approach of English law has been to adopt the *indirect duty* approach, which has enabled the question of animal welfare to be dealt with in a variety of contexts without the need to conclude that the animals concerned have any morally relevant interests or rights.

For nearly a century, the principal statute relating to animal welfare was the Protection of Animals Act 1911 (as subsequently amended on a number of occasions). This statute was, however, replaced by the Animal Welfare Act 2006. Without embarking on a detailed comparison of the old and new legislative schemes, it can be said that they both (albeit with rather more detail in the case of the 2006 Act than in the case of its predecessor), largely reflect the proposition that 'cruelty is uncivilized'. (This phrase is, of course, borrowed from Lord Templeman's speech in *R v Brown* [1993] 2 All ER 75, which concerned sado-masochism and is discussed at pp. 194–195.)

Although many (and perhaps most) people will consider it obvious that a society which considers itself to be civilized will enact laws prohibiting cruelty to animals, the point is nevertheless worth careful consideration, because it indicates that such laws may be seen as protecting an interest which is vested in society itself, rather than necessarily protecting the interests of the animals themselves. Therefore, the duty of avoiding cruelty which is placed on humankind may be classified as being *indirect*. However, the 2006 Act goes further than this by creating, for example, an offence of failing to 'take such steps as are reasonable in all the circumstances to ensure that the needs of an animal for which... [the defendant]... is responsible are met to the extent required by good practice'; and proceeding to indicate that those needs include matters such as the animal's 'need to be able to exhibit normal behaviour patterns'. (See s. 9.) Since restrictions which prevent an animal from exhibiting its normal behaviour pattern may well fall short of cruelty as commonly conceived, it can be said that the Act is recognizing the *direct* view of animal interests (and, possibly, rights).

On 1 March 2012, the Minister of State for Agriculture and Food made a written statement in the House of Commons, saying that the government planned to introduce primary legislation to ban the use of performing animals in travelling circuses. He said the government was acting on ethical grounds and that the government intended to use powers that it already possessed under the 2006 Act to introduce a new, strict scheme of licensing in order to protect animal welfare during the period before the planned legislation could be passed.

The law relating to charities provides a further illustration of the *indirect* view. In *Re Moss* [1949] 1 All ER 495, a testator left money to a woman who had cared for stray cats over a period of many years. The gift was stated to be 'for her to use at her discretion for her work for the welfare of cats and kittens needing care and protection'. Holding the gift to be charitable, the judge said that

'care and consideration for animals which through old age or sickness or otherwise are unable to care for themselves are manifestations of the finer side of human nature, and gifts in furtherance of these objects are calculated to develop that side and are, therefore, calculated to benefit mankind.'

In passing, it is worth mentioning that a superficial reading of the Charities Act 2006 may suggest that this view has acquired statutory backing. However, a more careful reading of the Act shows that the relevant charitable purpose has two independent elements, namely advancing animal welfare *and* serving the public interest, rather than seeing one as a consequence of the other (see s. 2(1) (a) and (b) and (2)(k)).

Another illustration of the law's adoption of the *indirect duty* view may be found in one aspect of the decision in *R v Somerset County Council ex parte Fewings and Others* [1995] 1 All ER 513. The local authority was under a statutory duty to use certain land in ways relating to the 'benefit, improvement or development' of the local authority's area as a whole. The issue for the court was whether the local authority could lawfully ban stag hunting with hounds on the land. Although the Court of Appeal held that, in all the circumstances of the case, the ban was unlawful, the court did accept that preventing cruelty to animals falls within the concept of public benefit, and that the local authority had been entitled to have regard to that factor. In the words of Simon Brown LJ:

'The concepts of benefit to the area, and public interest and good, invite consideration first of the council's human community, rather than its wildlife. But the two considerations are not discrete: human well-being for many will depend upon their satisfaction as to animal welfare.'

On the other hand, the law may conclude that society's interest in the morally elevating consequences of being kind to animals must be weighed in the balance against society's other interests. In *National Anti-Vivisection Society v Inland Revenue Commissioners* [1948] AC 31, the House of Lords refused to hold that the National Anti-Vivisection Society was a charity because, *inter alia*, the argument that the protection of animals elevates the moral character of humankind is not decisive where the consequence, in terms of restricting medical research, would have results which Lord Simonds characterized as 'injurious ... to the whole human and animal creation'.

We will return to a closer consideration of the consequentialist view of things which lies at the heart of this judgment when we consider the first limb of the *direct duty* view (see below). However, before doing so, it is worth noticing that the licensing scheme which controls experimentation on live animals under the Animals (Scientific Procedures) Act 1986, is also consequentialist in nature. Briefly, the grant of a licence under this scheme will depend on two requirements being satisfied. First, the likely benefits of the research must have been assessed against the likely suffering of the animals involved. Secondly, there must be no alternatives which would either replace the use of animals entirely; reduce the number of animals involved; or refine the experiment in order to keep the animals' suffering to a minimum. The first requirement is clearly an example of the utilitarian felicific calculus (see p. 165), while the second requirement (known for obvious reasons as the 3Rs) is equally clearly intended to reduce the amount of animal suffering, so that the assessment contained in the first requirement is more likely to be resolved in favour of humankind. (For a useful overview of the use of animals in scientific experiments, see Richard D. Ryder, *Speciesism in the Laboratory*, in *In Defense of Animals: the Second Wave*, 2006, Peter Singer (ed.).)

The 'direct duty' view: the first limb

You will recall (from p. 197) that the first limb of the *direct duty* view is based on the argument that animals have *interests* (but not *rights*) which have *directly* relevant moral consequences for human behaviour. This limb is best approached by considering Singer's argument, which begins with the proposition that the fundamental ethical *principle of equality*, in whatever context it may be applied, involves *equal consideration of interests*. (See, particularly, *Practical Ethics*, 2nd edn, 1993, Chapter 2.) Thus, for example, modern Western societies, based on the principles of liberal democracy, do not ascribe greater value to the interests of one sex rather than the other, nor to those of one racial group rather than another. In other words, theoretically at least, such societies are neither sexist nor racist; and those individuals who do in fact discriminate on grounds of sex and race are characterized as acting in ways which are morally wrong. Of course, ideas and perceptions of equality may develop over time. In the Victorian era, discrimination on the grounds of sex and race was commonplace and would seldom be regarded as morally wrong. From the latter part of the 20th century onwards, there has been an increasing awareness of the extent to which longstanding attitudes to the elderly and to the disabled may breach the principle of equality, and are, therefore, morally wrong.

Singer then proceeds to say that, just as sexists and racists act in a way which is morally wrong by breaching the principle of equality, people act in a way which is morally wrong if they breach the principle of equality by prioritizing the interests of their own species over those of other species. Furthermore, he adopts the term *speciesism* (which had been invented by Richard D. Ryder, a prominent worker on behalf of animals, following the linguistic precedents of *sexism* and *racism*), in order to emphasize the extent to which he thinks such conduct is repugnant. However, Cohen objects to this terminology, saying that

'the analogy drawn between "speciesism" and "racism" is insidious... [because]... the emotional overtones injected by the insinuating words interfere with sound moral thinking.' (Cohen and Regan, *The Animal Rights Debate*, 2001, p. 63.)

Indeed, Cohen turns Singer's terminology on its head by saying that

'speciesism, which asserts straightforwardly that all species are not equals, is not a vice but a demand of morality.' (*Op. cit.*, p. 66.)

Returning to Singer in a little more detail, and by way of example, he argues that the interests of humankind in advancing medical research must be weighed against the interests of the animals which are used in medical research laboratories. Conceptually, therefore – and not surprisingly in view of

Singer's utilitarian credentials – the moral decision-making process is seen as an example of the *felicific calculus* (which is discussed at pp. 165–166). In other words, it is necessary to quantify both the pleasure resulting from extending the duration (and/or enhancing the quality) of human lives and the pain suffered by animals in medical research laboratories. This quantification then enables us to weigh the one against the other, and the outcome of this process will, in turn, enable us to decide whether that use of those animals is morally acceptable.

Singer's conclusion that the application of the felicific calculus must, having regard to the amount of animal suffering involved in medical research, result in the issue being clearly resolved in favour of the animals, is not universally shared. In the present context, however, in addition to the standard problems arising from the felicific calculus (see p. 166), specific difficulties arise concerning the mental and emotional lives of animals. For example, while we may regard it as obvious that laboratory rats may feel pain, how are we to know whether they also experience the fear and frustration which human beings would experience if deprived of their freedom and subjected to experimental procedures?

To take another example, is it simply sentimental anthropomorphism to regard the extent to which an animal mother will protect her young from external danger as being an illustration of motherly love? Although such behaviour may be pure instinct, as would seem to be suggested by the fact that an adult animal will not recognize its own offspring once they have grown to adulthood, many people find greater emotional satisfaction in the anthropomorphic alternative. Even if this behaviour is purely instinctive, does this necessarily mean that animals which are unable to act on their instincts (perhaps because their young have been taken from them), do not experience feelings which are the same as (or at least akin to) the sort of emotional trauma which their human counterparts would experience in similar circumstances?

If, as seems likely, the answers to questions such as these will vary from one species to another, do we not need hard, scientific evidence before we can formulate satisfactory answers in relation to specific contexts? For example, we may *assume* that, say, spiders and dogs are materially different from each other for these purposes; but unless we have relevant *evidence* to that effect, are we not distinguishing between species on an arbitrary (rather than a rational) basis; and are we not, therefore, falling prey to a variety of speciesism – albeit not the variety which prioritizes the interests of humankind over those of animals?

Lawyers would see questions such as these in terms of *burden of proof*: in any situation where an assumption must be made one way or another, which side is assumed to be right unless and until the other side proves that it is not? In the present context, do we assume that, say, medical experimentation on animals is morally wrong unless and until it is proved, in respect of a particular species involved in a specific experimental regime, that its members *do not* experience the same sort of suffering as human beings? Or do we assume that using all animals in this way is morally acceptable, unless and until it is proved, in respect of the particular species involved in a specific experimental regime, that its members *do* experience the same sort of suffering as human beings?

Although individuals will often answer these questions very largely as a result of their own intuitions, which they subsequently dress up in rational clothing, both sides will be able to present supporting arguments.

Those who argue for the assumption in favour of animals will point out that the constant repetition of their argument makes it more likely that alternatives to animal research will be adopted wherever possible. Thus even if their arguments fail to stop animal research continuing in the quest for a cure for cancer, they may nevertheless be (and indeed largely have been) effective in persuading the cosmetic industry that, for example, the dermatological effects of new shampoos can be tested without pouring their products into the eyes of rabbits and monkeys. Similarly, those who argue for the assumption in favour of humankind will be able to point to drugs which could not have been developed as quickly as they were developed (and perhaps in some cases could not have been developed at all) without the use of laboratory animals. For those who support this position, the issue is just as clearly resolved as it is for Singer: but in the diametrically opposite direction.

Perhaps the most interesting aspect of the discussion so far is that we have not yet been required to address the question of whether animals have *rights*. Of course, there is nothing very startling in this. As we have seen, the *indirect duty* view does not really address itself to the animals at all, while the first limb of the *direct duty* view proceeds on the basis of the standard utilitarian reliance on *consequences* as the criteria for moral quality, in which context the question of whether animals have *rights* simply does not arise.

We must, therefore, now turn to the second limb of the *direct duty* view, which is unquestionably based on the argument that (at least some) animals do have moral status, which gives them moral rights.

The 'direct duty' view: the second limb

Before looking more closely at the question of animal rights, it will be useful to deal with one commonly encountered argument to the effect that animals quite clearly cannot have responsibilities and therefore it follows that they cannot have rights. The untenable nature of this argument becomes apparent as soon as we apply it, by analogy, to very young children and to any adult who is mentally incompetent. Would anyone seriously suggest that an individual within either of these categories has no rights, merely because they are unable to discharge any responsibilities?

Turning now to the question of animal rights, Regan, who accepts that 'few [moral issues] are more controversial than the one which asks whether animals have rights' (*op. cit.*, p. 207), presents an argument which may be summarized as follows.

We all 'bring to our life the mystery of consciousness', which makes each of us 'a subject-of-a-life', to use the phrase which Regan coins specifically to underpin his conception of morality. (*Op. cit.*, p. 201.) Each subject-of-a-life will have 'an experiential welfare' (*op. cit.*, p. 202), by which Regan means experiences of varying kinds, which will bring with them varying benefits and detriments. Furthermore, while recognizing that our relationships with other people may have a major impact on the quality of our own lives, Regan argues that an individual's experiential welfare is 'logically independent of whether that individual is valued by others' and concludes that 'the subject-of-a-life criterion' is 'a basis for determining who has inherent value'. (*Op. cit.*, pp. 201–202.)

From this starting point it is only a short step to the conclusion that animals which have consciousness and experiential welfare are subjects-of-a-life; and therefore that they have inherent value. The final stage of Regan's argument is that 'all those who, as subjects-of-a-life, have an experiential welfare – possess inherent value – thus are owed the direct duty to be treated with respect, thus have a right to such duty'. (*Op. cit.*, p. 202.)

Of course, it is logically fallacious to argue that if A owes a duty to B, it follows automatically that B has a right to the performance of that duty. Many moral codes, both religious and secular, would say that we have a duty to help the needy, but few, if any, would suggest that the needy have any right to that support. (If I choose not to give money to a beggar in the street, or to give to one beggar and not to another, can it credibly be argued that I am *infringing the rights* of those to whom I do not give?)

Regan meets this point by conceding that his conclusion as to the existence of animal rights is not universally true. More particularly, he accepts that different species possess different experiential capacities; and, therefore, that some primitive forms of animal life do not have rights, even if he cannot say with certainty which forms of life those are. To the objection that his core argument is invalidated by his inability to identify a dividing line below which animals have no rights, Regan responds that 'we do not need to know everything before we can know something'. (*Op. cit.*, p. 215.)

Furthermore, having asked himself whether his argument can be said to 'constitute a strict proof of animal rights', Regan replies that

> '"strict proofs" are not possible in these quarters [but my argument does] explain how the ascription of rights to animals is supported by a way of thinking that is principled, non-arbitrary, non-prejudicial and rationally defensible … [with the result being] to shift the burden of proof to those who favour some other view [so that it is now for those] who disagree with the conclusions I reach to explain where and why my argument goes wrong.' (*Op. cit.*, p. 212.)

11.7.3 Preserving public decency

Introduction

The argument that the law may legitimately intervene in individual morality in order to preserve public decency may be illustrated by the law relating to soliciting for the purposes of prostitution, homosexual conduct in public places, and indecent displays of articles such as magazines. We will consider each in turn.

Soliciting for the purposes of prostitution

The type of conduct which does and does not constitute the offence of soliciting in the street for the purposes of prostitution, which was created following the *Wolfenden Report* (see p. 185), may be illustrated by the following three decisions of the High Court.

First, in *Smith v Hughes* [1960] 1 WLR 830, several prostitutes who were either behind the windows, or on the balconies, of buildings overlooking the street, were attracting the attention of men who were in the street. In the words of the case stated relating to one of the prostitutes:

'The defendant's method of soliciting the men was (i) to attract their attention to her by tapping on the window pane with some metal object as they passed in the street in front of her and (ii) having so attracted their attention, to invite them in for a price which she indicated by extending three fingers of her hand and indicating the correct door of the premises. On one occasion the price so indicated was agreed and the man entered the premises, leaving some 15 minutes later. On another occasion, the price so indicated by the defendant was not agreed by the man concerned who, in his turn, made a counter-proposal as to price by extending two fingers of his hand. That counter-proposal was not accepted by the defendant and that man walked away.'

Leaving aside the question of whether the action of extending two fingers was genuinely intended to convey a counter-offer rather than some other message, the issue for the High Court was whether the facts disclosed a contravention of s. 1 of the Street Offences Act 1959. The precise wording of the section is that it is an offence for a prostitute 'to solicit in a street... for the purpose of prostitution'. This can, of course, be read in two ways. If the section is interpreted strictly, in favour of the defendant, a prostitute cannot commit the offence unless she is in a street. On the other hand, the section could simply mean that it is an offence to solicit men who are in the street. The High Court upheld the second interpretation, with Lord Parker CJ saying:

'Everybody knows that this was an Act intended to clean up the streets, to enable people to walk along the streets without being molested or solicited by common prostitutes.... For my part, I am content to base my decision on that ground and that ground alone.'

On the other hand, in *Weisz v Monahan* [1962] 1 WLR 262, Lord Parker CJ, in the High Court, held that a mere written advertisement, displayed on a board outside a newsagent's shop and indicating a prostitute's availability, did not constitute an offence under s. 1(1) of the 1959 Act because

'soliciting in that connection involves the physical presence of the prostitute and conduct on her part amounting to an importuning of prospective customers.'

On the basis of *Weisz v Monahan*, in *Behrendt v Burridge* [1976] 3 All ER 285, a magistrates' court acquitted a prostitute who had been sitting motionless, scantily clad and bathed in red light, in the window of premises in Southampton's red-light district. However, the High Court allowed an appeal by the prosecution, with Boreham J saying:

> 'It is clear in my judgment that she was soliciting in the sense of tempting or luring prospective customers to come in for the purpose of prostitution and projecting her solicitation to passers-by.'

The key factor in such cases appears, therefore, to be whether the prostitute is visible from the street, which is, of course, consistent with the legislative purpose of preserving public decency.

Finally, it is worth noticing that Parliament has subsequently intervened, if only on a limited basis, in the matter of advertising by prostitutes. More particularly, s. 46(1) of the Criminal Justice and Police Act 2001 creates the offence of placing an advertisement relating to prostitution on, or in the immediate vicinity of, a public telephone, provided there is an intention that the advertisement should come to people's attention. (It is difficult to imagine why any advertisement for anything should be displayed without such an intention.) Since such advertisements are commonly expressed in a form of coded language (albeit a code which no man or woman of the world should have any difficulty in deciphering), subs. (3) enacts a presumption that an advertisement is an advertisement relating to prostitution if a reasonable person would consider it to be such.

Homosexual conduct

Following the view of the *Wolfenden Report* (see p. 185) that the law on homosexuality should be relaxed, the Sexual Offences Act 1967 decriminalized homosexual conduct between consenting male adults in private (with the age of consent being reduced to 18 by the Criminal Justice and Public Order Act 1994, and a further reduction to 16 being effected by the Sexual Offences (Amendment) Act 2000 (see p. 126). Liberal though the 1967 Act was as to the result, it is worth noticing in passing that its promoter, the Labour Member of Parliament Leo Abse, clearly regarded homosexuals as being deficient. Thus, in his speech opening the second reading debate on the Bill which became the 1967 Act, he spoke of the removal of criminal sanctions as easing the 'terrible fate' of being homosexual, and of the need to 'reduce the number of faulty males in the community'. (This speech is quoted at length by Blom-Cooper and Drewry (eds), *op. cit.*, pp. 107–111.)

The 1967 Act deals only with conduct in private, and it is still possible to use public order legislation to punish public displays of male homosexual affection, on the grounds that they may be insulting to those who witness them. For example, in *Masterson and Another v Holden* [1986] 3 All ER 39 two men were kissing, cuddling and fondling each other while standing at a bus stop in London's Oxford Street at 1.55 a.m. Although they appeared to be unaware that there was anyone else in the vicinity, they were in fact seen by two couples of mixed sex, all aged in the region of 20 to 21. Initially, the young men appeared not to notice the homosexual conduct, but their female companions drew their attention to it, as a result of which one of the young men approached the homosexuals and said, 'You filthy sods. How dare you, in front of our girls?'. The police then arrived.

In due course, the magistrates' court convicted the homosexuals of 'insulting behaviour... whereby a breach of the peace may be occasioned', contrary to s. 54(13) of the Metropolitan Police Act 1839. The crucial issue was whether their conduct was 'insulting'. The High Court dismissed their appeals on the basis that it was open to the magistrates to conclude that passers-by, especially if young and female, would be insulted at the implicit suggestion that they would find overt homosexual behaviour in public to be acceptable. (The general proposition that the meaning of an ordinary word of the English language is a question of fact for the tribunal of fact, and the more specific proposition that ordinary people know an insult when they see it, are both clearly established by the decision of the House of Lords in *Brutus v Cozens* [1972] 2 All ER 1297.)

It is, of course, open to question whether, in the climate of public opinion prevailing more than 25 years after the decision in *Masterson v Holden*, a court would still consider public displays of homosexual affection to be 'insulting' where they are of a kind which would be considered to be, at worst, in bad taste if they were heterosexual in nature; but the law continues to allow the possibility to exist.

Finally, it may be worth mentioning the offence, created by s. 71 of the Sexual Offences Act 2003, of engaging in sexual activity in a public lavatory. While there is nothing in the statute limiting this offence to homosexual activity, the sexually segregated nature of public lavatories suggests that this is the context in which it is most likely to be committed.

Indecent displays

The *Williams Report* (see p. 190) as a whole was not implemented, but a Private Member's Bill, which gained government support, did take up the recommendation relating to the display of material, as a result of which Parliament passed the Indecent Displays (Control) Act 1981. The gist of the Act is that it is an offence to display 'any indecent matter', other than 'the actual human body' in any place which is visible from a place to which the public has, or is permitted to have, access, whether on payment or otherwise. There are exemptions for art galleries, museums and plays within the meaning of s. 18 of the Theatres Act 1968. Additionally, there is no offence if payment is made specifically for the viewing of the material in question, or if it is visible only in a shop or part of shop to which access cannot be gained without passing a warning notice in a form prescribed by the Act. Although based on the *Williams Report*, the 1981 Act relates only to the material which is publicly visible (for example, a magazine's cover) and not to the whole of the material.

The Act does not define the key word 'indecent', which accordingly has its ordinary meaning. In each case, of course, this will be a question of fact for the tribunal of fact (see *Brutus v Cozens* [1972] 2 All ER 1297), but a useful starting point may be the *Oxford English Dictionary* (2nd edn, 1991), which gives the principal meaning of indecent as 'unbecoming; highly unsuitable or inappropriate; contrary to the fitness of things; in extremely bad taste; unseemly' with a second, albeit obsolete meaning of 'uncomely; inelegant in form' and a third, extant, meaning of 'offending against the recognized standards of propriety and delicacy; highly indelicate; immodest; suggesting or tending to obscenity'. When these definitions are considered in the light of the principle in *Brutus v Cozens* (above), it is clear that the Act leaves a significant discretion in the hands of the court in each case. Although this may be useful in allowing different standards to be applied in different localities, it does increase the difficulty of predicting judicial outcomes.

Finally, it is worth noticing that the Act does not refer to *premises*, and therefore it will be an offence, for example, to wear a T-shirt with an indecent photograph or legend printed on it. This is particularly problematic, since such items are commonly intended to be primarily amusing rather than indecent. For example, it is an open question whether, by parity of reasoning with *Masterson v Holden* [1986] 3 All ER 39, discussed at pp. 205–206) a court could legitimately convict someone of an offence under the 1981 Act for wearing a T-shirt carrying the legend:

> Sticks and stones
> May break my bones;
> But leather and chains
> Excite me.

Finally, it is worth recalling in the present context the provisions of s. 46 of the Criminal Justice and Police Act 2001 (see p. 205), since prostitutes' advertisements commonly include pictures which might be considered to be 'indecent'.

Decency as a constraint on broadcasters

At this point it may be permissible to consider the case of *R (Pro-Life Alliance) v British Broadcasting Corporation* [2002] 2 All ER 756, although it has to be conceded that the facts (arising as they did from the public broadcasting of material which is then received privately) do not fit altogether squarely within the heading of preserving *public* decency.

The issue was whether an obligation to refrain from broadcasting material which offended against good taste and decency (contained in statute in the case of the independent broadcasters and in an agreement with the Secretary of State for National Heritage in the case of the BBC) justified the censoring of a Party Election Broadcast. More particularly, the broadcast would have contained explicit video material showing, among other things and in the words of Laws LJ, 'the products of a suction abortion: tiny limbs, bloodied and dismembered, a separated head, their human shape and form plainly recognizable'.

Taking the view that the case was (again in the words of Laws LJ) 'concerned with bedrock principles... with the protection of free expression in the context of political debate' and that 'the courts owe a special responsibility to the public as the constitutional guardian of the freedom of political debate... [which]... is most acute at the time and in the context of a general election', the Court of Appeal held that the broadcast should have been permitted.

In due course, however, the House of Lords, by a majority of four to one, reversed this decision. (See *R (Pro-Life Alliance) v British Broadcasting Corporation* [2003] 3 WLR 705.) Noting that the applicants had not sought a declaration, under s. 4 of the Human Rights Act 1998, to the effect that the relevant statutory provisions were incompatible with their right to freedom of expression under art. 10 of the European Convention on Human Rights, the majority held that the only question which fell to be determined was whether the broadcasters had exercised their discretion lawfully; and then held that there were no grounds for deciding that they had not done so. On the other hand, Lord Scott, in the minority, robustly criticized his colleagues' decision, saying that

> 'it treats ... [the voting public] ...like children who need to be protected from the unpleasant realities of life [and] seriously undervalues their political maturity.'

11.7.4 Paternalism

Introduction

The argument that the law may legitimately intervene in individual morality on a paternalistic basis may be illustrated by reference to the law relating to obscene publications and extreme pornography, and the compulsory wearing of crash helmets by motorcyclists. We will consider each in turn.

Obscene publications and extreme pornography

Introduction

The justification for classifying the law relating to obscene publications as paternalistic lies in the fact that, as we shall shortly see, the law defines *obscenity* in terms of a tendency to deprave and corrupt, even though there can be no doubt that many users of obscene publications enjoy rather than endure whatever effect that material may have upon them.

The law relating to obscenity was originally controlled by the ecclesiastical courts, but from at least the early part of the 18th century the common law courts also became involved by recognizing the offence of obscene libel. (*R v Curl* (1727) 2 Stra 788.) However, the modern law, the bulk of which may be found in the Obscene Publications Acts 1959 and 1964, has developed significantly beyond its original scope. Indeed, it even appears that s. 2(4) of the 1959 Act abolishes the common law offence of obscene libel, although the section is not explicit on the point and even if the substantive offence no longer exists, it is clear from *Shaw v DPP* [1961] 2 All ER 446 (see p. 193) that the offence of *conspiracy* to publish an obscene libel remains.

The meaning of 'obscenity'

The *Oxford English Dictionary* (2nd edn, 1991), having noted that the Latin word *obscenus* meant 'adverse, inauspicious or ill-omened' and having described the etymology of the English word *obscene* as 'doubtful', proceeds to give its principal meaning as 'offensive to the senses, or to taste or refinement; disgusting, repulsive, filthy, foul, abominable, loathsome'. There follows a second meaning of 'offensive to modesty or decency; expressing or suggesting unchaste or lustful ideas; impure, indecent, lewd' and a final meaning, returning to the Latin root, of 'ill-omened, inauspicious'. One citation in support of the second meaning is taken from s. 1(1) of the Obscene Publications Act 1959, which provides:

> 'For the purposes of this Act an article shall be deemed to be obscene if its effect or (where the article comprises two or more distinct items) the effect of any one of its items is, if taken as a whole, such as to tend to deprave and corrupt persons who are likely, having regard to all relevant circumstances, to read, see or hear the matter contained or embodied in it.'

In *R v Calder & Boyars Ltd* [1968] 3 All ER 644, the Court of Appeal interpreted this definition as meaning that the Act required a significant proportion of the people who are likely to be exposed to the material to be at risk of depravity and corruption. However, it is clear from the speech of Lord Cross in *DPP v Whyte* [1972] 3 All ER 12, that, in this context, a *significant proportion* may be much less than half, provided it is not so small as to be negligible.

The meaning of 'tend to deprave and corrupt'

There is no statutory definition of the key concepts of *depravity* and *corruption*, but in practice most prosecutions will be heard by the Crown Court, where it will be for the jurors to decide whether the material in question falls within the statutory wording, by reference to their perceptions of prevailing standards. Where the proceedings are brought before the magistrates' court under s. 3 of the Act for an order of forfeiture in respect of obscene material, it will fall to the magistrates to exercise this function. Whoever decides the question must do so without the help of expert evidence, except in respect of material which is directed at very young children, where expert evidence may be admitted to show the likely effect of the material in question on the juvenile mind. (*DPP v A and BC Chewing Gum Ltd* [1967] 2 All ER 504.) Even more fundamentally than the issue of whether or not the material will tend to deprave and corrupt, however, is the question of the meaning of the material in the first place. The point may be illustrated by an anecdote recounted by John Mortimer QC, in *Murderers and Other Friends* (Penguin edition, 1995, p. 35). The issue for a provincial magistrates' court was whether the law permitted the public display of the title of a record made by a punk rock group called the Sex Pistols. The title was *Never Mind the Bollocks*. Mortimer recalls how he called a clergyman, who was a lexicographer from the local university, who gave evidence that

'the word *bollocks* might well have been used to describe the rigging of an eighteenth-century man-of-war. [The magistrates] nodded wisely, appeared to accept this definition, and the record was inflicted on the public.'

(In fact, the *Oxford English Dictionary*, 2nd edn, 1991, gives a somewhat wider meaning to *bollocks*, namely 'either of two blocks fastened to the top-sail yard for the top-sail ties to reeve through'. However, whatever the nautical niceties might be, the basis of the magistrates' decision in the Sex Pistols case may prompt the observation that the same dictionary gives an alternative meaning of *bollocks* as 'nonsense'.)

Although most cases of alleged obscenity involve material of a sexual nature, the scope of human depravity and corruption is by no means confined to such matters. For example, in *DPP v A and BC Chewing Gum Ltd* (above) the material in question consisted of pictures of non-sexual violence contained in packets of bubble-gum, while *Calder (John) Publications Ltd v Powell* [1965] 1 All ER 159 involved a novel about drug abusers. In the latter case, Lord Parker CJ, in the High Court, said that

'[a book which highlighted] the favourable effects of drug-taking... [raised]... a real danger that those into whose hands the book came might be tempted at any rate to experiment with drugs and get the favourable sensations highlighted by the book.'

The case of *Powell* plainly envisages depravity in terms of subsequent conduct, but it is clear from the decision of the House of Lords in *DPP v Whyte* (above) that an article may be obscene even if its effects are limited to the stimulation of purely private fantasies, unaccompanied by any overt activity of any kind. In other words, *depravity* and *corruption* may be simply a state of mind.

It is important to remember that s. 1(1) of the 1959 Act deals with a tendency to deprave and corrupt *persons who are likely, having regard to all relevant circumstances, to read, see or hear the matter*. In the light of this, it is sometimes argued that since the only people who are likely to come into contact with obscene materials are devotees of that kind of material anyway, it follows that they are already depraved and corrupted, and that therefore the tendency required by the statute cannot be established. Plausible though this argument may seem, it has been rejected by the House of Lords. As Lord Wilberforce said, in *DPP v Whyte* (above):

'The Act is not merely concerned with the once and for all corruption of the wholly innocent, it equally protects the less innocent from further corruption, the addict from feeding or increasing his addiction.'

Offences and defences

There are offences of publishing an obscene article for gain, and having an obscene article for publication for gain, but simple possession is not an offence.

In respect of the offence of having an obscene article for gain, there is a defence which may be summarised as innocent possession.

In respect of an offence of publication for gain, s. 4(1) of the 1959 Act provides that it shall be a defence to prove that:

'publication of the article in question is justified as being for the public good on the ground that it is in the interests of science, literature, art or learning, or of other objects of general concern.'

Section 4(2) provides that:

'the opinion of experts as to the literary, artistic, scientific or other merits of an article may be admitted... either to establish or to negative the said ground.'

The legislative policy underlying the defence of public good seems to be that the harm to individuals who are depraved and corrupted may be outweighed by the wider consideration of the enhanced good of the public as a whole which will arise from living in a more scientifically sophisticated or culturally elevated society. This argument is plainly utilitarian in nature (see pp. 164–167), and therefore it raises the classic utilitarian problem of quantification. More particularly, a court which decides that the article in question has a tendency to deprave and corrupt persons who are likely, having regard to all relevant circumstances, to read, see or hear the matter contained or embodied in it, and that it possesses the necessary merits to bring it within the s. 4(2) defence, must then proceed to quantify both considerations in order to establish on which side the balance comes down.

There is little case law on the defence of public good, but in *DPP v Jordan* [1976] 3 All ER 775 the House of Lords held that expert evidence is not admissible to show that people who are sexually repressed or deviant may benefit from using obscene publications as a means of relieving their sexual frustration, which may otherwise manifest itself in antisocial conduct. The short point is that if the defence were allowed to operate in these circumstances, the effect would be to justify publication *because* of the material's obscenity, whereas the statutory intention is to justify publication *despite* its obscenity.

Extreme pornographic images

Possession of extreme pornographic images is an offence (see s. 63, Criminal Justice and Immigration Act 2008). Section 63 applies to images (irrespective of the means by which they are produced) and to data (stored by any means) which is capable of conversion into images (s. 63(8)). It is worth emphasising that an image does not come within s. 63 unless it is *both* pornographic *and* extreme.

As the change of terminology suggests, *pornographic* under the 2008 Act does not have the same meaning as *obscene* under the 1959 Act. More particularly, an image is *pornographic* 'if it is of such a nature that it must reasonably be assumed to have been produced solely or principally for the purpose of sexual arousal' (s. 63(3)).

An image is *extreme* if it is

'grossly offensive, disgusting or otherwise of an obscene character' [(s. 63(6)(b)) and it portrays] in an explicit and realistic way, any of the following–
'(a) an act which threatens a person's life,
'(b) an act which results, or is likely to result, in serious injury to a person's anus, breasts or genitals,
'(c) an act which involves sexual interference with a human corpse, or
'(d) a person performing an act of intercourse or oral sex with an animal (whether dead or alive),
'and a reasonable person looking at the image would think that any such person or animal was real (s. 63(7)).'

There are defences which may be summarised as dealing with possession which is legitimate or unintentional (s. 65); and situations in which the defendant 'directly participated' in the acts portrayed and those acts 'did not involve the infliction of any non-consensual harm on any person', provided that, if something appears to be a human corpse, it was not in fact so (s. 66).

The offence under s. 63 cannot be committed in relation to a work which has been granted a certificate under the Video Recordings Act 1984 (s. 64).

There is no defence of public good.

These provisions are based on a curious view of public policy since they are basically sex-related, with any violence having to be portrayed in one of a number of sex-related ways. By way of contrast, the ambit of the Obscene Publications Act 1959 includes non-sexual violence and drug abuse (see, respectively, *DPP v A and BC Chewing Gum* [1976] 2 All ER 504 and *Calder (John) Publications Ltd v Powell* [1965] 1 All ER 159, discussed at p. 210). Furthermore, the fact that these provisions are based on paternalism is clear from the fact that the offence is limited to possession (so only the person who views the images can be guilty), rather than extending to one or more of sale, supply and publication.

Crash helmets

The law requiring motorcyclists to wear crash helmets provides another illustration of the law's paternalism, and it was on precisely this basis that Enoch Powell opposed its introduction when the House of Commons debated the Motor Cycle (Wearing of Helmets) Regulations 1973. Having considered a variety of arguments, Powell concluded:

'The last and most beguiling argument... is that if this crime is created there will be fewer road casualties from this cause...

'That argument is the most dangerous because it is the most beguiling. When one bastion after another of individual freedom, of independence, is breached, it does not happen in an unpopular context. It does not happen when the reasons for doing so are unattractive. It does so when sentiment and emotion and the feelings of all of us are engaged...

'The abuse of legislative power by this House is far more serious and far more far-reaching in its effects than the loss of individual lives through foolish decisions...

'We are sent here to make laws and to preserve liberties. If we allow this regulation to stand, we shall have failed in the duties we were sent here to perform.'
(Quoted in Blom-Cooper and Drewry (eds), *op. cit.*, 1976, pp. 30–31.)

The Regulations were supported by 54 votes to 13.

11.8 Matters of life and death

11.8.1 Introduction

While there are many contexts within which the law deals with matters of life and death, this section of this chapter begins by considering various aspects of the right to live and the right to die, including abortion and the problem of *capacity* (or *competence*) (see pp. 219–220) to make relevant decisions for one's self as well as on behalf of people who lack the capacity to make such decisions for themselves. Having also considered the problem of assisted suicide, it concludes by contrasting two theoretical perspectives, before considering the problem of the allocation of scarce resources.

11.8.2 Abortion

Introduction

As a preliminary, it must be conceded that some people will argue that abortion falls squarely within the scope of the right to life and that its natural place within the structure of this chapter is, therefore, within the sub-heading of *choosing between life and death for other people*, under the sub-sub-heading of *choosing for children* (see pp. 231–233). These people will, therefore, consider its discrete treatment here to be inappropriate. However, as we shall see, to proceed on the assumption that abortion involves the right to life is to beg the question (using that expression in its original sense of pre-supposing the answer before considering the question). The interests of clarity are, therefore, best served by discussing abortion discretely.

Turning to the discussion itself, we shall begin by identifying two typical positions. Towards one end of the scale of possible positions there is the classic conservative view, as part of which it will be necessary to comment on the relevance (or irrelevance) of the Hippocratic oath. Towards the other end of the scale there is the classic liberal position. We shall then conclude by considering Dworkin's version of the liberal position.

The classic conservative position

The classic conservative position comes in both secular and religious versions. Both begin with the proposition that a newly born infant is plainly a moral subject, and both argue that that status must begin at the moment of conception. More particularly, the argument is that there is no magic moment, subsequent to conception, which can be credibly identified as the origin of status as a moral subject, and therefore no line may be drawn in order to determine when abortion is morally acceptable. The religious version of the argument will (at least, in the case of those religions which have a concept of the soul), typically advance an essentially similar additional argument, to the effect that the newly born infant plainly has a soul, and therefore the soul must inhere in the embryo from the moment of conception.

While religious belief generally reflects the kind of attitudes and values which are not amenable to rational criticism (recall, for example, the comments of Reynolds and Holmes, quoted at pp. 25 and 26), the same is not so generally true of the secular versions of the argument, against which two standard arguments may be advanced.

First, it is often necessary, for practical purposes, to draw lines which may accurately be described as arbitrary. For example, there is nothing intrinsically right or safe about driving in a built-up area at 29 mph, or intrinsically wrong or dangerous in driving at 31 mph. It follows that a speed limit of 30 mph can no more be justified than any other specific figure, but it does not follow from this that there should be no speed limit at all. Similarly, therefore, the argument is that there can be no rational objection to fixing some arbitrary point in pregnancy before which abortion is morally right and after which it is morally wrong.

Secondly, the emphasis on the relevance of continuous development from conception to birth may be challenged by means of an argument known as the *faded fabric analogy*. This argument assumes that a piece of coloured fabric is left in the sun until it fades to the point at which it is white. While there will be no single moment at which the fabric ceases to be coloured and becomes white, it is obviously untrue to say that it must therefore have been white at the start.

Some adherents of the conservative position seek to support their argument by reference to an oath which Hippocrates (*c.* 465–370 BCE) formulated by way of ethical guidance to physicians. (It is interesting that the oath distinguishes between physicians and surgeons, with the latter – presumably – being outwith its scope.) Even at this stage, therefore, it is obvious that the Hippocratic oath cannot apply to abortions performed by people who are not physicians. Furthermore, while the oath as formulated by Hippocrates plainly prohibits the procuring of abortions, it is practically impossible, even for physicians, to rely on this version of the oath in the modern context. Two points arise.

First, in its original form, the taker of the oath swears by 'Apollo the physician, by Æsculapius, Hygeia, and Panacea, and... [takes to witness]... all the gods, all the goddesses'. Therefore it cannot be binding on the conscience of anyone who does not believe in those pagan deities.

Secondly, another part of the oath requires the physician to teach, without payment, the art of medicine to the children of the person who taught him. Nobody ever suggests that this aspect of the oath binds the modern conscience, nor for that matter that it has any practical application in the world of modern medical schools.

It follows that reliance on the original Hippocratic oath as a prohibition on procuring abortions requires both a commitment to pagan gods and a talent for selective quotation.

However, not all physicians take an oath of any sort, and those that do are almost certain to take one of a number of modern versions of the Hippocratic oath. These modern versions generally differ significantly from the original (which is hardly surprising since if they did not do so there would be little or no point in formulating them). More particularly, a version which is widely used in modern American medical schools mentions neither the prohibition on abortion nor the obligation to provide free tuition to the offspring of one's teachers. The relevant part of this version, which was written in 1964 by Louis Lasagna, Academic Dean of the School of Medicine at Tufts University, says:

> 'If it is given to me to save a life, all thanks. But it may also be within my power to take a life; this awesome responsibility must be faced with great humbleness and awareness of my own frailty. Above all, I must not play at God.' (For the full version, see http://www.pbs.org/wgbh/nova/doctors/oath_modern.html.)

The emphasis on the responsibility involved in taking life, rather than an express prohibition on doing so is significant. The prohibition on playing God not only appears to reinforce this emphasis (since an all-powerful God is not *responsible*, in the literal sense of *answerable* to anyone), but also underlines the modern view of patient autonomy. (See, for example, the case of *Re B*, which is discussed at p. 221.)

The classic liberal position

Returning to the range of opinions on the morality of abortion, and going to the other end of the scale, the classic liberal position tends to support the morality of abortion, at least in the earlier stages of gestation. Views differ as to where the line should be drawn. One common view is that the test should be whether the foetus is viable independently of the woman who is carrying it, but this is problematic since the fact of viability depends on the level of medical care which is available to deal with premature births. So, for example, applying the viability test, it would be morally acceptable for a pregnant woman, who normally lives in a fully developed part of the world, to have an abortion while travelling in a Third World country at a later stage of pregnancy than if she had stayed at home. An alternative test, which we shall shortly encounter when we consider Dworkin's position, is that the foetus's capacity for sense-experience is the crucial factor.

However, leaving aside the question of precisely where to draw the line, the classic liberal position is based on the autonomy of women in respect of their own bodies.

In the American legal system, the leading case of *Roe v Wade* 410 US 113 (1973) expressed this in terms of the constitutional right of privacy. As O'Connor, Kennedy and Souter JJ subsequently said, in *Planned Parenthood of Southeastern Pennsylvania et al v Casey* 112 S Ct 2791 (1992):

'[Decisions about abortions involve] the most intimate and personal choices a person may make in a lifetime... [and]... at the heart of liberty is the right to define one's own concept of existence, of meaning, of the universe and of the mystery of human life.'

In that case the Supreme Court upheld both the principle of *Roe v Wade* and the constitutionality of a Pennsylvania statute which required 24 hours to elapse between the receipt of advice by a pregnant woman and the performance of an abortion. More particularly, the court held that the existence of a constitutional right to abortion did not preclude the law from seeking to ensure that the exercise of that right is 'thoughtful and informed'.

One standard objection to the argument based on autonomy in respect of one's own body is that such autonomy does not confer unlimited freedom to harm other people's interests. However, this objection begs the question by assuming that the foetus is a person with interests. It is the personhood and interests of the foetus which Dworkin specifically addresses.

Dworkin's version of the liberal position

Dworkin suggests a way of approaching the issue which relies on neither of the arguments we have just considered. He summarizes the problem thus:

'We have been persuaded the central issue is a metaphysical one – whether a foetus is a person – about which no argument can be decisive and no compromise acceptable, because for one side the question is whether babies may be murdered and for the other whether women should be victimized by religious superstition. When we look more closely at what ordinary people actually feel about abortion... almost no-one who supports anti-abortion laws really believes that a just-conceived foetus is a person, and almost no-one who opposes them really believes that the argument against abortion rests only on superstition.'

If the common perceptions do not accurately represent the real views of most proponents on each side (which, it must be noted, Dworkin merely asserts to be the case without producing any proof), it follows that some other analysis is required.

Reduced to its simplest, Dworkin's argument is as follows. First, the issue should be seen in terms of 'the sanctity or inviolability of every stage of every human life'. (*Life's Dominion*, 1993, p. 238.) (Dworkin uses the terms *sanctity* and *inviolability* interchangeably, recognizing that people whose view of the world is exclusively secular will find the latter more congenial than the former.)

However, proceeding on a constitutional basis, Dworkin argues that the key question is not whether a foetus is a person, but whether a foetus is a *constitutional* person. In other words, does a foetus have rights which are protected by the constitution? In the absence of an explicit constitutional statement either way, this question may usefully be approached by asking whether the foetus has *any* rights. This in turn leads to a consideration of the interests (if any) of the foetus and the legitimacy of the law's claim to be entitled to protect those interests to the detriment of another person, namely the pregnant woman who is plainly a constitutional person.

In this context, Dworkin distinguishes between the law asserting *derivative* claims and *detached* claims. (*What the Constitution Says*, in *Freedom's Law: the Moral Reading of the American Constitution*, 1996, p. 4.) The former category consists of those interests which *derive* from the pre-existence of other interests, while the latter category consists of those interests which are *detached* from (in the sense that they exist independently of) pre-existing interests. On the ground that 'nothing has interests unless it has or has had some form of consciousness' (*op. cit.*, p. 91), Dworkin then concludes that the foetus has no interests until it is capable of sense-experience. It follows that, in the early stages of gestation at least (with the limits to be determined by expert medical opinion), any claim that the law may assert to prohibit abortion cannot be derivative. If, on the other hand, the law successfully asserts a detached interest (which it can do only if it treats human life as an objective or intrinsic good, a value in itself, quite apart from its value either to the person whose life it is or to anyone else), the consequence is that a new category of constitutional person is being created with interests which are competitive with those of a pre-existing category, namely women.

Dworkin then embarks on a digression which is made necessary by the structure of the American constitution: can a state legislature which wishes to restrict or prohibit abortion create a new category of constitutional person? He concludes that it cannot do so. (The fact that this particular constitutional consideration is plainly inapplicable within the United Kingdom context does not detract from the main thrust of the argument that it is the *constitutional* status of the foetus which is of central importance.)

Dworkin's conclusion that the law cannot legitimately assert a detached interest in prohibiting abortion will, of course, be easily rejected by those who belong to the constitutive tradition of natural law (see p. 19) and who share the commonly held view within that tradition that human life is an objective good (see, for example, Finnis's version of natural law, which is discussed in Chapter 6). Others may find his analysis provides a usefully structured way of thinking about the question, irrespective of whether they are convinced by his detailed reasoning.

English law

Turning to English law, where a child in the womb is capable of being born alive but is prevented from being so born by the infliction of pre-natal injury, there may be the offence of procuring a miscarriage under s. 58 of the Offences Against the Person Act 1861, or of child destruction, under s. 1 of the Infant Life Preservation Act 1929. In the historical context it is interesting to note the old Common Law rule that sentence of death on a pregnant woman was not to be carried out until after the child was born. This rule was abolished by the Sentence of Death (Expectant Mothers) Act 1931, which substituted life imprisonment for death in such cases.

The basis of the current law is the Abortion Act 1967, which avoids the imposition of criminal liability, provided the pregnancy has not exceeded its twenty-fourth week, and two registered medical practitioners, acting in good faith, form at least one of the following opinions, namely that either its continuance would involve greater risk to the physical or mental health of the woman, or her existing children, than its termination or that the termination is necessary to avoid grave permanent injury to the woman's physical or mental health; there is a greater risk to the woman's life from continuance than from termination; or there is a substantial risk that the child, if born alive, would be seriously handicapped, either mentally or physically.

Finally, according to the European Commission on Human Rights (a body which no longer exists but which used to perform a filtering function in respect of cases, as a result of which some cases did not proceed to the European Court of Human Rights), art. 2(1) of the European Convention on Human Rights does not require states to prohibit abortion.

'The "life" of the foetus is intimately connected with, and cannot be regarded in isolation of, the pregnant woman. If art. 2 were held to cover the foetus and its protection were, in the absence of an express limitation, seen as absolute, an abortion would have to be considered as prohibited even where the continuance of the pregnancy would involve a serious risk to the life of the pregnant woman. This would mean that the "unborn life" of the foetus would be regarded as being of a higher value than the life of the pregnant woman. The "right to life" of a person already born would thus be considered as subject not only to the express limitations [set out in art. 2(2), which deals with killing in the course of defence against unlawful violence, or effecting lawful arrests and preventing the escape of persons lawfully detained, or action lawfully taken in quelling riots and insurrections] but also to a further, implied limitation.' (*Paton v United Kingdom* (1980) 19 DR 244.)

11.8.3 Choosing between life and death

Introduction

While many people agree that, for most of the time at least, life is intrinsically good and that, therefore, living as long as possible is greatly to be desired, it is also true that many people conclude that there is a time to die, even though their bodies are capable (whether with or without medical intervention) of continuing to function. Indeed, there are even some people who doubt the basic goodness of life itself, as illustrated by Sophocles' words 'not to be born is best' (see *Oedipus at Coloneus*), which an unknown versifier subsequently developed into:

'Never to be born is best', the ancient sages say;
Never feel the glow of dawn nor see the light of day;
The second best's a swift 'good night'
And softly steal away.

For our purposes, the question which arises is how the law approaches the problems, and sometimes the conflicts, which arise when people wish either to live as long as possible or to die before they need to do so. A subsidiary question arises where the person involved is incapable of managing their own affairs, with the result that someone else must make the decision for them. The topic appears, therefore, to fall naturally under two main headings, namely *choosing between life and death for one's self*, and *choosing between life and death for other people*. However, clarity of exposition will be aided by also treating three other matters discretely, namely *capacity and competence generally*, as well as *two theoretical perspectives* and the question of *who makes resource decisions*? We will begin with the first of these topics, before dealing with both aspects of choosing between life and death, and concluding with the theoretical perspectives and the question of resource decisions.

Capacity and competence

The law requires that any individual who makes a decision about their own affairs (including, crucially, for the present purposes, their own medical affairs) must have the *capacity*, or be *competent*, to do so. In terms of their meaning in this context, *capacity* and *competence* are interchangeable at common law, although the drafter of the Mental Capacity Act 2005 (see below) opted for the former.

Beginning with the common law, in *Re C (Adult: Refusal of Medical Treatment)* [1994] 1 All ER 819, the High Court held that, on the facts, a paranoid schizophrenic patient had capacity to refuse to consent to the amputation of a gangrenous foot, even though this decision gave him only a 15% chance of survival. More particularly, Thorpe J held that the hospital authorities had failed to rebut the presumption of capacity because the evidence showed that the patient had understood and retained the advice he had been given, and had been able to weigh it in the balance when making his decision. Therefore, it would be unlawful to proceed with the amputation.

Similarly, in *Re MB (An Adult: Medical Treatment)* [1997] 2 FCR 541 (where the issue was consent to a Caesarian section), in the Court of Appeal Butler-Sloss LJ emphasized that while each decision must always depend on the specific facts of the case, the court should approach each case in the light of certain basic principles. More particularly, there is a presumption of capacity, which is not rebutted simply because a decision is based on religious or other factors, or is irrational, or is based on no reasons at all, even though (in the context of impending child birth) the consequence may be that the child will die or be seriously handicapped. However, the more serious the consequences, the greater the level of competence which will be required (or, to put it the other way round, the easier it will be to rebut the presumption of capacity).

Turning to the Mental Capacity Act 2005, two introductory points may usefully be made.

First, in common with most statutes, the Mental Capacity Act 2005 does not operate retrospectively. The practical consequence of this is that cases (including appeals) arising from fact situations occurring before the Act came into force, will continue to be decided in accordance with the common law authorities, so both they and the Act (in relation to later cases) will operate alongside each other for many years.

Secondly, in general terms, the Mental Capacity Act 2005 applies only to people aged at least 16 (s. 2(5)). However, s. 18(3) provides that this restriction does not apply in relation to the personal welfare or property and affairs of a person under 16 if the Court of Protection considers it likely that that person will still lack capacity in respect of the relevant matter when he or she has reached the age of 18.

Turning to the scheme of the Act itself, s. 1 states the following principles relating to capacity to make decisions. A person is presumed to have capacity until the opposite is established. Furthermore, a person must not be treated as being unable to make a decision (a) unless all practicable steps have been taken to help him or her to do so and have failed; and (b) merely because he or she makes an unwise decision. An act must not be done, nor a decision made, on behalf of a person who lacks capacity unless (a) regard has been had to whether there is an equally effective alternative which would be less restrictive of his or her rights and freedom of action; and (b) it is done, or made, in his or her best interests.

A person lacks capacity in relation to a matter if, at the material time, he or she is unable to make a decision in relation to that matter because of an impairment of, or a disturbance in the functioning of, the mind or brain: and it is irrelevant whether the impairment or disturbance is permanent or temporary. In other words incapacity is issue-specific and time-specific, so at any given time a person may have capacity in relation to some matters and lack capacity in relation to others; or may alternate, from time to time, between capacity and incapacity in relation to a single matter (see s. 2(1) and (2)).

Having the capacity to make a decision depends on being able to (a) understand the information relevant to that decision; (b) retain that information; (c) use or weigh that information as part of the process of making that decision; and (d) communicate that decision by any means (including, for example, sign language) (see s. 3(1)).

When anyone other than the person who lacks capacity is considering that person's best interests, consideration must be given to whether (and if so, when) that person is likely to have capacity in relation to the matter in question in the future (see s. 4(3)). Other factors relevant to the question of best interests are (a) the person's wishes, feelings, values and other factors that he or she would be likely to consider if able to do so, with particular weight being given to any written statement he or she has made (see s. 4(6)); (b) the views of (i) anyone named by the person as someone who ought to be consulted, (ii) the person's carers and those interested in the welfare of the person; (iii) anyone holding a lasting power of attorney on behalf of the person; and (iv) any deputy appointed by the Court of Protection (see s. 4(7)). But where the issue involves life-sustaining treatment, the decision must not be motivated by a desire to bring about the death of the person who lacks capacity (see s. 4(6)).

For the first time in English law, the Act gives legal effect to *advance decisions* (also known as *advance directives* or, more informally, as *living wills*). More particularly, a written statement, signed by the person making it (when he or she had the capacity to do so) in the presence of a witness, to the effect that that person does not wish specified treatment to be given or continued, even if withholding or withdrawing that treatment will put his or her life at risk, has the same effect when the person who made it lacks capacity, as a statement of the same wish would have if that person had capacity at that time, (see s. 24(1) and (2)). An advance decision may be altered or withdrawn (not necessarily in writing) at any time when the person who made it has capacity to do so (see s. 24(3) and (4)).

Choosing between life and death for one's self

Introduction

The principal concern of this section of this chapter is assisted suicide, although it begins with one case about turning off a life-support system and another one about its polar opposite, namely prolonging life beyond the point at which it would normally, in standard clinical practice, be allowed to end.

The first of these two cases is *Re B (Adult: Refusal of Medical Treatment)* [2002] 2 All ER 449, where Dame Elizabeth Butler-Sloss P, sitting in the Court of Appeal, held that a fully competent adult, who was paralyzed from the neck down and who was being kept alive on a ventilator, was entitled to decide that she did not wish to continue to be ventilated even though she knew that turning off the ventilator would result in her death. Her doctors refused to comply with her wishes. On the question of the patient's competence (or capacity – see p. 219) the judge was careful to point out that when a patient's doctors disagree with their patient, 'the view of the patient may reflect a difference in values rather than an absence of competence and the assessment of competence should be approached with this firmly in mind'. (The statutory presumption in favour of capacity, which was introduced by the Mental Capacity Act 2005 (see p. 220), has reduced the need to rely on this dictum, but it nevertheless remains a useful reminder that there may be basic disagreements about the most fundamental questions of life and death.) Returning to the facts of *Re B*, the unwillingness of the patient's doctors to act on her wishes, even despite the court's decision, resulted in her being transferred to another hospital where her wishes were respected and she died.

The second case is *R (Burke) v General Medical Council* [2005] EWCA Civ 1003. Mr Burke suffered from an untreatable, progressive, degenerative, and ultimately fatal, neurological condition, although all the indications were that he still had several more years to live. He sought a number of declaratory orders, the most important of which was that, irrespective of the degree to which his condition deteriorated, his doctors should never withdraw artificial nutrition and hydration (ANH), because he did not wish to die of starvation and thirst. (In practice, of course, a patient in this position will be sedated to prevent suffering, but it may still be thought to be an undignified way of dying.)

Munby J, having considered a substantial body of case law, made a number of declaratory orders. However, the Court of Appeal, in a judgment to which all three members contributed but which Lord Phillips MR delivered, disagreed with him in a comprehensive manner. The following points are worth emphasizing.

First, the court did 'not think it possible to attempt to define what is in the best interests of a patient by a single test, applicable in all circumstances' and it expressly recognized that

> 'where the patient is dying, the goal may properly be to ease suffering and, where appropriate, to "ease the passing" rather than to achieve a short prolongation of life ... [while always being careful to avoid] treating the life of a disabled patient as being of less value than the life of a patient without disability.'

While expressly rejecting the test of the 'intolerability' of the patient's life as a means of deciding when ANH could properly be withdrawn, the court did think

> '[the idea of *best interests* should be restricted to] an objective test, which is of most use when considering the duty owed to a patient who is not competent and is easiest to apply when confined to a situation where the relevant interests are medical.'

The court also rejected the view that, as a matter of law, the authorization of a court was required before life-prolonging treatment could be withheld. The court pointed out that Munby J's conclusion to the contrary had been based on the view that in cases of this sort the court is authorizing something which would otherwise be unlawful, whereas all the court actually has any power to do is to say whether or not the proposed course of action is lawful. While it may, therefore, be good medical practice to seek the view of the court in some, more difficult, situations, this would never be a legal requirement.

Despite the fact that the relationship between patient and doctor can never be one where the former gives orders which the latter is bound to obey, the Court of Appeal did acknowledge that a doctor who overrides a patient's express wishes by withdrawing ANH which would keep the patient alive will be guilty of murder, provided the withdrawal was done with the intention of killing the patient. (This proviso brings into play the doctrine of double effect, which is discussed below in the context of the case of *Bland*.)

Finally, the Court of Appeal rejected arguments that there had been any infringement of Mr Burke's Convention rights under arts 2 (right to life), 3 (prohibition of torture or inhuman or degrading treatment or punishment), 8 (right to respect for private and family life) and 14 (prohibition of discrimination in enjoyment of rights under the Convention), of the European Convention on Human Rights, as applied in English law by the Human Rights Act 1998. The correctness of the court's decisions on these aspects of the case is reinforced by the fact that, in due course, the European Court of Human Rights ruled that Mr Burke's application to that court was 'manifestly ill-founded' and, therefore, inadmissible. (See the decision dated 11 July 2006 on Application No. 19807/06 *Burke v United Kingdom*.)

Suicide and assisted suicide

Straightforward suicide, undertaken by people who are fit enough to accomplish the act on their own, has raised neither practical issues of law nor conceptual issues of legal theory since the Suicide Act 1961 decriminalized suicide. However, this decriminalization of suicide itself is only part of the story, because s. 2 of the Act continued to criminalize aiding, abetting, counselling and procuring suicide. After very nearly 50 years, s. 2 was amended by s. 59 of, and Sch. 12 to, the Coroners and Justice Act 2009, which abolished the offences of aiding, abetting, counselling and procuring suicide and substituted the new offences of doing an act which was *both* capable of encouraging or assisting suicide or attempted suicide and was intended to do so. We will return to this topic shortly but before doing so it is worth clearing up a potential source of confusion.

The problem is that a patient who insists that a life-support system is turned off may appear to be committing suicide. If this appearance reflects the legal reality of the situation, it would follow that anyone who turns off a life-support system would be committing the offence of assisting the patient to commit suicide. However, the appearance does not reflect the reality because turning off the life-support system does not cause the patient's death: all it does is to cease to continue to postpone the natural death which it then allows to occur (and which would have already occurred if the life-support system had never been used). The correctness of this alternative analysis may be reinforced by considering the contrasting case of a patient who is paralysed from the neck down but who is still able to suck liquid in and to swallow it. In this case anyone who, for example, holds a cup of fatally toxic medication to the lips of the patient, who then drinks it, is clearly assisting the patient to commit suicide. The difference between the two types of intervention is, therefore, clear; and, in purely practical terms, it is the difference between innocence and guilt in relation to an offence under s. 2 of the 1961 Act. Of course, a doctor or other medical professional may object to turning off a life-support system, but this objection would be ethical rather than legal.

Having cleared up that potential source of confusion, we can now consider the situation which arises when someone who is, or is likely to become, physically incapable of committing suicide wants to be helped to do so, or know that they can be helped to do so when the time comes; and also wants to know that, in either case, anyone who provides the help will not be exposed to the risk of prosecution.

In *R (Pretty) v Director of Public Prosecutions* [2001] UKHL 61, [2002] 1 All ER 1, the House of Lords held that the DPP had acted lawfully in refusing to give an undertaking that he would not prosecute the husband of a fully competent, adult patient suffering from motor neurone disease, if he assisted her to commit suicide when she was incapable of doing so unaided. (The offence would have been one of aiding and abetting her suicide.)

The House of Lords took the view that art. 2 of the European Convention on Human Rights (the right to life) reinforces the sanctity of human life by guaranteeing that no one should be deprived of life through the intentional intervention of another person. This is clearly the exact opposite of the state of affairs which Mrs Pretty wished to bring about. Moreover, even if s. 2 of the Act were *prima facie* incompatible with a Convention right, it had been enacted for the protection of vulnerable people and could be said to be a proportionate response to the need to balance rights of individuals against the legitimate interest of the state in protecting the lives of its citizens. Nor could the prohibition on inhuman or degrading treatment under art. 3 of the Convention be interpreted as requiring a state to guarantee a right to die through the assistance of another person.

Furthermore, Mrs Pretty could gain no support from art. 8 of the Convention (which deals with respect for private and family life) because this article is concerned with how people live their lives and is not properly applicable to the question of how they might choose to die. Similarly, although art. 9 of the Convention plainly guarantees freedom of thought, conscience and religion, it does not guarantee the right to act in whatever way might be required by an individual's thought, conscience or religion. For example, in *Arrowsmith v United Kingdom* (1981) 3 EHRR 218, the European Commission on Human Rights accepted that pacifism was a belief within the scope of art. 9; but also held that distributing leaflets to English soldiers, urging them to refuse to serve in Northern Ireland, was not simply a manifestation of pacifist beliefs. In reality, it was a manifestation of a political belief about the correct way to deal with the Northern Ireland problem; and, as such, was not protected by art. 9.

Finally, the 1961 Act does not create or recognize a right to commit suicide, neither does s. 2 of the Act involve any unequal treatment before the law (and, therefore, it is not incompatible with the guarantee of freedom from discrimination contained in art. 14 of the Convention).

Mrs Pretty also failed in the European Court of Human Rights (see *Pretty v United Kingdom* [2002] 35 EHRR 1) but on the basis of different reasoning. More particularly, the House of Lords had held that none of Mrs Pretty's Convention rights had been engaged, whereas the European Court of Human Rights accepted that art. 8 had been engaged but went on to hold that a total prohibition of assisted suicide was not disproportionate, bearing in mind that the prohibition had been imposed in order to protect vulnerable members of society.

The issue of assisted suicide came before the courts again in *R (Purdy) v Director of Public Prosecution (Society for the Protection of Unborn Children Intervening)* [2009] UKHL 45, [2009] 3 WLR 403. Ms Purdy suffered from an incurable condition, namely primary progressive multiple sclerosis. She feared that at some future time her condition would deteriorate to the extent that she would find life intolerable. At that stage she would wish to kill herself, but the nature of her condition would be such that she would be physically unable to do so. Her wish then would be to travel to a country where assisted suicide was lawful and her husband was willing to assist her to do so. However, she also feared that her husband might be prosecuted for assisting her (see s. 2 of the Suicide Act 1961, as amended); and, on the basis of this fear, Ms Purdy felt that the most likely practical outcome would be that she would take her own life significantly sooner than she would otherwise do, in case she left it too late to do so unaided. In other words, the availability of assisted suicide would, from her point of view, prolong life rather than shortening it.

The DPP's *Code for Crown Prosecutors* set out in general terms the considerations by reference to which the discretion to prosecute would be exercised but it offered practically no guidance which would either confirm or allay Ms Purdy's fears. She therefore sought judicial review on the basis that this state of affairs constituted a breach of her Convention right (under the Human Rights Act 1998) to respect for her private life, other than in accordance with the law (see art. 8 of the European Convention on Human Rights). The DPP responded that it was impossible to predict, in a very specific way, how the discretion to prosecute would be exercised without having the context of a real case presenting real factors for consideration; and, the existing regime of a blanket prohibition, coupled with flexible enforcement, should be maintained.

The High Court and the Court of Appeal both dismissed Ms Purdy's claim but the House of Lords allowed her appeal.

On the technical matter of the application of the doctrine of binding precedent, the House took the view that the interests of human rights law would not be well served if the House regarded itself as being bound by its own decision (in *Pretty*), to the effect that the facts of cases of the kind under consideration did not engage any Convention rights, when the European Court of Human Rights had subsequently held that they did do so.

On the substance of Ms Purdy's claim, the House held that unless Ms Purdy could identify the principles governing the exercise of the discretion to prosecute her husband for an offence contrary to s. 2 of the 1961 Act, the apparent protection of art. 8 was illusory, since it did not enable her to decide how she should live her life (or, in her case, when she should terminate it). In other words, in the absence of such principles, the interference with the art. 8 right which s. 2 constituted was not 'in accordance with the law'. It followed, therefore, that the DPP should publish guidance as to the basis on which the discretion to prosecute would be exercised in cases of assisted suicide.

In September 2009, the DPP issued an interim policy, together with a consultation paper inviting public participation in the formulation of his final policy. In February 2010, the DPP issued his final policy which, following the style of its interim predecessor, contains two lists of public interest factors (see paras 43 and 45 respectively). The lists contained in the final policy specify 16 factors which make a prosecution more likely and six factors which make a prosecution less likely. We will consider each list in turn, but before doing so two preliminary points are worth making.

First, the final policy provides (just as the interim policy provided) a gloss on the general Code for Crown Prosecutors (which is also available on the CPS's web page (see above)). Reduced to its simplest, the Code requires a two-stage approach to the exercise of the discretion to prosecute, in the form of an *evidential test* and a *public interest test*. (See para. 4.5 of the Code.) The evidential test requires that the prosecutor must be satisfied that there is sufficient evidence to provide a realistic prospect of conviction. Unless this test is satisfied, no prosecution should be brought. But, even if the evidential test is satisfied, a prosecutor must still consider whether the public interest requires that a prosecution should be brought. In other words, even though there is sufficient evidence, a prosecution will not always be brought. The policy in relation to cases of assisted suicide deals only with the public interest test.

Secondly, the final policy follows its interim predecessor in dealing only with the exercise of the discretion to prosecute. It emphatically does not, either actually or effectively, decriminalize conduct which the 1961 Act, as amended, characterizes as being criminal. The fact that there have been no prosecutions for this offence since the interim policy was introduced is simply an indication that the circumstances of all the cases which have come to the DPP's attention during that time have been such as to merit no prosecution and thus to allow a series of sensitive, compassionate and humane outcomes to be achieved.

Returning to the factors which are relevant to the exercise of prosecutorial discretion, those which render a prosecution more likely may be summarized as follows.

- ▶ The victim was under the age of 18.
- ▶ The victim had not made a voluntary, clear, settled and informed decision to commit suicide and, even if the victim had made such a decision, he or she had not clearly communicated that decision to the suspect.
- ▶ The suspect was not wholly motivated by compassion (for example, the suspect stood to gain from the victim's death). (The question of gaining from the victim's death must be answered in a common sense way, with the critical consideration being the suspect's motive. Taking an example which the policy does not take, it will be commonplace for spouses and civil partners to be co-owners of the houses or flats where they live; and for the survivor to inherit the victim's share when the victim dies and so become sole owner. This outcome need not negate a conclusion that the suspect was motivated wholly by compassion. (See para. 44.)

▶ The suspect had a history of violence or abuse towards the victim. (The DPP's *Introductory Remarks on Assisted Suicide Policy*, 25 Feb 2010 – which were published on the DPP's web page alongside his final policy – make it clear that this factor is designed to reflect the possibility that violence and abuse may have contributed to the victim's decision to commit suicide.)

▶ The suspect encouraged or assisted two or more victims who were not known to each other.

▶ The suspect was a healthcare professional and was acting as such.

▶ The suspect was involved in the management, or was employed by, an organisation or group which provided facilities for assisted suicide.

On the other hand, all the factors rendering a prosecution less likely may be summarized as follows.

▶ The victim had made a voluntary, clear, settled and informed decision to commit suicide.

▶ The suspect was wholly motivated by compassion.

▶ The actions of the suspect provided only minor or reluctant encouragement or assistance; and the suspect had tried to dissuade the victim from committing suicide.

▶ The suspect had reported the victim's suicide to, and had fully cooperated with, the police.

Without descending to a detailed, point-by-point comparison between the interim policy and the final one, two points may usefully be made.

First, and more generally, the DPP's *Introductory Remarks* (see above) make it clear that one outcome of the public consultation on his interim policy was that the focus shifted from 'the behaviour and characteristics of the victim' to 'the actions and role of the suspect'.

Secondly, and more specifically, the final policy omits a factor which appeared in both lists in the interim policy, namely whether or not the victim had 'a terminal illness; or a severe and incurable physical disability; or a severe degenerative physical condition from which there was no possibility of recovery'.

Finally, the *DPP's Introductory Remarks* (see above) clearly indicate that applying the policy is neither a 'tick box' exercise, nor a 'numbers game': 'It is quite possible that one factor alone may outweigh a number of other factors which tend in the opposite direction'. Although these comments are important they are by no means novel in the context of the exercise of discretion in the field of public law. More particularly, it has long been established that discretions must be exercised in the light of all the relevant considerations and that automatic implementation of any policy is unlawful. (See, respectively, *Associated Provincial Picture Houses Ltd v Wednesbury Corporation* [1947] 2 All ER 680 and *British Oxygen v Minister of Technology* [1970] 3 All ER 165.)

Before leaving the topic of assisted suicide, it is worth noticing that in 2012, Dignity in Dying (www.dignityindying.org.uk), a charity which campaigns for the legalization of assisted suicide, facilitated the establishment of a Commission on Assisted Dying and obtained donor funding to cover its operating costs. The Commission and its secretariat functioned entirely independently of Dignity in Dying. It had the following terms of reference:

▶ to investigate the circumstances under which it should be possible for people to be assisted to die;
▶ to recommend what system, if any, should exist to allow people to be assisted to die;
▶ to identify who should be entitled to be assisted to die;
▶ to determine what safeguards should be put in place to ensure that vulnerable people are neither abused nor pressured to choose an assisted death;
▶ to recommend what changes in the law, if any, should be introduced.

The Commission was chaired by Lord Faulkner QC (a former Lord Chancellor and Secretary of State for Justice) and had 10 other members drawn from the fields of academic medicine and medical practice (including palliative care and hospice work), members of the House of Lords with an interest in the Commission's work (including a former Commissioner of the Metropolitan Police), a Conservative MP and an Anglican priest with experience as a hospital chaplain. The Commission concluded (in its Report published in January 2012), that it would be possible to devise a legal framework consisting of eligibility criteria for seeking assisted suicide. Two essential elements of the framework were that it would set out strictly defined circumstances in which terminally ill people might be assisted to die. Crucially, people seeking assisted suicide would be supported by health and social care professionals and 'robust upfront safeguards' would be put in place to 'prevent inappropriate requests that did not meet the eligibility criteria going ahead'. (See p. 25 of the Commission's Report, which is available as a free download from http://www.demos.co.uk/publications/thecommissiononassisteddying.)

The three eligibility criteria were as follows.

▶ The person seeking assisted suicide must be aged 18 or over and must have been diagnosed as suffering from a 'terminal illness', namely 'an advanced, progressive, incurable condition that is likely to lead to the patient's death within the next 12 months'. (*Op. cit.*, p. 27.) This criterion was designed to send a clear message that disabled people's lives are of equal value with everyone else's. (Of course, it would not prevent a disabled person, who was also suffering from a terminal illness, from seeking assisted suicide.) The omission of any requirement of 'unbearable suffering' (or any similar phrase) was intentional on the basis that any such requirement would inevitably be subjective and the best person to decide what is unbearable is the person who is suffering. (*Ibid.*)

▶ A decision to seek assisted suicide must be 'settled' and must be 'a genuinely voluntary and autonomous choice, not influenced by another person's wishes, or by constrained social circumstances, such as lack of access to adequate end of life care and support'. (*Ibid.*) The requirement that the decision must be 'settled' should be met by requiring at least two weeks to elapse between the request for assistance to commit suicide and the death itself . (*Op. cit.*, p. 30.)

▶ Despite the presumption of capacity contained in the Mental Capacity Act 2005 (see p. 220), the Commission concluded that the seriousness of a decision to seek assisted suicide is such that a specific assessment of capacity should be undertaken by two doctors. The doctors must be independent of each other, but one of them should, wherever possible, know the person who wishes to die. It would be a matter for the relevant professional bodies to devise appropriate codes of conduct for doctors undertaking assessments. (*Op. cit.*, pp. 27–28.)

Among the Commission's other recommendations were that there is a 'need for continuing government investment in improving end of life care' and a 'need for continuing use of the policy of the Director of Public Prosecutions... for prosecutors in non-terminal cases. (*Op. cit.*, p. 21.)

The only dissenting voice among the members of the Commission was that of the Reverend Canon Dr James Woodward (the Commissioner who was an Anglican priest), in whose view there is a

'need to engage further with the social and ethical reflections on experiences of death and dying. The ethical debate is not over and it is the responsibility of all "sides" of the debate to listen more carefully to the questions and concerns of one another... I am particularly concerned about the adequacy of UK health and social care where dignity and compassion are values that are universally affirmed but often not part of the day to day practice of those who are tasked to care.... I understand that my particular view is a minority one and I both respect and admire my fellow Commissioners in their views and recommendations. I hope that the Report will be read carefully – it is an important contribution to the debate.'

Choosing between life and death for other people

Choosing for adults

Beginning with the common law, the classic situation is that of a patient in a persistent vegetative state. Here, the law is that withdrawing life support, including ANH, is not necessarily unlawful and that each case must be considered on its merits. The leading case is *Airedale National Health Service Trust v Bland* [1993] 1 All ER 821, where the House of Lords unanimously agreed that the doctors having the care of a young man who had been in a persistent vegetative state for over three years, throughout which time he had been fed through tubes, could lawfully withhold food even though the inevitable result was that he would die of starvation. While agreeing with the decision, Lord Browne-Wilkinson expressed his puzzlement thus:

'How can it be lawful to allow a patient to die slowly, though painlessly, over a period of weeks from lack of food but unlawful to produce his immediate death by a lethal injection, thereby saving his family from yet another ordeal to add to the tragedy that has already struck them? I find it difficult to find a moral answer to that question. But it is undoubtedly the law...'

At a more general level, he adopted the standard test in relation to allegations of medical negligence (as formulated in *Bolam v Friern Hospital Management Committee* [1957] 2 All ER 118), under which

'[the court will not question the exercise of clinical judgment, provided] the doctor's decision... is in accordance with a respectable body of medical opinion and is reasonable.'

Furthermore, Lord Goff specifically endorsed the principle commonly called the *doctrine* (or *principle*) *of double effect*. This doctrine deals with the situation in which it is known that certain treatment which will have a justifiable medical effect will also have the effect of shortening the patient's life. The key distinction here is between *intention* and *foresight*, in the sense that if the intention of those who administer the treatment is medically justifiable, it is legally irrelevant that they can also foresee the additional effect of hastening the patient's death. As Lord Goff put it:

'The established rule [is] that a doctor may, when caring for a patient who is, for example, dying of cancer, lawfully administer painkilling drugs despite the fact that he knows that an incidental effect of that application will be to abbreviate the patient's life. *Such a decision may properly be made as part of the care of the living patient, in his best interests; and on this basis, the treatment will be lawful.*' (Emphasis added.)

The approval of the doctrine of double effect is particularly interesting, because although many people accept it as a valid ethical principle, many others do not. For example, Peter Singer (whose views on the ethical status of animals we have already encountered – see p. 196), who is a prominent consequentialist philosopher, says:

'The distinction between directly intended effect and side-effect is a contrived one. We cannot avoid responsibility by directing our intention to one effect rather than another. If we foresee both effects, we must take responsibility for the foreseen effects of what we do. We often want to do something but cannot do it because of its other, unwanted consequences.' (*Practical Ethics*, 3rd edn, 2011, p. 212.)

Choosing for children

The obvious major difference between choosing between life and death for adults and children is that in the case of the latter, the individuals will (at least in the case of young children) lack the capacity to make their own decisions, or to express relevant wishes to guide those who may make a decisions on their behalf. The second major difference is that, basically (but see p. 220), the Mental Capacity Act applies only to people over the age of 16. However, the common law principles are well developed, and may be illustrated by two cases.

The first case is *Re A (Children) (Conjoined Twins: Surgical Separation)* [2000] 4 All ER 961, which involved a pair of conjoined twins (or, in other words, what were, at one time, popularly known as Siamese twins). Mary, the weaker twin, was capable of surviving only because the heart of her sister, Jodie, was capable of pumping enough blood through the whole of their conjoined bodies to keep both babies alive. However, it was clear that this position could not continue indefinitely and that, without surgery, Jodie's heart would fail and both babies would die within about six months or so. The difficulty was that if the artery carrying the blood to Mary were cut and clamped, Mary would inevitably die. The parents, being devout Roman Catholics, took the view that their children's predicament was a manifestation of God's will, and they were accordingly willing to leave the matter in God's hands. The medical authorities, on the other hand, wished to operate in order to save Jodie's life. In cases like this, parents will normally make decisions on behalf of their children – provided, of course, that the parents are competent. However, as cases such as the present one show, the courts will be willing to override parental wishes in respect of a child, even though they would uphold the same wishes if they related to the life or death of the parents themselves. The same proposition applies equally to cases where an adult patient lacks capacity, with the result that decisions on matters of life and death have to be made by another adult on the patient's behalf. The key issue in all such cases, assuming the wishes of the patient are unknown – as will always be the case with young children – will be the patient's best interests.

The Court of Appeal, upholding the High Court's decision that surgery to separate the twins would be lawful, even though it would inevitably result in Mary's death, approached the matter on the basis of having to choose the lesser of two evils: performing surgery would result in the survival of one baby, while withholding it would result in the death of both. Additional elements in the judgments included an acceptance that, in the very special circumstances of the case (and distinguishing *R v Dudley and Stephens* (1884) 14 QBD 273, which is discussed at p. 32), a defence of necessity should be allowed if the operation proceeded and was followed by a murder trial; that there was an element of quasi-self-defence, with the doctors acting on behalf, and in defence, of Jodie; and that the proposed surgery would not contravene art. 2 of the European Convention on Human Rights, because the intention would be to save Jodie's life, and therefore the death of Mary, even though it was foreseeable to the point of certainty, would not be brought about intentionally. This last point is an application of the doctrine of double effect which the House of Lords accepted in *Airedale National Health Service Trust v Bland* (see p. 229).

The second case is *Re Wyatt (A Child) (Medical Treatment: Continuation of Order)* [2005] EWCA Civ 1181, [2005] 1 WLR 3995. The facts involved a baby who, having been born at 26 weeks and weighing only 458 grams, was severely disabled. The case came before the High Court and the Court of Appeal on a number of occasions because her parents, contrary to medical advice, wanted everything possible to be done to prolong her life. The issue was what orders (if any) the court should make and the period of time for which any such orders should remain in force. On one occasion when the case came before the Court of Appeal, Wall LJ delivered the judgment of the court, from which the following propositions of principle emerge.

First,

'it is nearly always a matter of regret when the debate relating to the treatment of a seriously disabled or sick child... needs to be conducted in a courtroom, rather than a hospital or a consulting room... [but where the venue is a courtroom]... the forensic debate should... be unfettered by any potentially contentious glosses on the best interests test, which are likely either inappropriately to shift the focus of the debate, or to restrict the broad exercise of the judicial discretion involved in balancing the multifarious factors in the case.'

Secondly,

'the intellectual milestones for the judge in a case such as the present are... simple, although the ultimate decision will frequently be extremely difficult. The judge must decide what is in the child's best interests. In making that decision, the welfare of the child is paramount, and the judge must look at the question from the assumed point of view of the patient.... There is a strong presumption in favour of a course of action which will prolong life, but that presumption is not irrebuttable.... The term 'best interests' encompasses medical, emotional, and all other welfare issues.... The court must conduct a balancing exercise in which all the relevant factors are weighed.... and a helpful way of undertaking this exercise is to draw up a balance sheet... [and]... any criteria which seek to circumscribe the best interests tests are... to be avoided.... At the end of the day.... it is for the judge to strike the balance between benefit and harm.'

Thirdly, there is

'[a need for] caution in the application to children of factors relevant to the treatment of adults, although some general statements of principle plainly apply to both... [so, for example, *Burke*]... was not concerned with what was meant by "best interests" in the context of the treatment of an incompetent child.'

Fourthly,

'[while "intolerability" is not the single, defining factor] it is ... a valuable guide in the search for best interests in this kind of case.'

The case of *T and T v An NHS Trust and OT (A Child)* [2008] EWCA Civ 409, provides an example of circumstances in which the 'strong presumption in favour of a course of action which will prolong life' was rebutted. The facts concerned a child aged 10 months at the date of the judgment, who suffered from a congenital defect as a result of which his body failed to generate the energy which was necessary for its proper functioning. He had also suffered a number of strokes, as a result of which various parts of his brain had ceased to function. More particularly, he was entirely dependent on artificial ventilation; and, owing to his inability to swallow, was also dependent on gastro-nasal feeding, as well as needing extremely frequent suctioning to remove secretions from his mouth, nose and throat. His eyes, on the other hand, did function, but his brain was unable to make sense of the signals which it received from them. His parents wished his life to be prolonged, but the medical evidence before the court was unanimously to the effect that he would probably die before reaching the age of three and would certainly die before reaching the age of five; and that, as long as he continued to live, his waking time would amount to experiencing a mixture of distress, discomfort and pain, with no countervailing benefit.

Parker J, in the High Court, held that, even in the absence of the parents' consent, it would be lawful for the child to be allowed to die if the hospital authorities considered that to be in his best interests.

The Court of Appeal refused to grant the parents permission to appeal, on the basis that (see para. [28] of the Court of Appeal's judgment) 'the only proper programme for... [the child]... in his interests was, as his... [guardian *ad litem*...] contended, entirely obvious'. The child died the day after the Court of Appeal's decision. (The substance of the argument on appeal was that the parents had been given insufficient time to obtain independent medical evidence, even though they refused to disclose such independent medical evidence as they already had; but, in the light of all the facts, the Court of Appeal, finding that the parents had known for some time that legal proceedings would be likely, rejected this argument.)

Finally, the European Court of Human Rights has held that it is a breach of art. 8 of the European Convention on Human Rights (respect for private and family life) to administer treatment to a child whose parent has expressly forbidden it. (See *Glass v United Kingdom* (2004) 39 EHRR 15.)

Having identified the approaches to various end-of-life problems adopted by both the common law and the Mental Capacity Act 2005 (and having noticed that, in essence, the latter supplements, rather than changes, the former) we now consider two theoretical perspectives.

Two theoretical perspectives

The theoretical perspectives which we will consider here are those of Dworkin and Keown.

When considering the question of euthanasia, Dworkin continues his concern for 'the sanctity or inviolability of every stage of every human life' (see above).

'People who want an early, peaceful death for themselves or their relatives are not rejecting or denigrating the sanctity of life; on the contrary, they believe that a quicker death shows more respect for life than a protracted one. Once again, both sides in the debate about euthanasia share a concern for life's sanctity; they are united by that value, and disagree only on how best to interpret and respect it.'

He goes on to say that

'["dignity" in the sense of] respecting the inherent value of our own lives... argues decisively... for individual freedom... for a regime of law... that encourages each of us to make mortal decisions for himself.'

In passing, it should be noted that although euthanasia is simply homicide in the eyes of English law, convictions for manslaughter rather than murder are not uncommon with the practical consequence being that the sentence becomes discretionary and leniency is frequently exercised by the passing of a non-custodial sentence.

The second, and more traditional, view is presented (probably as persuasively as it can be, assuming the reader is open to persuasion) by Keown in an article entitled *Restoring Moral and Intellectual Shape to the Law after Bland* (1997) 113 LQR 481. Briefly, Keown's argument is that there are three possible positions, namely *vitalism*, the *sanctity of life* and the *quality of life*.

According to *vitalism*, human life is an absolute moral value, and therefore it is morally wrong to shorten it, or fail to lengthen it, as the case may be. Since life must be preserved at all costs, the pain, suffering or financial expenditure which may be involved are all irrelevant. Keown rejects this view, saying that it is

'as ethically untenable as its attempt to maintain life indefinitely is physically impossible. Its error lies in isolating the genuine and basic good of human life, and the duty to respect and promote that good, from the network of standards and responsibilities which make up our ethics and law as a whole; and its neglect of concepts and distinctions (such as between intention and foresight) vital to that network.' (*Op. cit.*, p. 482.)

At the other extreme lies the quality (or Quality as Keown prefers to call it, in this context, in order to make a distinction which will shortly become apparent) of life position, which holds that a life which is not worth living need not be preserved or extended. Keown objects to this position thus:

'It denies the ineliminable value of each patient and engages in discriminatory judgments, posited on fundamentally arbitrary criteria such as physical or mental disability, about whose lives are "worthwhile" and whose are not. The arbitrariness is highlighted when it is asked which disabilities, and to which degree, are supposed to make life not worth living.' (Original emphasis. *Op. cit.*, p. 487.)

Between the extremes, there lies the *sanctity* (or *inviolability*) *of life* position, which holds that 'one ought never to kill an innocent human being'. (*Op. cit.*, p.

483.) Pausing only to note that Keown explains the limitation to those who are innocent as taking account of killing in self-defence, in the course of a just war and in execution of a judicial sentence of death, we can progress to the essence of his position, which he explains as follows.

> 'The dignity of human beings inheres because of the radical [i.e. basic] capacities, such as for understanding and rational choice, inherent in human nature. Some human beings such as infants, may not possess the ability to exercise these radical capacities. But radical capacities must not be confused with abilities: one may have, for example, the radical capacity but not the ability to speak Swahili. All human beings possess the capacities inherent in their nature even though, because of infancy, disability or senility, they may not yet, not now, or no longer have the ability to exercise them.'

Although the sanctity of life position holds life to be a *basic* good (in the sense that it is worthwhile in itself and not merely as a means to an end) it is *not* an *absolute* good. By way of contrast, the prohibition on intentional taking, or shortening of innocent life *is* absolute. Thus

> 'intentionally shortening a patient's life by withholding treatment, or food, water or warmth, is no less wrong than injecting a lethal poison.' (*Op. cit.*, p. 485.)

For example, a treatment may legitimately be withheld if either the risks or the suffering entailed would outweigh the benefits, even though withholding the treatment will cause or accelerate death. This illustrates the distinction between *intention* and *foresight* (which is discussed above in the context of the doctrine of double effect, and which you will recall *vitalism* does not recognize), and allows treatment to be withheld where it would not be worthwhile. However, the essential point in Keown's argument is that it is the treatment, and not the patient's life, which is being adjudged as being 'not worthwhile'. In other words, the assessment of the worthwhileness of the treatment may involve a consideration of its impact on the quality of the patient's life, but this is the only way in which the quality of life becomes relevant. It should now be clear how Keown's distinctive use of quality and Quality reflects his differentiation between quality of life, which he recognizes as an acceptable, and sometimes inevitable, aspect of the sanctity of life position, and Quality of life which he sees as a morally indefensible position.

Who makes decisions on the allocation of resources?

In purely practical terms, it can be argued that ethical arguments which focus on individual patients cannot realistically ignore the fact that long-term healthcare can be very expensive and that public funds which are spent on one patient cannot be spent on others. The courts recognize the intrinsic difficulty of making this kind of resource decision, while emphasizing that it is not a matter within their jurisdiction. For example, in *R v Cambridge Health Authority ex parte B* [1995] 2 All ER 129, Lord Bingham MR said:

'I have no doubt that in a perfect world any treatment which a patient, or a patient's family, sought would be provided if doctors were willing to give it, no matter how much it cost, particularly when a life was potentially at stake. It would however, in my view, be shutting one's eyes to the real world if the court were to proceed on the basis that we do live in such a world. It is common knowledge that health authorities of all kinds are constantly pressed to make ends meet.... Difficult and agonizing judgments have to be made as to how a limited budget is best allocated to the maximum advantage of the maximum number of patients. That is not a judgment which the court can make.'

This view is, of course, wholly consistent with the constitutional doctrine of the Separation of Powers, as evidenced by the traditional approach of the courts in judicial review proceedings that decisions as to the allocation of scarce resources are matters for the decision-maker which Parliament has designated as the provider of the services in question.

Summary

▶ Discussion of the legal regulation of morality usually deals principally with the criminal law.

▶ Mill's *harm condition*, which states that the law is entitled to intervene to prevent harm to others, but not to protect people from themselves, is commonly taken as being the basis of one side of the argument, with the other side resting on the proposition that all immorality harms, and is therefore the legitimate business of, society as a whole.

▶ The exchange of views between Devlin and Hart, prompted by the *Wolfenden Report on Homosexual Offences and Prostitution*, presents a good example of the arguments both for and against the legal regulation of morality.

▶ Dworkin argues for a liberal position, based on identifying and protecting the purposes for which society exists.

▶ Consideration of English law shows that, in some circumstances, the law may intervene to protect the fabric of society, or to protect public decency or to prevent people from harming themselves.

▶ Opinions vary widely as to the acceptability (or otherwise) of abortion, but Dworkin's version of the liberal argument for freedom of choice in relation to abortion and euthanasia is an important contribution to the debate.

▶ The DPP has issued his policy in relation to cases of assisted suicide.

▶ The Commission on Assisted Dying has made recommendations for legalizing assisted suicide in certain situations.

▶ The courts are likely to uphold a fully competent patient's wish to die, but it does not follow in all cases that other people will be absolved from criminal liability if they help to bring about that patient's death.

Summary cont'd

▶ The idea of a patient's *best* interests may be complex; and propositions of law formulated in cases concerning children are not necessarily applicable to cases involving competent adults.

▶ The Mental Capacity Act 2005 defines *capacity* and makes extensive provision for people who lack capacity.

Further reading

Blom-Cooper, Louis and Drewry, Gavin (eds), *Law and Morality*, 1976

Cohen, Carl and Regan, Tom, *The Animal Rights Debate*, 2001

Devlin, Patrick, *The Enforcement of Morals* (1959) 45 *Proceedings of the British Academy*, reprinted as *Morals and the Criminal Law* in *The Enforcement of Morals*, 1965

Dworkin, Ronald, *What The Constitution Says* in *Freedom's Law: the Moral Reading of the American Constitution*, 1996

Dworkin, Ronald, *Liberal Community* (1989) 77 Calif Law Rev 479, included in a shortened form in *Communitarianism and Individualism*, Avineri, Shlomo and de-Shalit, Avner (eds), 1992

Dworkin, Ronald, *Life's Dominion*, 1993

Hart, H.L.A., Law, *Liberty and Morality*, 1963

Hart, H.L.A., *The Concept of Law*, 2nd edn, 1994

Honoré, Tony, *Herbert Lionel Adolphus Hart, 1907–92: In Memoriam* (1993) 84 *Proceedings of the British Academy* 295

Keown, *Restoring Moral and Intellectual Shape to the Law after Bland* (1997) 113 LQR 481

Lacey, Nicola, *A Life of H.L.A. Hart*, 2004

Lasagna, Louis, http://www.pbs.org/wgbh/nova/doctors/oath_modern.html

Mill, John Stuart, *Essay on Liberty*, 1859

Mortimer, John, *Murderers and Other Friends*, 1995

Report of Commission on Assisted Dying, 2012

Singer, Peter, *Animal Liberation: a New Ethics for our Treatment of Animals*, first published 1975, revised edition 1990, republished with a new preface 1995.

Singer, Peter (ed), In *Defense of Animals: the Second Wave*, 2006

Singer, Peter, *Practical Ethics*, 3rd edn, 2011

Stephen, James Fitzjames, *Liberty, Equality, Fraternity*, 1873

Williams Report, 1979 Cmd 7772

Wolf, Naomi, *The Beauty Myth*, 1990

Wolfenden Report, 1957 Cmd 247

Selected further reading

Although reading lists are included with each chapter, and without seeking to dissuade students from consulting the primary sources wherever possible, it may be worth indicating some other textbooks and commentaries to which further reference may usefully be made.

The most comprehensive collection of materials and commentary remains *Lloyd's Introduction to Jurisprudence*, M.D.A. Freeman, 8th edn, 2008, Sweet & Maxwell. However, it is rather daunting for all but the most committed of students, and many will find a more accessible resource in the form of *Jurisprudence and Legal Theory: Commentary and Materials*, Penner, Schiff, Nobles *et al.*, 2002, Butterworths. Although the materials which this book reproduces are less comprehensive than those contained in *Lloyd*, they are nevertheless very substantial and have the advantage of being fully integrated into the text, rather than being appended to it.

Turning to conventional textbooks, the leading modern examples of works which survey more or less the whole field (subject to minor variations) include *Legal Philosophies*, J.W. Harris, 2nd edn, 1997, Oxford University Press; *Understanding Jurisprudence*, Raymond Wacks, 3rd edn, Oxford University Press; *Textbook on Jurisprudence*, Hilaire McCoubrey and Nigel D. White (ed. J.E. Penner), 4th edn, 2008, Oxford University Press; and *Jurisprudence*, J.G. Riddall, 2nd edn, 1999, Oxford University Press. An excellent text with a narrower scope than any of these books, but correspondingly more detailed analysis of what it does cover, is *Central Issues in Jurisprudence*, N.E. Simmonds, 3rd edn, 2008, Sweet & Maxwell.

An invaluable treatment of the specifically American dimension may be found in *Patterns of American Jurisprudence*, Neil Duxbury, first published in 1995, but reprinted with corrections, in 1997, Oxford University Press.

Students wishing to pursue the topic of postmodernism in general and critical legal studies in particular will find useful points of departure in *Postmodern Legal Movements: Law and Jurisprudence at Century's End*, Gary Minda, 1995, New York University Press, and *An Introduction to Critical Legal Theory*, Ian Ward, 2nd edn, 2004, Routledge. Much of the literature on feminism is contained in the journals, and especially those published by American universities, a combination which inevitably gives rise to problems of physical accessibility. However, Hilaire Barnett's *Sourcebook on Feminist Jurisprudence*, 1997, and *Introduction to Feminist Jurisprudence*, 1998, both Routledge Publishing, and *Feminist Perspectives on Law*, Jo Bridgeman and Susan Millns, 1998, Sweet & Maxwell, are all very useful.

Students who find that studying legal theory stimulates their interest in philosophy more generally will find a wealth of introductory titles available, but it would be difficult for beginners to do better than *Philosophy: the Basics*, Nigel Warburton, 5th edn, 2012, Routledge. Similarly, for a short study of ethics which is eminently suitable for beginners, it would be difficult to improve on *Being Good*, Simon Blackburn, 2001 (paperback 2002), Oxford University Press.

Index